A Forensic Linguistic
Legal Disclosures

This book is a scholarly work of forensic linguistics that demonstrates how the principles of Gricean pragmatics and their recent elaboration in Information Manipulation Theory (IMT) can be of use to courts faced with deciding cases of allegedly fraudulent disclosure documents. The usual goal of legal rules for disclosure documents is not merely to prevent lying but other forms of deception as well. In particular, the goal of these rules is to force the communicator to reveal information that could cause material harm to certain receivers, harms that the communicator, for various reasons of self-interest, might prefer to keep secret or hidden. Because IMT and the Gricean framework have seldom been used in published studies to investigate legally mandated disclosure documents aimed at laypersons, this book seeks to enrich current explications of the rhetorical 'workings' of deceptive disclosures within the broader Gricean tradition of pragmatics. The book questions the fundamental relationships among Grice's maxims as well as the much-circulated notion that violation of some maxims is more deceptive and more immoral than violations of others. In addition, the book also attempts to show how various other theories and research in discourse linguistics and reading comprehension can be used to support IMT analyses in addressing the discourse-processing issues unique to legally required disclosure texts. In this way the book contributes to the larger dual mission of the field of forensic linguistics, which is both to understand and to improve courts' impact on social justice.

James F. Stratman is associate professor in the Department of Communication at the University of Colorado Denver, USA.

Routledge Studies in Linguistics

1 **Polari—The Lost Language of Gay Men**
Paul Baker

2 **The Linguistic Analysis of Jokes**
Graeme Ritchie

3 **The Irish Language in Ireland**
From Goídel to Globalisation
Diarmait Mac Giolla Chríost

4 **Conceptualizing Metaphors**
On Charles Peirce's Marginalia
Ivan Mladenov

5 **The Linguistics of Laughter**
A Corpus-assisted Study of Laughter-talk
Alan Partington

6 **The Communication of Leadership**
The Design of Leadership Style
Jonathan Charteris-Black

7 **Semantics and Pragmatics of False Friends**
Pedro J. Chamizo-Domínguez

8 **Style and Ideology in Translation**
Latin American Writing in English
Jeremy Munday

9 **Lesbian Discourses**
Images of a Community
Veronika Koller

10 **Structure in Language**
A Dynamic Perspective
Thomas Berg

11 **Metaphor and Reconciliation**
The Discourse Dynamics of Empathy in Post-Conflict Conversations
Lynne J. Cameron

12 **Relational Semantics and the Anatomy of Abstraction**
Tamar Sovran

13 **Language Contact and the Origins of the Germanic Languages**
Peter Schrijver

14 **Metonymy and Language**
A New Theory of Linguistic Processing
Charles Denroche

15 **A Forensic Linguistic Approach to Legal Disclosures**
ERISA Cash Balance Conversion Cases and the Contextual Dynamics of Deception
James F. Stratman

A Forensic Linguistic Approach to Legal Disclosures

ERISA Cash Balance Conversion Cases and the Contextual Dynamics of Deception

James F. Stratman

Routledge
Taylor & Francis Group
LONDON AND NEW YORK

First published 2016
by Routledge

2 Park Square, Milton Park, Abingdon, Oxfordshire OX14 4RN
711 Third Avenue, New York, NY 10017

Routledge is an imprint of the Taylor & Francis Group, an informa business

First issued in paperback 2018

Library of Congress Cataloging-in-Publication Data
Stratman, James F., author.
A forensic linguistic approach to legal disclosures : ERISA cash balance conversion cases and the contextual dynamics of deception / by James F. Stratman.
pages cm — (Routledge studies in linguistics)
Includes bibliographical references and index.
1. Pension trusts—Law and legislation—United States. 2. United States. Employee Retirement Income Security Act of 1974. 3. Disclosure of information—Law and legislation—United States. 4. Pension trusts—Law and legislation—United States—Language. 5. Forensic linguistics—United States. 6. Discourse analysis—United States. I. Title.
KF3512.S76 2015
345.73'0263—dc23 2015021675

ISBN: 978-1-138-92005-7 (hbk)
ISBN: 978-0-367-02349-2 (pbk)

Typeset in Times New Roman
by Apex CoVantage, LLC

For my father, Anthony F. Stratman

Contents

Tables

Acknowledgments

I would first like to thank Mr. Stephen R. Bruce (Stephen R. Bruce Law Offices, Washington, DC) not only for providing invaluable critical comments and detailed suggestions on the first draft of this project but more deeply for the many stimulating conversations about Employment Retirement Income Security Act (ERISA) disclosure rules, cases, and disclosure documents that we have shared over the years. Stephen's encyclopedic scholarly work, *Pension Claims: Rights and Obligations* (2nd ed., 1993) is well-known and respected by thousands of ERISA advocates and researchers. Much of what I hope I have gotten right in the present work is due to his perception and experience, whereas any missteps are all my own. I would also like to thank Mr. David Steelman (of Steelman, Gaunt & Horsefield, in Rolla, Missouri) for similar help in reviewing my first draft and for offering thoughtful and candid appraisals of my arguments. I know that my work is much better for his advice and insights. The late Peter M. Tiersma, Honorable William Matthew Byrne chair and professor of law at the Loyola of Los Angeles School of Law, and his scholarly publishing partner, Professor Lawrence Solan, Don Forchelli professor of law and director of graduate education at the Brooklyn School of Law, must also be acknowledged for the inspiration they have both (albeit unknowingly) provided to me and to an entire generation of researchers in forensic linguistics, not only in the U.S. but around the world. To the anonymous scholarly reviewers who were recruited on my behalf by Routledge/Taylor & Francis, I also owe a debt of thanks for their insightful comments on my initial project proposal and draft chapters. I would be remiss if I also did not acknowledge my former professors and mentors in Carnegie Mellon University's doctoral program in rhetoric during my formative years as a writer and researcher, especially Professors Linda Flower, David Kaufer, and John R. Hayes, whose insistent focus on the interdisciplinary foundations of rhetorical theory and discourse analysis is one that I hope I have brought meaningfully to bear in the present work. I am grateful as well to the University of Colorado Denver for the Dissemination Grant Award that made the indexing of this work possible. Finally, I would like to thank Margo Irvin and Kathleen Laurentiev at Routledge/Taylor & Francis first, for believing in this book and my initial proposal concerning it, and second, for their professional assistance in further guiding my editing of the manuscript.

Neoptolemus: What do you bid me do but to tell lies?
Odysseus: By craft I bid you to take him, Philoctetes.
Neoptolemus: And why by craft rather than persuasion?

Sophocles, *Philoctetes*
(Lines 101–102, translation by David Grene)

1 Introduction

Consider the following scenario: you have worked in a managerial position for MultiNatCorp for 32 years, and you are now in the last week of your employment with the firm. You have raised a family, held your marriage together through some turbulent times, and raised three children, with two now in college and the third about to enter at the end of the year. You are really looking forward to retirement, especially given that you were diligent about saving and are feeling secure. On Thursday before your last day, some 100 people are gathered at your office for your bon voyage party, including top company officials who have flown in for the event. Everyone is in high spirits—it's been great to work with so many talented and dedicated people. As it happens, you are chatting and sipping wine with two vice presidents (VPs) from human resources. That conversation ends with their congratulations, and then a lawyer you also know from the firm approaches. She looks a bit somber and is trying to smile. "John," she says, "you'd be sick if you knew about the wear-away factor your retirement account has been under for the last nine years." She nods toward the VPs who just left.

You look into her eyes, puzzled. "Wear away? What do you mean?" She looks down at the floor, obviously sorry that she said anything. But then she opens up a little and explains that ever since the company changed its pension plan from a final pay average plan to a cash balance plan nine years ago, you have not, in fact, been earning any additional retirement benefits. Indeed, during those years, you have not earned one more penny for your pension—when you believed you were earning at a nice rate of accrual.

"But," you stammer, "I read all of the notices the company sent me about the transition; they were all reassuring that I would continue to earn quarterly pay and interest credits in my new cash balance account." The attorney shakes her head and is suddenly whisked away by another VP. An anxious feeling comes over you. "Have I made a terrible mistake?" you ask yourself. The people in the room around you disappear in a fog as you try to remember all of the many official company documents you received—all of them, you vividly recall, stating that your pension benefits were "protected" and that your "benefit earnings would continue under the new plan." Will you in fact need to continue working somewhere else? How will you explain this catastrophe to your family?

This scenario is not entirely hypothetical. It closely resembles a recent federal district court case in which a retiring employee at her going-away party made exactly the same painful discovery about her retirement, a case that landed in the U.S. Supreme Court in May 2011 (*Amara v. CIGNA Corp.* 2008, 2012, 2014; *CIGNA Corp. v. Amara*, 2011. See also Schultz, 2011, pp. 29–38.). And across the U.S. over the last two decades, the same basic story has played out for tens of thousands of older, longer-service workers whose companies ended their defined pension plans and replaced them with cash balance plans.

Under the Employment Retirement Income Security Act (ERISA) of 1974, any pension plan benefits that a vested participant has already earned cannot be taken away or reduced (29 U.S.C. §§ 1001–1461 (1982). However, except where prevented or limited by collective bargaining agreements, employers have long had the right to change the type of plan they offer to employees and to reduce or even terminate their employees' future pension benefits without employee consent or approval (Bruce, 1993; Muir, 1999, 2004; Wiedenbeck, 2008; Wooten, 2004). As a condition on this right, ERISA requires employers to provide their employees with 'plain language' descriptions of their pensions and of the conditions under which future pension benefits might be reduced or terminated. Depending upon the circumstances, these descriptions must be provided to employees in a Summary Plan Document (SPD), a Summary of Material Modifications (SMMs), or what is known as a § 204(h) notice (29 U.S.C. § 1022(a) and (b); 29 C.F.R. § 2520.102–1, 102–2; 102–3; 29 C.F.R. 2520.104(b)(3); and 29 U.S.C. § 1054(h)(1)). Since ERISA's original passage, the composition of all of these documents has grown ever more complicated and evolved to become a major and quite profitable outsource industry. At the same time, ERISA's disclosure rules governing these documents have confronted courts with myriad interpretive difficulties in expensive and complex class action litigation that continues up to the present time. Some cases filed by plaintiff–employees in the mid and late 1990s are still awaiting trial or settlement, and hundreds of millions of dollars are still at stake (e.g., see Schultz, 2010, 2011).

Some of the most controversial ERISA disclosure litigation has challenged employers' conversion of their pension plans from so-called defined pension plans to a very different type of pension plan, termed 'cash balance' plans. As the previous scenario suggests, such conversions can be especially painful for older, longer-service employees who may see catastrophic pension reductions—reaching more than 50 percent—to their future pension benefits (U.S. General Accounting Office, 2000a, 2000b, 2005). Recent cash balance conversion lawsuits often involve employees' complaints that employers not only deceived employees that any significant future pension reductions would occur but also that employers concealed a notorious effect of these conversions: many employees, and especially older, longer-service employees, may work for many years following the plan conversion during which they earn no additional pension benefits at all, a phenomenon known as 'wear away' (*Bilello v. JPMorgan Chase Ret. Plan*, 2009; *Custer v. Southern New England Telephone Company*, 2008; *Register v. PNC Financial Services Group, Inc.*, 2007; *Frommert v. Conkright*, 2006; *In re*

Citigroup Pension Plan ERISA Litigation, 2006; *Hirt v. Equitable Retirement Plan for Emples., Managers & Agents*, 2006; *Charles v. Pepco Holdings, Inc.*, 2006; *Engers v. AT&T and AT&T Management Pension Plan*, 2006; *Richards v. FleetBoston Fin. Corp.*, 2006; *Burstein v. Retirement Account Plan for Employees of Allegheny Health Education Research Fund*, 2003.)

Despite the extensive and ongoing critical attention that cash balance conversion cases have received in the law review literature, almost no research has closely or critically examined features of the disclosure documents and messages employers have actually distributed in these cases and analyzed how these might be understood by ordinary employees (Anand, 2000; Flint, 1995; Forman & Nixon, 2000; Jefferson, 2001; Noel, 2005; Muir, 2004; Rodine, 2001; Saxinger, 2000; Schulstad, 2001; Sennott, 2001; Stover, 2001; Sulentic, 2000, 2007; Zelinsky, 2000). In particular, no linguistic or communication research investigates the ways in which their alleged textual and rhetorical deceptiveness or communicative adequacy may be assessed. As its primary purpose, this book explores one potentially useful approach to analyzing these messages—Information Manipulation Theory (IMT), which draws heavily upon natural language philosopher H. P. Grice's original theory of cooperation in spoken conversation and his four maxims of quality, quantity, relation, and manner (Castelfranchi & Poggi, 1994; Dynel, 2011; Galasinski, 2000; Grice, 1989, 1975; McCornack, 1992, 1997, 2008).

Within IMT, violations of Grice's four maxims are theorized to fairly exhaust the ways a communicator may verbally deceive a communication recipient. First, the maxim of *quality* is violated when the communicator tells a falsehood: suppose a blind person is attempting cross a busy intersection and asks the person next to her if the crossing light is green, and the person, seeing that the light actually just turned red, replies, "Yes, it's green." Thus, knowing the truth, the communicator states or implies the very opposite, producing deceit by commission. In contrast, the maxim of *quantity* is violated when a communicator omits stating information a receiver would reasonably want or need to know. For example, a husband asks his spouse what she did at lunchtime, and she replies she had lunch out with a friend (which is true) but neglects to add that the friend is her former husband, and she had previously promised not to see her former spouse any more. A violation of the maxim of *relevance* occurs when a communicator contrives to appear to answer a question asked by the receiver but actually does not do so and instead answers a subtly different question. For example, a person seeking a new home mortgage asks the mortgager if the future interest rate on the mortgage is subject to change, and the mortgager, knowing interest rates on the specified mortgage could actually increase at any time, replies: "At ACME Finance we make every effort to prevent that from occurring, and at this time we do not anticipate that the rate will change for at least eight years." The mortgager's reply violates the relevance maxim because what the mortgager says is a response to a question that the person seeking the mortgage did not ask; that is, the person did not ask what the mortgager would try to do or what the mortgager "anticipated."

Finally, the maxim of *manner* (or *clarity*) is violated when a communicator responds to a receiver's question in a way that equivocates, involves ambiguity or vagueness, or utilizes some combination of these that makes coherent interpretation of the communicator's meaning onerous and uncertain. Consider a patient whose pain medication has recently been changed by her health maintenance organization (HMO). She asks her HMO physician if the new medication will prevent her pain as effectively as the previous, cancelled medication. The physician has reasons for believing that the new medication, although helpful, may not be as effective as the old medication; the physician then tells the patient the following: "This type of new medication generally is very different from the old medication you have been taking. Future pain you experience may be greater than, the same as, or less than what you would likely be experiencing using the previous medication depending somewhat on your age, length of time you have had your infection, and the dosage amount you have been taking with the old medication." Then he says nothing further. The maxim of clarity appears violated because the provider's statement, although it does address the question the patient asked, is rather vague and amounts to an equivocation; that is, anything could happen. Unless the provider specifically discusses the impact that the variables mentioned could have on the particular patient's experience of pain, the provider's response simply puts the problem of figuring out how these variables will affect her body's response to the new medication upon the message receiver herself.

PURPOSES OF THE BOOK

IMT and these four Gricean maxims have shown promise for describing and explaining how conversational utterances may deceive. However, so far they have rarely been extended to analyses of naturally occurring written discourse, particularly in formal, mass-distributed legal and financial disclosures whose deceptiveness versus communicative adequacy is often litigated in court. As a primary purpose of this book, I will generally argue that courts wrestling with ERISA's complex statutory framework for deciding cash balance disclosure lawsuits may find IMT and the Gricean maxims of conversation to be valuable tools, particularly when experimentally obtained data regarding readers' comprehension of actual disclosure language is not available as evidence (Ainsworth, 2006; Solan, 1999, 2010; Howald, 2006; Tiersma & Solan, 2002; cf., Stratman, 1988). To be sure, other approaches to the analysis of legal disclosure discourse are possible, such as speech act theory (Searle, 1969, 2001; Vanderveken & Kubo, 2001), speech event theory (Gumperz, 1999; Gumperz & Levinson, 1996), and schema theory in cognitive psychology and reading comprehension research (Arbib, Conklin, & Hill, 1987; Bartlett, 1932; Brewer, 2000; Mandler, 1984; Richgels, 1982; Whitney, 1987), to name only some alternatives. Although I do draw upon schema theory at various points, especially when discussing disclosure readers' comprehension, IMT and the Gricean maxims seemed the best initial, overall approach, particularly in view of the way that legal disclosure rules under ERISA are framed and the nature of the communication and contractual problems they are intended to address.

To explore IMT's potential applicability, this book analyzes in detail the disclosure documents and messages that were contested in one ongoing and one recently decided cash balance transition case: *Amara v. CIGNA Corp.* (2008) and *Tomlinson v. El Paso Corporation* (2008, 2009, 2011). These two cases were chosen because although the harmful effects of the cash balance conversions on employees' future pension benefits in both were quite similar, the case outcomes and judicial approach to analyzing disclosure language for its adequacy or deceptiveness are markedly different. After a seven-day bench trial the district court in *Amara* ultimately found defendant CIGNA's disclosures to be deceptive, whereas the *Tomlinson* court, although looking at somewhat different disclosures produced by El Paso Corporation, found no deception at all, and in a summary judgment concluded that the disclosures provided by El Paso were entirely adequate.[1]

As will be explained, the differences in case outcome and judicial analytic approach to the disclosures between these cases expose challenging interpretive issues for courts regarding the nature and definition of deception, issues that may be helpfully clarified with concepts from IMT and thus potentially help future adjudication processes.

In addition to this primary purpose, the book has four important secondary theoretical purposes as well.

1. First, because IMT and the Gricean framework have seldom been used in published studies to investigate legally mandated disclosure documents, this book seeks to enrich current explications of the rhetorical "workings" of deception within the broader Gricean tradition of pragmatics. A concern commonly expressed about the Gricean maxims is that explications of them are often limited to very short examples (or else contextually limited or 'sanitized,' hypothetical examples) excerpted from larger, ongoing conversational exchanges of which they were a part in natural discourse situations. The surrounding discourse elided from these examples, however, is often critical because it may influence (and greatly complicate) how the specimen passages themselves are perceived as well as explanations concerning how maxim violations involved in these specimens occur (e.g., see Sarangi & Slembrouck, 1992).

For instance, in expert forensic linguistic testimony, short specimen statements excerpted from formal written documents, such as ERISA-mandated pension disclosures, might be presented and dissected by the Gricean analyst apart from both their surrounding relevant text and their larger situational context with the result that the analyst risks oversimplifying and even distorting how the specimen passages may function and be understood. After all, although some instances of deceptive discourse occur in single sentences, others only become manifest across many sentences, passages, or even multiple documents. Litigants disputing the adequacy of employer disclosures, as well as judges called upon to decide such disputes, can ill afford to simply ignore the surrounding textual, spatial, and chronological contexts in which disputed passages appear. Thus, one purpose of this book will be to suggest how other theoretical principles, especially those developed in cognitive studies of reading comprehension, persuasion, and in studies of the problem of expert hindsight bias, can be usefully integrated with IMT and the Gricean maxims to explicate the workings of allegedly deceptive communication. The relevance of principles from these additional areas becomes manifest in documents that are of greater length and technical complexity than one typically finds explicated in the deceptive discourse and forensic linguistics literature.

2. A second, closely related theoretical purpose is to explore the functional relationships and dependencies that may exist among violations of the quality, quantity, relation, and manner maxims. It has been observed that a given conversational utterance may, in fact, simultaneously violate more than one maxim. One specific issue that has been raised is whether or not a communicator's violation of the maxim of quality necessarily means the communicator also violates one or more of the three remaining maxims as well, if only thereby to make the falsehood being told either more invisible or persuasive to the receiver (Dynel, 2011; Galasinski, 2000). For instance, when a communicator tells a falsehood of the sort mentioned in the crosswalk example, does the communicator also necessarily violate the maxim of quantity? After all, the bystander who falsely answers the blind person's question about the color of the crosswalk light can also be argued to omit the truthful information that the light is red rather than green. Similarly, in such a case it might also be argued that by violating the maxims of quality and quantity, the bystander has also violated the maxim of relevance: is telling the blind person that the light is green when it is actually red also providing an irrelevant response? This seems a more difficult claim. Indeed, the extent to which one maxim violation necessarily entails violation of a different maxim remains controversial, and examples of naturally occurring ('real-world') discourse rather than hypothetical examples should be examined in pursuing an understanding of such relationships.

In McCornack's work (1992, 1997) and that of other deception researchers such as Galasinski (2000), complex, simultaneous violations of the maxims are sometimes shown to occur through implicatures. A common, simple example of an implicature is the question, "Can you pass the salt?" i.e., while we are sharing dinner. Literally understood, the question is not a request for some salt but instead a question about the receiver's capability. However, this question in such a context is commonly understood as a cooperative, face-saving way to ask for some salt. In effect, although what the speaker says is potentially deceptive in relation to what the speaker actually means, the receiver nonetheless clearly perceives what the speaker means and is not deceived. A great many expressions in English involve implicatures that have this cooperative interpretation, and they pass both conversational partners with little notice. But some deviations between what speakers say and what they actually mean may not be so innocent. In these situations, implicatures may sometimes serve as 'masks' behind which the communicator attempts to hide either a violation of the quantity or quality (or both) maxims, while nonetheless seeming to speak in a fully cooperative manner toward receivers and in a way that makes them seem worthy of the receivers' trust.

For instance, consider the mortgage example introduced above. The mortgager's failure to answer the question that was asked is a 'two-way' violation of the quantity maxim, in that the mortgager's answer provides both too much and too little information at the same time. The mortgager avoids providing an answer to the particular question the applicant most wants answered (Will my future mortgage interest rate increase?) while simultaneously encouraging the applicant to mistakenly believe that no change in the interest rate will occur for at least eight years and that the mortgager can predict when future rates will rise. This encouragement actually helps to mask the fact that key information the applicant is asking for is omitted: "We make every effort to prevent [rate increases] from occurring, and at this time we do not anticipate that the rate will change for at least eight years." Note that the mortgager's reply is at least partially relevant semantically to the extent that it preserves the topic of "changes to the future interest rate," which the applicant focused upon in her question. But the reply also strategically and covertly reframes the applicant's original question as one asking what the mortgager anticipates and what the mortgager will do, thereby creating a deceptive implicature. We can see that the reply speciously implies that the finance company is somehow on the mortgage applicant's side and potentially capable of preventing future interest rates on the loan from rising or is capable of predicting when rises will occur. No false statement per se is made, but the reply invites the inaccurate interpretation that the customer's interest rate will not increase for at least eight years.

The present study of contested pension benefit disclosures attempts to identify and explicate these sorts of deceptive implicatures and the ways they are contextualized in the peculiar author–reader relationship that is constructed by the employer. As close examination of the *Amara* and *Tomlinson* case disclosures will reveal, deceptive implicatures can be generated not only through strategic contextual and syntactic positioning of facially and partially truthful statements but also through framing devices such as frequently asked questions (FAQs), section headings, and visual spacing, among others (Ewald & Vann, 2008; Schriver, 1997). In this way, the study attempts to show how the dependencies and functional relationships among the four maxims can be much more complex than many treatments of IMT and the Gricean maxims relying upon hypothetical examples may suggest.

3. A third theoretical purpose is to explore and critically assess arguments concerning whether or not a moral hierarchy exists among the four Gricean maxims (Carson, 2012; DeScioli, Christner, & Kurzban, 2011; Green, 2001; Hancock, Curry, Goorha, & Woodworth, 2008; Tiersma, 1990; Van Swol, Braun, & Malhotra, 2012). Some experimental studies have suggested that ordinary observers see different degrees (or 'stair steps') of moral wrongfulness when each of the different Gricean maxims are violated, such that it is often perceived less wrongful to commit omissions (quantity violations) than to tell or imply falsehoods (quality violations) even where the material harms to persons resulting from these

violations turn out to be the same (Spranca, Minsk, & Baron, 1991; see also Ornatowski, 1998). In turn, relevance violations are perceived as less wrongful than deceptions by omission, and deceptive clarity (manner) violations are perceived as less wrongful than relevance violations (e.g., McCornack, Levine, Solowczuk, Torres, & Campbell, 1992). These hypothesized relations can be schematized in Table 1.1:

Table 1.1 Hypothesized Moral Hierarchy among Gricean Maxims

More Deceptive, More Immoral	Quality violations (lies)
↓	
↓	Quantity violations (omissions)
↓	
↓	Relevance violations (topic shifts, evasions,
↓	'red herrings')
↓	
Less Deceptive, Less Immoral	Manner/clarity violations (ambiguity, vagueness, equivocation)

IMT currently does not offer any coherent grounds or rationales for differentiating degrees of wrongfulness among the four maxim violations; nor, for that matter, has Grice done so. However, if one is to hypothesize a decrease in the moral wrongfulness across these four maxim violations as suggested in Table 1.1, a key premise for that hypothesis would be that clarity or manner violations involve the least deception (if, indeed, any deception at all), whereas quality violations would involve the most. The notion, in other words, is that the relative moral wrongfulness of each violation correlates strongly with its inherent degree of deceptiveness, that is, the degree to which each violation confounds receivers' reasonable expectations or leads them to mistaken understandings about some reality. Thus, it seems important to consider the question of degrees of deceptiveness per se across the maxim violations without immediate regard for the consequent degree of material harm these violations may also cause to receivers. Unquestionably, material harm is important in the ERISA context as in other areas of law where concepts or definitions of deception are involved. But the degree of material harm resulting from each violation is only a second-order correlate, if you will, of the degree of moral wrongfulness attaching to each maxim violation. For instance, depending upon the situation, a violation of the maxim of relevance may confound a receiver's accurate understanding of a situation just as much as an outright lie and therefore prove just as morally wrongful, regardless of the degree of material harm that each violation occasions.

Nor should one confound the degree of deceptiveness of a particular maxim violation with the degree of intent to deceive that may be present in the communicator because all four violations may be equally intentional. That is, a person can intend to introduce an irrelevancy in a response to a question just as much as one can intend to introduce a lie. Thus, like material harm, degree of intent to deceive may only be a second-order correlate of deceptiveness. As Galasinski (2000, pp. 17–26) argues, we rarely have foolproof means for ascertaining *to what degree* a communicator intends to deceive because intent is ultimately a mental state or attribute of consciousness. We are left to infer a communicator's degree of intent from various direct and indirect signs and evidence, for example, from witnesses, documents, communicator self-disclosure, and so on. Intent to deceive is, however, perhaps the most widely shared constituent of all attempts to define deception as a language behavior: deception is commonly theorized not to occur where there is no such intent at all.

Given this understanding, the first-order correlate of moral wrongfulness is the relative or comparative degree of deceptiveness. That is, the deceptiveness of a given maxim violation should be evaluated in terms of the degree of misunderstanding that a maxim violation works upon a receiver's comprehension of a situation or event or the extent to which the violation defeats the receiver's expectation of truthfulness in a communication. At least, in any debate about the general soundness of the moral differentiation hypothesized to exist among the four different maxim violations, it seems more important as a first step to focus attention on the functional dynamics of the different maxim violations and their likely consequences for receivers' thinking and beliefs *per se* rather than focus upon the degree to which the speaker intended to deceive.

Questions about the existence of a moral hierarchy attaching to different violations of the Gricean maxims are clearly relevant to courts' interpretations concerning what ERISA's rules proscribe in employers' disclosures. As will be discussed in Chapter 3 of this book, although ERISA's provisions might straightforwardly appear to proscribe all four of the maxim violations, ERISA itself offers no how-to guide for detecting or categorizing these violations as they might actually occur in employers' disclosure documents. Nor does ERISA illustrate its proscriptions with examples.[2] Even to the limited extent that ERISA 'names' communication strategies that employers must not use, it does not clearly state or imply whether all of these proscribed strategies are to be viewed as equally unacceptable or whether some are more unacceptable than others. Worse, attempts to synthesize consistent interpretations of these proscriptions across the extant ERISA case law open to view a broken, inconsistent patchwork of distinctions about what constitutes deceptive versus nondeceptive disclosure. For instance, ERISA statutory and regulatory sources do not set forth any grounds for determining whether or not deception by omission (quantity violations) and deception by commission (quality violations) in disclosures are to be judged equally unacceptable and equally compensable. Nonetheless, in litigation over the disclosure strategies that employers use, it seems entirely possible (if not probable) that courts would need to consider explicitly the grounds upon which they differentiate (or do not differentiate) degrees of deceptiveness among the types of maxim violations previously illustrated.

Currently, several theories to explain differential judgments of deceptiveness in verbal communication (and, consequently, degrees of moral wrongfulness) involving the four maxim violations have been suggested, and they involve somewhat different factors and rationales (e.g., Carson, 2012; Spranca et al., 1991). One is that the three non-lying violations (quantity, relevance, and manner/clarity) are potentially more *detectable* by receivers than outright lies, which in many circumstances, may not be detectable at all. The underlying idea in this theory seems to be that the more undetectable to receivers one has made the lie or the misleading nature of a message, the more deceptive and therefore more dishonest or immoral that lie or message is—again, regardless of the fact that the material harms caused by different maxim violations or the degree of intent to deceive may be the same. Thus omissions of information are theorized to be potentially more detectable by receivers than false statements; irrelevancies in messages (sometimes labeled 'red herrings') are theorized to be more detectable than omissions of information; and ambiguities, equivocations, or vagueness as means of misleading receivers are theorized to be still more detectable than introducing irrelevancies into a message. This theory thus tries to move attention away from both the intent of the communicator and away from the material consequences to receivers of any particular violation. Instead, it looks at the implications of each type of maxim violation for receivers' information processing, especially the conclusions or inferences receivers can and cannot draw when faced with them.

Another similar theoretical basis for differentiating degrees of deceptiveness among maxim violations is that a communicator's non-lying violations are perceived as being less *causally responsible* for receivers' mistaken beliefs or understandings than are outright lies. In some ways this theory seems simply to state reciprocally what the detectability theory of differentiation states. Be that as it may, proponents of the causal involvement view stress that it is entirely reasonable to expect receivers of messages to pay careful attention to any seeming incompleteness, vagueness, ambiguity, or irrelevancy in messages presented to them. The reasonableness of this expectation is offered as grounds for asserting that responsibility for violations of the three non-lying maxims is shared between the communicator and receiver to some degree, much the way that legal negligence may potentially be distributed among persons involved in an auto accident. Indeed, some scholars theorize that when violations of the non-lying maxims occur in the absence of a violation of the maxim of quality (i.e., when no lie or falsehood is told), receivers of messages that involve these non-lying violations can be said to be at least partially complicit in their own deception—a complicity that has been captured in the phrase *'caveat auditor'* (Green, 2001). In contrast, complete causal responsibility and thus moral culpability for violations of the maxim of quality (lying) is argued to rest solely with the communicator.

Finally, still another theory to explain the perceived differential (or decreasing) degrees of deceptiveness among the four maxim violations is based on the notion of *foreseeability*. In particular, a communicator is thought to be progressively less able to predict the possible consequences of the violation for the receiver's thinking or understanding. Thus, intentional, outright liars are theorized to have the greatest foreknowledge of the nature and scope of the 'mistake' they may inflict on their receivers' thinking or understanding, whereas persons communicating incomplete, vague, ambiguous, or irrelevant messages are theorized to have less accurate or precise foreknowledge about the cognitive consequences these sorts of messages will have. When telling outright lies, the communicator is thought to exercise far more precise control over the receiver's cognition than when committing the other three maxim violations. Conversely, it is theorized that a communicator cannot be quite so confident about the ultimate effect of a strategic omission of information—that is, about what the receiver may infer from a message involving that omission—compared to the confidence the communicator can have about the specific effect upon the receiver if a completely false statement is presented.

All three of these explanations are controversial, and they are perhaps most intensively debated in response to the claim that communicators who violate the quantity maxim (omitting reasonably expected information) should be considered less deceptive, and therefore less morally blameworthy, than those who violate the maxim of quality (telling falsehoods). Green (2001), for example, has argued that this particular differentiation in culpability is reflected across a number of laws that govern various crimes of deception. He grounds his argument for a general, moral differentiation between violations of the quality and quantity maxims in part on the fact that many people intuitively seem to judge even provably intentional omissions of reasonably expected information as less deceptive or dishonest than lies (e.g., see McCornack et al., 1992). But otherwise, Green does not offer a full explanation as to why many people hold this view, that is, either in terms of the detectability, shared causal responsibility, or foreseeability of cognitive consequence rationales. Significantly, in the context of many ERISA disclosure cases, including the *Amara* and *Tomlinson* cases, which are the focus of this book, whether lying and omission can be differentiated in terms of their deceptiveness is often an implicit if not explicit issue, one for which, again, ERISA's disclosure rules provide little guidance.

The subtle and complex nature of this controversy over degrees of deceptiveness involved in omission of information versus the telling of falsehoods can perhaps be better appreciated by returning to and elaborating upon the crosswalk case. Consider these four permutations of that situation where, in each one, the material consequences to the receiver are held constant:[3]

1. A blind person wants to cross a street where there is a steady volume of traffic and is aware of a bystander next to her. She does not, however, ask him whether the light is green. The bystander sees that the light is red and that the blind person seems uncertain, but he remains silent and does not inform her. She steps into the intersection and is struck by a vehicle.
2. A blind person wants to cross a street where there is a steady volume of traffic and, aware of a bystander next to her, asks him if the light is green. The bystander sees that the light is red and that the blind person seems uncertain, but he does not answer her question and instead remains silent. She steps into the intersection and is struck by a vehicle.
3. A blind person wants to cross a street where there is a steady volume of traffic and, aware of a bystander next to her, asks him if the light is green.

Knowing that the light is red, he nevertheless replies, "I think it's safe to cross now." She steps into the intersection and is struck by a vehicle.

4. A blind person wants to cross a street where there is a steady volume of traffic and, aware of a bystander next to her, asks him if the light is green. Knowing that the light is red, he nevertheless replies, "Yes, it's green." She steps into the intersection and is struck by a vehicle.

At first glance, both the first and second cases might be considered violations of the maxim of quantity. The bystander does not tell any lie; he sees the potential danger to the blind person and her apparent uncertainty and yet says nothing. However, Grice (1975) himself does not refer to such silences as violations of the quantity maxim. He proposes that the bystander's silence is not necessarily uncooperative in either case, and he thus does not view these silences as forms or acts of deception. Instead, he views them as instances of the speaker simply opting out of conversation altogether, quite as if the blind person was not there. In not construing cases like 1 and 2 as quantity violations, what seems crucial for Grice is that such silences, as omissions of information, are not in any sense covert or hidden but are instead known to the receiver. But this viewpoint might well be questioned in case 2 where, unlike case 1, silence is also an unexpected conversational response. Should leaving someone in ignorance through silence about a situation that she plainly cannot address herself and that she directly asks about be considered deceptive? What, if anything at all, might the blind person reasonably infer based upon this silent response? One way to think about these questions might be to further ask: would the bystander's silence in case 2 impact the blind person's belief about the color of the crossing light in the same way that the bystander's silence in case1 might impact her beliefs, or would the impact of these two silences on her beliefs about the light be different? Unlike the silence in case 1, would the bystander's silence in case 2 make her more inclined to believe the light was green?

Turning to the third and fourth cases, these can both be argued to constitute violations of the maxim of quality, because in both, the bystander either implies or directly voices (respectively) a falsehood. However, assuming that there is deception in both of these, is there less deception involved in case 3 than in case 4? And, if so, is it clear that there is more deception involved in both of these cases than in case 2? Or, alternatively, assuming that the silences in cases 1 and 2 both represent quantity violations, do these cases involve the same degree of deceptiveness as cases 3 and 4, thus making the bystander equally morally culpable for what happens to the blind person in all four cases? What little experimental research exists suggests that most observers would consider the bystander to be morally culpable to some degree for what happens to the blind person in all four cases but to be only behaving or communicating deceptively in cases 3 and 4 (e.g., Spranca et al., 1991; McCornack et al., 1992).

To explore these issues a bit further, let's first compare the 'silent bystander' cases in 1 and 2 (together) to those in which the bystander speaks (cases 3 and 4) in terms of the 'detectability' explanation for moral differentiation. A bystander who sees the danger (i.e., the crossing light is red) and simply remains silent or who does not answer the blind person's direct question may be argued to be less deceptive than a bystander who misleadingly or falsely answers her direct question. Observers taking this position contend that the silent, nonresponsive bystanders in cases 1 and 2 cannot and should not be criminally or civilly prosecuted for practicing any deception, whereas those in 3 and 4 perhaps could or should be.[4]

The detectability explanation for the claim that there is no deception in cases 1 and 2 is that in both, the blind person herself has a responsibility to ask about the crossing light, to repeat her question even after receiving no reply (as in case 2), and to simply wait until answered or until other help arrives. It is further argued that her responsibility for her own thinking and decision-making process must be 'subtracted from' (although it may not eliminate entirely) any responsibility that the silent, nonresponsive bystander has to inform her (e.g., see Green, 2001). Effectively, the bystander's silence in both situations is a perceivable cue whose significance any rational person must weigh and investigate before taking action. What is interesting and controversial about this argument is why the blind person's responsibility to ask (more) questions must be subtracted from the bystander's responsibility to speak up or answer in the first place. Could it be said, rather, that his responsibility to speak up or answer must be subtracted from her own responsibility to learn the color of the crossing light and stay put until she does? The latter view may gain some support from the fact that the bystander must know her blindness is a serious disability relative to most other people facing the same situation.

Considering cases 3 and 4 under the detectability explanation, it seems far less responsibility for being deceived, if any at all, can be attributed to her. With respect to case 3, the bystander's reply ("I think it's safe to cross now") can be argued to violate both the quantity maxim *and* quality maxim. It omits any direct or express information about the color of the crossing light, information she specifically requested, while simultaneously inviting her to make the false inference that the light is green. The bystander's reply could reasonably be understood as encouragement to enter the intersection; in particular, the bystander's omission of the most semantically relevant information (the color of the light) is masked by the fact that his reply is pragmatically relevant. That is, what he says appears relevant because it seems to acknowledge what motivates the blind person's question about the crossing light and what she ultimately needs to know, that is, whether it would be safe to cross the street. The detectability explanation thus proposes that unlike cases 1 and 2 in which the blind person can 'hear' the bystander's silence (which makes his omission of information overt rather than covert), the blind person in cases 3 and 4 *cannot* hear what is being omitted because the bystander is putting either a false implication (case 3) or false information (case 4) in its place.

Some observers who also rely on the detectability explanation for attributing different degrees of deceptiveness to the four types of maxim violations might view case 3 as closer to cases 1 and 2 than it is to case 4. They might argue that a reasonable blind person, upon receiving the pragmatically relevant but semantically deviant reply, "I think it's safe to cross," should attach no particular significance to it or form any inference about the color of the light based upon it. In other words, they argue that the blind person should be able to recognize that the bystander's reply omits (for her) a crucial point. If she enters the intersection without careful thinking about this omission or without asking again about the color of the light, this argument runs, she should be seen as at least somewhat complicit in her own deception and as sharing some responsibility for what happens to her, just as she should be seen in cases 1 and 2, where the silence of the bystander appears meaningless and conveys nothing. Effectively, then, in this argument the differentiation in deceptiveness is based upon how detectable the omission of information within a reply may be. In case 3, it could be argued, the omission of any information about the crossing light should be only slightly less detectable by her than it is in cases 1 and 2. In contrast, in case 4 where the bystander replies with an outright lie, neither any semantic irrelevance nor other signal of unreliability is considered readily detectable on the part of the receiver.

Another frequent argument in support of a general differentiation in deceptiveness between quality and quantity violations is that the bystander's silence in cases 1 and 2 is much less causally related to the ensuing mistake in judgment of the blind person (if related at all) than is the bystander's response in cases 3 and 4. In this argument, the silent bystander is claimed to have done nothing to influence the victim to enter the intersection, as if to say his silence makes the situation no different than if he was not present on the corner with her at all. In contrast, opponents of this view would dispute that it is wholly accurate to say that the bystander's silence in both cases 1 and 2 is not causally related to the blind person's mistaken judgment.

Considering this causal rationale, Dynel (2011) has proposed that deceptive versus nondeceptive omissions (in this case, silence) should be distinguished in the following way. Deceptive omissions, Dynel states, are those which are "meant to nurture a false belief" in the receiver, whereas nondeceptive omissions involve "mere ignorance fostering" in the receiver; that is, the omission is one that either leaves or encourages receivers to adhere to an existing belief or remain in the same state of doubt to the same degree as they have up to the present moment (p. 154). Indeed, on the basis of this distinction, it seems that Dynel, like Grice (1975), would likely not consider the bystander's silence in cases 1 and 2 to violate the quantity maxim and thus also not consider either silence to be deceptive.

But, as before, some questions might be raised about this position. First, even assuming that we can readily say of both cases 1 and 2 that they involve "mere ignorance fostering" (to use Dynel's phrase), why isn't a silent omission which "fosters" (or simply permits) another's existing ignorance deceptive? Is there a sense in which we commonly say that someone who is knowingly or intentionally left ignorant of something by others is also being deceived by those others?

For instance, Tiersma (1995) discusses a case somewhat similar to case 1 that involves a homeowner omitting mention to a potential buyer of the fact that her home is infested with termites. The potential buyer (like the blind person) never asked about the possibility of termites. On the one hand, Tiersma argues that courts have sometimes found such silences to constitute deliberate misrepresentations, but on the other he also asserts that "we cannot reasonably state that [the seller], by her silence, informed [the buyer] that the house had no termites" (p. 55). He further explains, "While silence in nondisclosure cases may not intentionally communicate that there are no termites . . . the silence carelessly allows the buyer to draw such an inference. Intentionally or carelessly creating a false impression [via silence] . . . is quite sufficient to support a [legal] cause of action for fraud, which is satisfied with allegations of negligent conduct" (p. 56).

Interestingly, after perhaps sensing difficulties with her distinction, Dynel (2011) then qualifies it. She further proposes that the difference between "deceptive" versus "mere ignorance fostering" omissions depends "on whether a particular matter is crucial for an individual" (p. 155). She thus appears to say that the seriousness of material consequences to a receiver that may follow upon a silent omission should be considered in weighing whether the silent omission is deceptive or not (p. 155). By this criterion, then, it appears her position regarding cases 1 and 2 would change, and she *would* view the bystander's silences in these cases as acts of deception. It could be argued in response, however, that this position lacks parsimony. That is, some observers might reasonably object that the question of the deceptiveness of silent omissions ought not to turn on the nature or extent of the material consequences (the degree of harm) that results; they could maintain this position because the degree of harm resulting to the receivers *per se* is conceptually orthogonal to the degree of deceptiveness. Instead, these observers could assert that the issue of whether a silence is deceptive should turn on the degree to which the beliefs 'fostered' (or simply permitted) in the receiver's thinking are mistaken or inaccurate.

To take another instance, consider a case that might be considered to lie somewhere between crossing light cases 1 and 2—call it case 1.5. As before, the bystander sees that the blind person seems uncertain of her surroundings and that she may be about to step into the intersection. The bystander sees the crossing light is red when the blind person asks him, "Have I reached Colfax Avenue?" The bystander truthfully says, "Yes, you have; this is Colfax," but then neither says nor does anything more. As before, the blind person steps off the curb and is struck by a vehicle. Dynel's revised proposal is that in these 'you didn't specifically ask, so I didn't tell' situations, the omission of information, which fosters (or simply permits) a person's existing ignorance, could nonetheless be considered deceptive because the omitted information proves seriously harmful. However, this conclusion should strike us as questionable because, unlike cases 2, 3, and 4, in case 1.5 the blind person's question does not suggest that the blind person seeks to cross the street at all or that she needs to know about the color of the light. The bystander, who may have felt that she may need to know the color of the light, shifts away from this thought about what she needs to know when he hears her ask, "Have I reached Colfax Avenue?" He answers this question forthrightly; but it would be unreasonable to conclude that he *also* should have *presumed* she needed or wanted to know about the light. At least, in the context of her express question, his silence about the color of the crossing light, although it still occasions her being struck, would not seem as deceptive as his silence in case 2 or even as deceptive as that in case 1. By virtue of her question, the informational value or meaning of his silence appears to change.

Perhaps the best one can say here is that, depending upon the precise situation, the line between silent omissions that are intended to "nurture" a false belief in another (and thus are deceptive) and those which "merely foster" (or permit) ignorance can seem quite thin. Context and conversational partners' prior experience and relationship with each other (if any) can and should weigh heavily in considering what kind of silent omission is involved. At the same time, it seems important to remember that both of the bystander's silences in cases 1 and 2 are types of social acts felt by and impacting the receiver to some degree. That is to say, these silences are quite different events than the silence the blind person might experience if there was no one on the corner with her at all. In both cases 1 and 2, the presumption is that she is aware that someone is standing near to her and that this person is not speaking. On the one hand, in both cases 1 and 2 the bystander's silence certainly has the potential merely to foster her ignorance about the color of the crossing light, that is, if she has no current belief, one way or the other, about what the color may be. But, on the other hand, to the extent she may already suspect the light to be green, the bystander's silence might also nurture this false belief: she may have the reasonable expectation that the bystander, knowing she was blind, would warn if the light were red and that his silence meant the light was green.

Finally, like the 'detectability' and 'shared causal responsibility' explanations, the 'foreseeability of cognitive consequences' rationale might also seem to lead to the conclusion that the bystander's behavior in cases 1 and 2 is less deceptive than in cases 3 and 4. In cases 3 and 4 the bystander can foresee the consequences of his statements on the blind person's beliefs, yet he cannot as clearly foresee the consequences of his silence upon her beliefs in cases 1 and 2. Using this lack of foreseeability as a premise, observers advocating the 'shared causal responsibility' rationale for moral differentiation among the maxim violations would thus conclude that violations of the quantity maxim through silence or omissions are inherently less morally blameworthy than quality violations.

In sharp disagreement with all three of these rationales, other observers argue that any difference in the degree of deceptiveness involved in violations of quality versus quantity is illusory, the result of an unconscious 'omission bias' that is often supported or accompanied by mistaken beliefs about causality (e.g., Spranca et al., 1991; Barnes, 1994; Bok, 1999, 1983; Davidson, 1980; Smith, 2004). First, these observers would argue that all five of the cases introduced do involve quantity violations (omissions of information) *in relation to what we would reasonably expect the bystander to communicate in this situation, whether expressly asked or not*. Indeed, they would argue that quantity violations rather than quality violations are the essential, shared property of all verbal deception.[5] Second, these observers argue that it is precisely the juxtaposition of cases 1 and 2 against cases 3 and 4 that makes the deceptiveness of the bystander's silence in cases 1 and 2 more difficult to see—the result of a contrast effect. They argue that cases 1 and 2 will be evaluated for deceptiveness more accurately by us if they are *not* framed against cases 3 and 4, as they are here. Ultimately, this position claims that the silence of the bystander, *as a form or type of communicative response to the blind person's situation*, irrefutably becomes a causal variable or factor in whatever occurs next and does so regardless of the bystander's intention.

In particular, this argument for equivalent deceptiveness rests on the claim that the bystander's silence inevitably enters into whatever thinking about her situation the blind person is pursuing and *does so in a way that is almost certainly different than if she was simply alone on the street corner*. As such, the bystander's silence in all five cases is seen as inherently deceptive and inherently consequential to the blind person's decision making because it confounds her reasonable expectation, given her evident disability, of some intervention or clear notice that the crossing light is red. Even if the silent bystander has no legal liability for failing to volunteer information or for not answering her direct question, these observers argue, the bystander's silence becomes a causal factor in whatever happens next. Indeed, this seems to be the interpretation brought to bear upon Tiersma's (1995) termite case noted above.

Although it is not the primary purpose of this book to resolve the debate about whether quantity violations are inherently less deceptive than quality violations, I will return to further explore this debate in the final chapter by examining disclosure discourse samples from the *Amara* and *Tomlinson* cases. And more generally, what I do wish to demonstrate is that IMT's Gricean maxims can provide functionally precise and therefore quite useful categories for demonstrating whether or not contested disclosures may be deceptive for ordinary readers or "average plan participants" (29 U.S.C. § 1022 (a) and (b)). In particular, as noted, the criteria that may be pertinent for distinguishing between deceptive versus nondeceptive omissions of information in employer disclosures are not elaborated in ERISA's plain English rules; thus, what criteria ought to be applied become hotly disputed in litigation. As I hope to show in the analysis of the *Amara* and *Tomlinson* cases, courts clearly struggle with the absence of such criteria as they try to explain why certain contested disclosures do or not satisfy those rules.

To further provide context for the disclosure cases that I will examine in this book, I will here again draw upon the crossing light cases to show how the specific issue of information omission in cash balance disclosure cases, although similar in certain basic respects to the crossing light case, is also different and more complex.

To begin, the blindness of the person on the street corner might plausibly be analogized to the ignorance that many or most employees have about transitions from defined pension plans to the newer cash balance plans. In this general sense, the two cases are broadly parallel: the blind person seeking to cross the street wants to know if she may safely cross without risk of harm, and similarly, employees want to know if 'crossing' to the new cash balance plan can cause them future financial loss or harm relative to what their present plan would provide if that plan were continued. Employees on the threshold of having their pension benefits altered by a cash balance plan are arguably just as 'blind' or as handicapped as the person seeking to cross the street, unless they happen to have specialized or advanced knowledge about cash balance plans and their differences. Employees need information about the actual effects of a cash balance transition to be in a position to protect themselves; at the same time, like the blind person, they do have some responsibility to ask further questions about the transition if they feel they do not understand it; and they need to persist in asking if their questions are not answered. So far, then, the crosswalk and cash balance transition situations appear at least broadly analogous.

But there are also salient differences. The most crucial difference is that, whereas no law requires the bystander to truthfully inform the blind person about the color of the light or even to speak to her at all, ERISA requires that employers inform employees about circumstances and conditions that would cause them to lose future pension benefits, and as Chapters 2 and 3 will discuss, it does so in seemingly exhaustive terms. In particular, unlike the blind person in cases 2, 3, and 4, who understands the danger of an intersection and seems to know what she needs to ask, employees on the cusp of a cash balance transition may simply not know enough about such transitions to ask those questions critical to their future financial welfare. Theoretically, this problem for employees, that is, not knowing what they do not know, is precisely the problem that ERISA's disclosure rules were intended to address. ERISA's rules require many specific types of content in employer disclosures, and they broadly identify the kinds of employee questions that disclosures must answer. Conversely, they also itemize kinds of disclosure communication in which employers must not engage. As Chapter 2 will suggest, however, the interpretations of these rules by the federal courts vary considerably and have led to widespread doubts about the courts' willingness or ability to protect employees from misleading disclosures (Amoroso, Flagg, Polisner, Rietz, Segal, 2002; Jefferson, 2001; Forman & Nixon, 2000; Noel, 2005; Muir, 2004; Rodine, 2001; Saxinger, 2000; Sennott, 2001; Sulentic, 2007; Valenza, 2011).

In addition to the difference that employees may not know what questions to ask, analogizing cash balance transitions to the crosswalk case is problematic for several other reasons. First, the bystander appears to have no direct conflict of interest in helping the blind person to learn the color of the crossing light. That is, the bystander would not appear to lose anything by helping her nor gain anything by either ignoring or misleading her. The same cannot be said in many, if not most, contested cash balance disclosure cases. Employers wishing to convert their defined benefit plans to cash balance plans often chiefly do so to save company pension expense, and they do not want employees to quit or engage in organized protests over the future pension benefit reductions that a new cash balance plan may entail. Company bottom-line interests thus potentially conflict with cooperative, candid communication with employees.

Second, it is crucial to recognize that employers planning cash balance transitions are almost never silent about the transitions in the stark and complete way that the bystander in the street corner case is silent (i.e., in cases 1 and 2). By law, they are required to communicate with employees, to send them messages other than complete silence. And in fact in most cash balance transitions, employers do put forward large amounts of technical information, across multiple documents, for their employees to consider.

Third, unlike the bystander who has no existing or prior relationship to the blind person, it must be remembered that employers and employees are not complete strangers. Employers are involved in an ongoing relationship with their employees, one that is governed not just by ERISA's disclosure rules but also by related and complex fiduciary rules and various treasury and labor regulations, among others. Notably, because of their existing relationship with their employees and certain conflicts of interest embedded in that relationship, employers may find themselves tempted to do something like the bystander in case 3 does: they may attempt to conceal crucial omissions of information about cash balance transitions by contextualizing them with encouraging, positively valenced statements designed to increase employee trust in both the transition and in the employer as communicator. That is, just as the bystander's remark that "I think it's safe to cross" may successfully elicit the blind person's trust so that she asks no further questions, employers' encouraging remarks about effects of the cash balance transitions—even when these remarks involve no lies or demonstrably false statements—may nonetheless be calculated to induce employees not to ask the very questions that the latter need to ask for their own protection.

Ultimately, for these reasons, distinguishing whether employers are strategically omitting information versus merely allowing the maintenance of inaccurate beliefs on the part of employees can confront courts in cash balance transition cases with a quite subtle analytic challenge. In one or both of the recent ERISA cases to be examined in this book, the employer's disclosures omit any express statements that (a) employees' future pension benefit accrual rates will be lower as a result of transition; (b) employees' opening account balances in the new plan will be significantly less than the total value of the pension benefits they have already earned under the old plan; and (c) employees will experience lengthy wear-away periods beginning on the date of plan transition during which they will earn no additional pension benefits at all. Thus what is critical is not only investigating whether such omissions exist in the disclosure materials but also, crucially, investigating *what are the likely interacting effects produced by the context in which these omissions occur*. It is an important task of this book to try to explicate how different kinds of contexts may affect the impact of specific omissions upon employee readers' understanding. I will take up the theoretical issue of contextual effects in more detail in Chapter 3.

Indeed, despite admitting that they omitted certain express statements, employers may nonetheless argue during litigation that their required disclosures cumulatively provided sufficient 'cues' that, when properly combined by the reader, clearly imply that employees could or would experience all three of the harmful transition effects previously enumerated. In effect, employers may argue that they should have the right to avoid express statements about possible material harms if the information thereby omitted can otherwise be conveyed or constructed through implicature and inference.

THE 'AVERAGE PLAN PARTICIPANT' STANDARD

This defense has at least facial plausibility given that, under ERISA's provisions, pension reduction disclosures must be made understandable to an 'average plan participant.' Importantly, this phrase has no statutory definition and only a tentative and variable definition in the ERISA case law. Nominally, an 'average plan participant' is one who has no formal actuarial education and no professional experience in designing pension plans or assessing their relative value. But, quite obviously, there could be a wide 'grey area' encompassing plan participants who, although lacking any formal pension and actuarial training, may nonetheless have been employed in positions in benefits management or human resources. Such positions arguably would provide them with much more information about pension plans than persons who work, say, in natural gas extraction or who sell furniture for a living. Thus, where a plan participant falls on a hypothetical 'bell curve' of prior knowledge about pension plans relates both theoretically and empirically to that participant's ability to detect partial informational cues in employer disclosures and then assemble them into accurate representations (Stygall, 2010). Some disclosure readers might be able to play this game of 'connect the pieces,' whereas others—presumably those on the lower end of the pension knowledge curve—may be oblivious that such a game even exists. I will argue that IMT's Gricean maxims can be useful in demonstrating the challenges that ordinary readers face in inferring consistent meaning from disclosures that deploy the equivalent of a jigsaw puzzle with no picture on the box to guide their understanding.

For instance, in *Amara* many CIGNA plan participants who sued the corporation were in fact managerial employees, and CIGNA's business was in part underwriting pension plans for other companies. Whether or not these managerial employees could be said to be average plan participants is open to debate: collectively, as a class, they probably knew somewhat more about pension plans than plaintiff–employees in a company like El Paso Natural Gas in the *Tomlinson* case would know. However, recent research investigating Americans' retirement and financial literacy over the last decade does not offer an encouraging picture regarding how much older as well as younger employees understand about pension plan types and their associated calculations (Eckerdt & Hackney, 2002; Lusardi, 2008; Lusardi & Mitchell, 2007, 2008; Lusardi, Mitchell & Curto, 2010). For instance, Eckerdt and Hackney (2002) found that 35 percent of respondents to their survey could not provide even a guess concerning how much their pension benefits would be in general, and some 38 percent could not guess how much their retirement benefits would be reduced if they took them early. At the same time, these researchers discovered that among employees who were 10 or more years away from retirement, 45 percent could not guess how much they would receive from their defined benefit plans, and 22 percent did not know their balances in these plans. Such figures do not bode well for the knowledge that the average plan participant might have about a relatively new type of plan like cash balance plans, which first began to appear and find increasing favor among employers in the late 1980s.

This uncertainty about what knowledge the average plan participant should be assumed to possess complicates the question of whether a defendant–employer's omission of express statements are actually deceptive. In other words, in what contexts and under what conditions are omissions of express statements about plan transition effects on the part of employers deceptive? When should full responsibility for effects of such omissions be laid squarely and unequivocally on the employer's doorstep rather than at least partially on the doorstep of the receivers' inferential processes? In view of the ERISA requirements concerning disclosure, what analytic tools and concepts concerning deceptive communication should courts use to evaluate omissions for employer liability? The ERISA concept of the average plan participant does not tell us much, and this circumstance makes assessing the degree of deceptiveness involved in quality versus quantity violations a multifaceted task. As I will discuss in detail in Chapter 3, the nature of the temporal and locative contexts in which omissions occur and the potentially interacting role played by other maxim violations (i.e., relevance or clarity/manner) within the employer's disclosure documents are crucial considerations. All of these issues haunt both the *Amara* and *Tomlinson* decisions about employer pension disclosures as well as more recent cash balance transition cases, such as *Mezyk v. U.S. Bank* (2009, 2012) and *Osberg v. Foot Locker* (2012, 2014), cases for which I also prepared written reports and gave oral depositions.

4. Finally, as a fourth theoretical purpose, I draw upon the analysis of the documents in *Amara* and *Tomlinson* to revisit the question as to what linguistics generally, and the field of written discourse pragmatics specifically, might contribute to judicial decision making in disclosure cases. As the well-known legal language scholar Clark Cunningham put it in a famous three-day symposium between lawyers and linguists in 1995, "Is there any aspect of judicial decision making where the judge ought to turn to a linguist and say, 'You have better information than I do'?" (Proceedings, 1995, p. 935).

In response to this question, I will make two basic arguments. First, I will argue that the maxims can help to identify which claims alleging deceptive and inadequate disclosure can be experimentally tested using surrogate readers and thereby either be supported or rejected with empirical data. A variety of reader self-report methods can help reveal readers' understanding of disclosure documents and move decision making in these cases away from sole reliance upon judges' non-experimentally based opinions about deceptiveness and ordinary readers' comprehension (Dumas & Redish, 1999; Howald, 2006; Pressley & Afflerbach, 1995; Stratman, 1988; Stratman & Dahl, 1996). Second, I will further argue that even in the absence of experimental reader comprehension data gathered in response to the particular texts in dispute, expert witnesses' analyses using IMT and the Gricean maxims can constructively support courts' analyses of the communicative adequacy or deceptiveness of contested cash balance plan disclosures (Ainsworth, 2006; Solan, 1999). Specifically, given their fundamental congruence with ERISA's disclosure rules, I will argue that IMT and Grice's maxims can help to reveal how and why certain disclosure text practices are likely to interfere with ordinary readers' processing and comprehension.

PLAN OF THE BOOK

To set the stage for the analysis and comparison of the disclosure messages and documents in *Amara* and *Tomlinson,* two important preliminary tasks are addressed in Chapters 2 and 3.

Chapter 2 overviews the basic mechanics of cash balance plan transitions. These mechanics have a number of far-reaching effects on employee pension benefits that are counterintuitive and potentially very difficult for ordinary employees without specialized pension and actuarial knowledge to comprehend. An explanation of these mechanics is necessary to understand the arguments concerning disclosure presented by plaintiffs and defendants in these cases. Additionally, this chapter puts these mechanics into legal perspective by discussing key interpretive uncertainties that courts face in ERISA's statutory and regulatory framework when they adjudicate allegations of deceptive disclosures in cash balance conversions. A fundamental uncertainty concerns the way courts may interpret the authoritative relationship between two sets of rules: ERISA's older 'plain language' rules for Summary Plan Descriptions (SPDs) and Summaries of Material Modifications (SMMs) (29 U.S.C §1022(a) and (b); 29 C.F.R § 2520.102–1, 102–2, and 102–3; and 29 C.F.R. 2520.104(b)(3)) and more recent regulations promulgated under ERISA by the Department of the Treasury for what are known as § 204(h) notices (29 U.S.C. § 1054(h)(1)). The latter are written notices that employers must provide to their employees when they formally amend their existing pension plans to reduce significantly employees' future rate of benefit accrual. As this chapter will illustrate, some district and circuit court decisions have been sharply divided over the interpretation to be given to the relationship between ERISA's older and newer disclosure rules and, as a result, also divided over what constitutes adequate versus deceptive disclosure. In particular, interpretation as to what content or messages are required in § 204(h) notices, and what the purposes of the notices should be, has been a frequent flashpoint in cash balance conversion cases.

Chapter 3 then overviews the strengths and limitations of IMT and Grice's four maxims as tools for categorizing and describing the workings of deceptive oral communication generally and then written pension reduction disclosures specifically. In particular, it will describe the dynamic contextual relationship between violations of the quantity and the other three maxims. It does so by applying certain additional principles drawn from the persuasion, reading comprehension, and expert hindsight bias research literatures and then concludes by discussing the basic congruency of IMT and Grice's maxims with ERISA's specific pension benefit disclosure requirements.

Following these preliminary but essential tasks, in Chapters 4 and 5, respectively, I draw upon IMT and Grice's maxims to provide a detailed critical comparison of the employer disclosure messages and language that were contested in the *Amara* and *Tomlinson* cases. In Chapter 4 I argue that although the *Amara* court's analysis of CIGNA's disclosure materials is largely consistent with one that can be reached utilizing IMT and Grice's maxims, the maxims do help focus problematic aspects of the court's approach in interpreting ERISA's complex statutory framework, particularly as regards what ERISA § 204(h) requires and prohibits in a plan amendment disclosure. Consideration of the maxims could have helped the *Amara* court to appreciate that the deceptiveness of omissions (violations of quantity) can be enhanced by statements and textual elements other than those that are demonstrably shown to be affirmatively misleading statements. In particular, Chapter 4 will argue that IMT's maxims help reveal how employer statements judged to be 'materially misleading' do not necessarily also have to assert something that is positively false to be sanctioned. Instead, statements judged to be materially misleading can, as suggested in this introduction, effect deception entirely through what such statements omit. This is a problem that the *Amara* court, for all of its care in examining CIGNA's disclosures, left unsatisfactorily addressed.

In contrast, Chapter 5 argues that the court's disclosure analysis in *Tomlinson* is disturbingly deficient because the court fails to recognize the following: (a) affirmatively misleading statements in the disclosures (quality violations); (b) omissions that are materially misleading (quantity violations); (c) potent joint or interacting effects of both of these kinds of maxim violations on employees' understanding; and (d) numerous contextual and semantic ambiguities about the effects of El Paso's cash balance conversion that would seem to seriously conflict with ERISA's requirement that disclosures must be "written in a manner calculated to be understood by the average plan participant." Thus, with respect to IMT and Grice's maxims, the *Tomlinson* court's analysis of El Paso's disclosure materials appears particularly egregious, especially when compared to the analysis undertaken by the *Amara* court.

In Chapters 6 and 7 I discuss the broader implications and issues raised by my analyses of the *Amara* and *Tomlinson* disclosure documents. In Chapter 6 I discuss how, guided by IMT's Gricean maxims, one may form and then experimentally test hypotheses about contested disclosure messages and the ways average plan participants would or would not understand them. Regarding such tests, I will discuss issues potentially raised by both the U.S. Supreme Court's *Daubert* benchmarks and Federal Rule of Evidence 702 for the admission of expert testimony when experimental and non-experimental testimony are compared (*Daubert v. Merrell Dow Pharmaceutical, Inc.*,1993). To help examine these issues, I will discuss a modest but still useful experimental study that I was able to conduct on contested disclosure statements in another recent cash balance conversion case, *Mezyk v. U.S. Bank* (2009, 2012). Drawing upon this experiment I argue that experimental evidence of surrogate readers' comprehension of disclosures, when it is feasible, is to be preferred to opinions based solely upon judicial intuition regarding average plan participant readers. At the same time I will further argue that just because linguistic, communication, or reading comprehension expert testimony does *not* include experimentally obtained surrogate reader data does not mean that the expert's analytic testimony must be worthless or no different than the analyses judges alone could produce. Judges tackling the question of deceptive disclosures typically do so in terms of precedent, not only without reader experimental data in hand but also without using theoretical categories and research findings available in in the fields of written discourse pragmatics and reading comprehension that could prove helpful.

Finally, in Chapter 7 I discuss how and why IMT and the Gricean maxims could be helpful to courts faced with deciding whether or not legally required disclosures are deceptive, even in the absence of experimental data collected from an appropriate sample of surrogate readers. Here I will make several related arguments. First, I discuss implicit assumptions on the part of some courts about the greater inherent deceptiveness of quality violations in comparison with the other three non-lying maxim violations—that is, quantity, relevance, and clarity or manner. This will entail revisiting the controversy explored in this introduction over what distinguishes omissions (quantity violations) that are "merely ignorance fostering" from those that in fact are deceptive or that, once combined with other textual features, contribute to readers' deception. My main thesis here is that both the discourse context and readers' prior knowledge are demonstrably critical considerations when evaluating the potency of an omission's contribution to deception. Especially where disclosures, as under ERISA, *are specifically required to aid the comprehension of nonexpert readers*, courts need to operate on different principles and assumptions about the effect of omissions than they would if they were dealing with texts mainly aimed at expert audiences. Second, I argue that cataloging the larger or overall pattern of maxim violations in a disclosure, including the ways that different types of violations may contribute to and amplify each other, is critical to clarifying whether and to what extent deception occurs and full disclosure of material harms may be confounded. That is, the emerging pattern of violations helps one to see what the disclosure texts do and do not communicate clearly and accurately relative to the plan conversion's actual material harms. Finally, I also discuss how and why IMT and the Gricean maxims, although certainly helpful in this effort, are not sufficient for resolving questions of alleged deception in a disclosure. I discuss why these conceptual tools must be used in combination with well-established principles and research findings in the areas of reading comprehension, graphical perception, persuasion, and especially, the phenomena of expert hindsight bias.

NOTES

1 I have had access to the disclosure documents contested in both cases as a result of having prepared and submitted expert reports in both for plaintiff's counsel. In *Amara*, which is now a landmark case in pension benefit disclosure law, I also presented expert testimony in U.S. District Court of Connecticut in 2008. *Amara* is an

extraordinary case, not least because it began more than 12 years ago and, as of this writing, is still not fully resolved; the size and nature of the remedy for CIGNA's violations of federal pension disclosure law are still in dispute.

2 In this respect, ERISA differs from another landmark disclosure statute enacted just three years later, the Fair Debt Collection Practices Act of 1977 (FDCPA), which enumerates and provides specific examples of some 16 different deceptive practices or statements that must not be used by debt collection companies in the debt notices they send to consumers (Public Law No. 95–109 Stat. 874 (1977). For discussion see Griffith (2008, 2012).

3 Basic assumptions common to all of these permutations are as follows: (a) both persons have excellent hearing and speech abilities; (b) the bystander knows that the person next to him is blind because he sees that her eyes are closed and she is using her contact stick; (c) the blind person knows there is a bystander next to her—she hears him step up; (d) the bystander has normal vision; (e) the blind person is not suicidal; (f) they are complete strangers; (g) unlike some crossing lights in modern cities, the crossing light on this particular corner does not have an audible signal indicating that it is safe to cross; (h) although one or two other persons are also on the corner, they are far from the bystander and the blind person and out of earshot; and (i) both the bystander and the blind person are native speakers of the same language (English).

4 An excellent discussion of the potential significance of silence in different areas of the law is provided in Tiersma (1995).

5 Dynel (2011, pp. 139–146), in fact, seems to agree with this position in her revised proposal.

REFERENCES

Ainsworth, J. (2006). Linguistics as a knowledge domain in the law. *Drake Law Review, 54*, 651–668.

Amara v. CIGNA Corp., 559 F. Supp. 2d 192 (D. Conn. 2008).

Amara v. CIGNA Corp., 925 F. Supp. 2d 242 (D. Conn. 2012).

Amoroso, V., Flagg, D., Polisner, D., Rietz, R., & Segal, D. (2002). ABCD cash balance letter: rephrasing the question. *Enrolled Actuaries Report, 27*(3), 1–7.

Anand, V. (2000, June 26). Potential reductions weren't disclosed. *Pensions and Investments, 20*, 20.

Arbib, M., Conklin, E., & Hill, J. (1987). *From schema theory to language*. New York: Oxford University Press.

Barnes, J.A. (1994). *A pack of lies: Towards a sociology of lying*. New York, NY: Cambridge University Press.

Bartlett, F. (1932). *Remembering*. Oxford, England: Oxford University Press.

Bilello v. J.P. Morgan Chase Ret. Plan, 649 F. Supp. 2d 142 (S.D.N.Y. 2009).

Bok, S. (1999). *Lying: Moral choice in public and private life*. New York, NY: Vintage Books.

Bok, S. (1983). *Secrets: On the ethics of concealment and revelation*. New York, NY: Pantheon.

Brewer, W. (2000). Bartlett's concept of the schema and its impact on theories of knowledge representation in contemporary cognitive psychology. In S. Akiko (Ed.), *Bartlett, culture and cognition* (pp. 69–89). New York, NY: Psychology Press.

Bruce, S. (1993). *Pension claims: Rights and obligations* (2nd ed.). Salem, MA: Bureau of National Affairs (BNA) Publishers.

Burstein v. Retirement Account Plan for Employees of Allegheny Health Education Research Fund, 334 F.3d 365 (3rd Cir. 2003).

Carson, T. (2012). *Lying and deception: Theory and practice*. Oxford: University of Oxford Press.
Castelfranchi, C. and Poggi, I. (1994). Lying as pretending to give information. In H. Parret (Ed.), *Pretending to communicate* (pp. 276–279). Berlin: Mouton de Gruyter.
Charles v. Pepco Holdings, Inc., 437 F. Supp. 2d 248 (D. Del. 2006).
CIGNA Corp. v. Amara, 131 S. Ct. 2900 (2011).
In re Citigroup Pension Plan ERISA Litigation, 470 F. Supp. 2d 323 (S.D.N.Y. 2006).
Custer v. Southern New England Telephone Company, 42 Employee Benefits Cas. (BNA) 2479 (D. Conn. 2008).
Daubert v. Merrell Dow Pharmaceutical, Inc., 509 U.S. 579 (1993).
Davidson, D. (1980). Deception and division. In J. Elster (Ed.), *The multiple self* (pp. 79–92). Cambridge: Cambridge University Press.
DeScioli, P., Christner, J., & Kurzban, R. (2011). The omission strategy. *Psychological Science, 22*, 442–446.
Dumas, J., & Redish, J. C. (1999). *A practical guide to usability testing*. Exeter, UK: Intellect Books Ltd.
Dynel, M. (2011). A web of deceit: A neo-Gricean view on types of verbal deception. *International Review of Pragmatics, 3*, 139–167.
Eckerdt, J. & Hackney, J. (2002). Workers' ignorance of retirement benefits. *The Gerontologist, 4*, 543–551.
Employment Retirement Income Security Act of 1974, 29 U.S.C. § 1054(h)(1) (Matthew Bender & Company 2009).
Employment Retirement Income Security Act of 1974, 29 C.F.R. 2520.104(b)(3) (Matthew Bender & Company 2008).
Employment Retirement Income Security Act of 1974, 29 U.S.C. § 1022 (a) and (b). (Matthew Bender & Company 2007).
Employment Retirement Income Security Act of 1974, 29 C.F.R. § 2520.102–1,102–2, 102–3 (Michie 1996).
Employment Retirement Income Security Act of 1974, 29 U.S.C. §§ 1001–1461 (1982).
Engers v. AT&T and AT&T Management Pension Plan, 428 F.Supp.2d 213 (D.N.J. 2006).
Ewald, H., & Vann, R. (2008). Deception by design: Figure ground and verbal illusion in direct mail. *Journal of Business Communication, 45*(4), 430–450.
Fair Debt Collection Practices Act (FDCPA), Public Law No. 95–109, 91 Stat. 874 (1977).
Flint, Jr., G. (1995). ERISA: Reformulating the federal common law for plan interpretation. *San Diego Law Review, 32*, 955–1062.
Forman, B., & Nixon, A. (2000). Cash balance pension plan conversions. *Oklahoma City University Law Review, 25*, 379–434.
Frommert v. Conkright, 433 F. 3d 254 (2nd Cir. 2006).
Galasinski, D. (2000). *The language of deception: A discourse analytic study*. Thousand Oaks, CA: Sage Publications.
Green, S. (2001). Lying, misleading, and falsely denying: How moral concepts inform the law of perjury, fraud, and false statements. *Hastings Law Journal, 53*, 157–212.
Grice, P. (1989). *Studies in the way of words*. Cambridge, MA: Harvard University Press.
Grice, P. (1975). Logic and conversation. In P. Cole & J. Morgan (Eds.), *Syntax and semantics* (Vol. 3, pp. 41–58). New York, NY: Academic Press.
Griffith, E. (2012). The search for better communication between the debt collector and the consumer under the Fair Debt Collection Practices Act. *Kansas Law Review* 61, 179–228.
Griffith, E. (2008). The peculiarity of language in the debt collection process: The impact of the Fair Debt Collection Practices Act. *Wayne Law Review, 54*, 673–734.
Gumperz, J. (1999). On interactional sociolinguistic method. In S. Sarangi & C. Roberts (Eds.), *Talk, work, and institutional order: Discourse in medical, mediation, and management settings* (pp. 453–471). Berlin, Germany: Mouton de Gruyter.
Gumperz, J., & Levinson, S. (1996). *Rethinking linguistic relativity*. Cambridge, England: Cambridge University Press.

Hancock, J., Curry, L., Goorha, S., & Woodworth, M. (2008). On lying and being lied to: A linguistic analysis of deception in computer-mediated communication. *Discourse Processes, 45*, 1–23.

Hirt v. Equitable Retirement Plan for Employees, Managers & Agents, 441 F. Supp. 2d 516 (S.D.N.Y. 2006).

Howald, B. (2006). Comparative and non-comparative forensic linguistic analysis techniques: Methodologies for negotiating the interface of linguistics and evidentiary jurisprudence in the American judiciary. *University of Detroit Mercy Law Review, 83*, 285–327.

Jefferson, R. (2001). Striking a balance in the cash balance plan debate. *Buffalo Law Review, 49*, 513–575.

Levi, J., Cunningham, C., Bennett, R., Eskridge, W., Greenawalt, K., Moore, M., & Sadock, J. (1995). Northwestern University/Washington University Law and Linguistics Conference. *Washington University Law Quarterly, 73*(3), 769–970.

Lusardi, A. (2008). Financial literacy: An essential tool for informed consumer choice. *National Bureau of Economic Research*. Retrieved April 12, 2015, from http://www.nber.org/papers/w14084 doi: 10.3386/w14084

Lusardi, A., & Mitchell, O. (2008). Planning and financial literacy: How do women fare? *American Economic Review, 98*(2), 413–417.

Lusardi, A., & Mitchell, O. (2007). Financial literacy and retirement preparedness: Evidence and implications for financial education. *Business Economics, 42*(1), 35–44.

Lusardi, A., Mitchell, O., & Curto, V. (2010). Financial literacy among the young. *Journal of Consumer Affairs, 44*(2), 358–380.

Mandler, J. (1984). *Stories, scripts, and scenes: Aspects of scheme theory*. Hillsdale, NJ: Lawrence Erlbaum.

McCornack, S.A. (2008). Information manipulation theory. In L.A. Baxter & D.O. Braithewaite (Eds.), *Engaging theories in interpersonal communication: Multiple perspectives* (pp. 215–226). Thousand Oaks, CA: Sage Publications.

McCornack, S.A. (1997). The generation of deceptive messages: Laying groundwork for a viable theory of interpersonal deception. In J.O. Greene (Ed.), *Message production: Advances in communication theory* (pp. 91–126). Hillsdale, NJ: Lawrence Erlbaum.

McCornack, S.A. (1992). Information manipulation theory. *Communication Monographs, 59*, 1–16.

McCornack, S.A., Levine, T.R., Solowczuk, K.A., Torres, H.I., & Campbell, D.M. (1992). When the alteration of information is viewed as deception: An empirical test of information manipulation theory. *Communication Monographs, 59*, 17–29.

Mezyk v. U.S. Bank Pension Plan, 48 Employee Benefits Cas. (BNA) 1118 (S.D. Ill. 2009).

Mezyk v. U.S. Bank Pension Plan, 2012 U.S. Dist. LEXIS 97762 (S.D. Ill. 2012).

Muir, D.M. (2004). Counting the cash: Disclosure and cash balance plans. *The John Marshall Law Review, 37*, 849–901.

Muir, D.M. (1999). The plan amendment trilogy: Settling the scope of the Settlor doctrine. *The Labor Lawyer, 15*, 205–229.

Noel, A.B. (2005). The future of cash balance plans: Inherently illegal or a viable pension option? *Alabama Law Review, 56*, 899–91.

Ornatowski, C. (1998). 2 + 2 = 5 if 2 is large enough: Rhetorical spaces of technology development in aerospace engine testing. *Journal of Business and Technical Communication, 12*(3), 316–342.

Osberg v. Foot Locker, Inc., 907 F. Supp. 2d 527 (S.D.N.Y. 2012).

Osberg v. Foot Locker, Inc., 57 Employee Benefits Cas. (BNA) 1921 (2d Cir. 2014).

Pressley, M., & Afflerbach, P. (1995). *Verbal protocols of reading: The nature of constructively responsive reading*. Hillsdale, NJ: Lawrence Erlbaum Associates.

Register v. PNC Financial Services Group, Inc., 477 F.3d 56 (3rd Cir. 2007).

Richards v. FleetBoston Financial Corp., 427 F. Supp. 2d 150 (D. Conn. 2006).

Richgels, D.J. (1982). Schema theory, linguistic theory, and representations of reading comprehension. *The Journal of Educational Research, 76*(1), 54–62.
Rodine, J. (2001). Does the cash ever balance after conversion? An examination of cash balance pension plan conversions and ADEA claims. *Elder Law Journal, 9*, 285–311.
Sarangi, S., & Slembrouck, S. (1992). Non-cooperation in communication: A reassessment of Gricean pragmatics. *Journal of Pragmatics, 17*, 117–154.
Saxinger, D. (2000). Cash balance plans: They work for employers but do they work for employees? *The John Marshall Law Review, 34*, 345–377.
Schriver, K. (1997). *Dynamics in document design*. New York, NY: John Wiley and Sons.
Schulstad, E. (2001). ERISA disclosure decisions: A pyrrhic victory for disclosure advocates. *Indiana Law Review, 34*, 501–528.
Schultz, E. (2011). *Retirement heist: How companies plunder and profit from the nest eggs of American workers*. New York, NY: Penguin/Porfolio.
Schultz, E. (2010, April 7). AT&T fights pension suit: Potential liability for retirees' plan conversion is estimated at $2.3 billion. *Wall Street Journal*, B2.
Searle, J.R. (2001). How performatives work. In D. Vanderveken & S. Kubo (Eds.), *Essays in speech act theory* (pp. 85–107). Amsterdam: John Benjamins.
Searle, J. (1969). *Speech acts: An essay in the philosophy of language*. London: Cambridge University Press.
Sennott, D. (2001). Finding the balance in cash balance pension plans. *University of Illinois Law Review, 4*, 1059–1084.
Smith, D. (2004). *Why we lie: The evolutionary roots of deception and the unconscious mind*. New York, NY: St. Martin's Press.
Solan, L. (2010). The forensic linguist: The expert linguist meets the adversarial system. In M. Coulthard & A. Jamison (Eds.), *Routledge handbook of forensic linguistics* (pp. 395–410). New York, NY: Routledge.
Solan, L. (1999). Can the legal system use experts on meaning? *Tennessee Law Review, 66*, 1167–1199.
Spranca, M., Minsk, E., & Baron, J. (1991). Omission and commission in judgment and choice. *Journal of Experimental Social Psychology, 27*, 76–105.
Stover, M. (2001). Maintaining ERISA's balance: The fundamental business decision v. the affirmative duty to disclose proposed change. *Washington and Lee Law Review, 58*, 689–733.
Stratman, J. (1988). Contract disclaimers in ERISA summary plans: A deceptive practice? *Industrial Relations Law Journal, 10*(3), 350–380.
Stratman, J., & Dahl, P. (1996). Readers' comprehension of temporary restraining orders in domestic violence cases: A missing link in abuse prevention? *Forensic Linguistics, 3*(2), 211–231.
Stygall, G. (2010). Complex documents/average and not-so-average readers. In M. Coulthard & A. Jamison (Eds.), *Routledge handbook of forensic linguistics* (pp. 51–64). New York, NY: Routledge.
Sulentic, A. M. (2007). Secrets, lies and ERISA: The social ethics of misrepresentation and omissions in summary plan descriptions. *The John Marshall Law Review, 40*, 731–766.
Sulentic, A. M. (2000). Promises, promises: Using the parol evidence rule to manage extrinsic evidence in ERISA litigation. *Journal of Labor and Employment Law, 3*, 1–64.
Tiersma, P. M. (1990). The language of perjury: 'Literal truth,' ambiguity, and the false statement requirement. *Southern California Law Review, 63*, 373–431.
Tiersma, P., & Solan, L. (2002). The linguist on the witness stand: Forensic linguistics in American courts. *Language, 78*(2), 221–239.
Tomlinson v. El Paso Corporation and El Paso Pension Plan, 132 S. Ct. 1574 (2012).
Tomlinson v. El Paso Corporation and El Paso Pension Plan, 653 F.3d 1281 (10th Cir. 2011).
Tomlinson v. El Paso Corporation and El Paso Pension Plan, 45 Employee Benefits Cas. (BNA) 2534 (D. Colo. 2009).

Tomlinson v. El Paso Corporation and El Paso Pension Plan, 43 Employee Benefits Cas. (BNA) 1932 (D. Colo. 2008).

U.S. General Accounting Office. (2005). *Private pensions: Information on cash balance plans* (U.S. General Accounting Office, Health, Education and Human Services Division, 06–42). Washington, DC: Author.

U.S. General Accounting Office. (2000a). *Cash balance plans: Implications for retirement income* (U.S. General Accounting Office, Health, Education and Human Services Division, 00–207). Washington, DC: Author.

U.S. General Accounting Office. (2000b). *Private pensions: Implications of conversions to cash balance plans* (U.S. General Accounting Office, Health, Education and Human Services Division, 00–185). Washington, DC: Author.

Vanderveken, D., & Kubo, S. (2001). *Essays in speech act theory*. Amsterdam: John Benjamins.

Valenza, M. (2011). CIGNA v. Amara: Supreme Court resolves several ERISA claims issues while leaving others for the lower courts. *Tennessee Journal of Business Law, 13*, 139–164.

Van Swol, L., Braun, M., & Malhotra, D. (2012). Evidence for the Pinocchio effect: Linguistic differences between lies, deception by omissions, and truths. *Discourse Processes, 49*(2), 79–106.

Whitney, P. (1987). Psychological theories of elaborative inferences: Implications for schema-theoretic views of comprehension. *Reading Research Quarterly, 22*(3), 299–310.

Wiedenbeck, P. (2008). *ERISA in the Courts*. Washington, DC: Federal Judicial Center.

Wooten, J. (2004). *The Employee Retirement Income Security Act of 1974: A political history*. Berkeley, CA: University of California Press.

Zelinsky, E. (2000). The cash balance controversy. *Virginia Tax Review, 19*, 683–762.

2 The Cash Balance Conversion Controversy

Dying, but Not Dead

The basic reason for ERISA's disclosure requirements is that because pension benefits are deferred compensation for employee labor, employees must be given information about any pending pension reductions so as to decide what they wish to do going forward. For instance, after learning of pending reductions, employees nevertheless might decide to continue working for the employer while making other investments to build their retirement and offset the employer's reductions; they might make adjustments to savings plans they set up for any dependents, for example, to pay for their children's college tuitions; they might simply decide to seek employment elsewhere, (i.e., in a company that offers pension benefits like their current benefits or better ones); or they might join with fellow employees to protest the employer's pending pension reductions and try to persuade the employer to cut company costs and improve revenue in other ways. In other words, employees facing future pension reductions might try to negotiate their future pension compensation just as new potential hires to the company might do before accepting an initial employment offer. ERISA's rules requiring 'plain language' disclosure are intended to facilitate a true 'meeting of minds,' which must be present to make any contract legally binding and valid.

Prior to actually implementing conversions from one type of pension plan to another, companies prepare what are known as the official 'plan' documents. Typically these documents are extremely technical, written for and used by professional actuaries, pension benefit managers, and lawyers. They describe mathematically and in exacting detail how the conversion from the old to the new plan will work, which age and service groups of employees will be affected and when, the specific formulae needed to determine these things, as well as an array of complex assumptions and conditions placed on the use of these formulae. Plan documents must be presented to and approved by the appropriate corporate board(s) before any conversion of an existing employee pension plan can be implemented. Employees do have the right to see these technical documents, but when ERISA was passed in 1974, Congress recognized that these documents would not be readily understood by readers without professional legal, accounting, and actuarial training—readers who fall within the term 'average plan participants.' Hence, depending upon circumstances, ERISA further requires employers to prepare one or more of the following plain language disclosures, which are discussed further in later sections: Summary Plan Descriptions (SPDs), Summary of Material Modifications (SMMs), and § 204(h) notices. The goal of all of these disclosures is to force the employer to reveal information that could signal material harm to certain employees, harms that the employer, for various reasons of self-interest, might prefer to keep secret or hidden.

To understand how employer conversions of defined benefit plans to cash balance plans result in reductions to employees' future pension benefits and the attendant ERISA requirement to disclose such reductions, it is necessary first to explain the basic similarities and differences between defined pension plans and cash balance pension plans.

DEFINED BENEFIT PENSION PLANS COMPARED WITH CASH BALANCE PLANS

Starting in the 1980s, U.S. companies began to realize that the defined benefit plans they were offering their employees were becoming very expensive relative to their expected revenue growth. During the same period, labor markets were changing dramatically, and it was becoming less and less appealing for workers to stay with a single employer for most or all of their working lives. Defined benefit plans proved to be an obstacle to attracting new employees because they were not mobile pension plans; if an employee wished to leave an employer offering this type of plan, the plan assets could not be rolled over into a new pension plan account with the new employer. If the employees' old plan assets could not remain on the employer's books, the employee might have to take them as a distribution when leaving the employer and possibly pay a tax penalty on them. Cash balance plans, although often requiring less money to fund than defined benefit plans, also have the advantage of being mobile plans, and employees can roll over the plan assets earned under one employer's cash balance plan into a new cash balance account with a new employer (Forman & Nixon, 2000, pp. 393–395; Jefferson, 2001, pp. 522–539).

Let's look more closely at key similarities and differences in how the two different types of plans accrue benefits over time.

In both types of plans, the company promises workers a specific amount of pension benefit at retirement (age 67) based upon a formula. For this reason, both types of plans are technically considered 'defined benefit' plans, even though each may use rather different benefit accrual formulas. Also, in both types of plans the employer rather than the employee carries the risk of the underlying investments. The employer must establish and manage trust fund investments so that the benefits promised to workers at retirement can be paid. Thus, in both defined plans and cash balance plans, the employee does not make individual investment decisions.

A key difference between defined benefit plans and cash balance plans is the period of employment during which workers earn most of their retirement benefits. Under a defined benefit plan, most of a worker's retirement benefit is earned in the later years of his or her employment, and relatively little is earned in the early and middle years, a practice known as 'back-loading' (Forman & Nixon, 2000, p. 388). Back-loading provides a strong incentive for workers to stay with an employer for their entire careers and discourages them from changing jobs, given that they earn the greatest part of their retirement benefit in the years just preceding their normal retirement date of 67. If workers in a back-loaded plan leave before those years, they stand to lose a lot of their potential retirement benefit. In contrast, a typical cash balance plan spreads out employees' benefit accrual more or less equally over all the years they work. The plan uses a different formula to compute the employee's retirement benefit, and it typically expresses this benefit as a lump sum rather than an annually paid benefit (or annuity). Cash balance plan formulae usually have two components, a benefit credit (also called a service, pay, or work credit, usually expressed as a percentage of annual salary) and an interest credit. As Saxinger (2000) explains, "The [benefit] credit is the employer's contribution . . . and is . . . [a] specific percentage of the employee's annual compensation. The interest on [this account] compounds like the interest on a 401(k) or any other interest-bearing account such as a personal savings account held at a bank" (p. 353). As a result of this compounding interest in the cash balance account, employees' overall rate of accrual remains nearly constant over their entire period of employment.

Because of this constant rate of benefit accrual, cash balance plans are argued to be much more attractive to workers who want to change employers more often and who want to build more of their retirement while they are younger (Forman & Nixon, 2000; Jefferson, 2001; Sennott, 2001; U.S. General Accounting Office, 2000a, 2000b). Companies' desire to attract such workers has meant that conversions to cash balance plans increased dramatically over the past 25 years, with the greatest number occurring in the decade between 1990 and 2000 (U.S. General Accounting Office, 2005). As Saxinger (2000) reports, "Since the Internal Revenue Service approved the first cash balance plan in 1985 an estimated 400 to 600 mid-sized and large companies have adopted cash balance plans, covering about seven million people" (p. 349). The number of companies now offering such plans is even greater.

EFFECTS OF CASH BALANCE CONVERSIONS ON OLDER, LONGER-SERVICE WORKERS

There is a broad consensus among economists and pension specialists that employer conversions from defined benefit plans to the newer cash balance plans can be quite harmful to older, middle-age employees. The harmful effects occur in several interrelated ways, and all of these effects are present in the *Amara* and *Tomlinson* cases, which are the subjects of this study. First, when companies convert, the rate at which older, mid-career employees' benefits accrue is greatly reduced compared to the rate of accrual they would have enjoyed under the old plan, in some cases by nearly 50 percent. The large increases in employer contributions that older employees would have enjoyed in the final 5 to 10 years of their employment are lost, and these losses mean that the older, longer-service employees' benefit accrual rates (over the full period of their employment) drops sharply. Jefferson (2001) notes that under defined benefit plans,

> [i]t is not unusual for employees who spend their entire working lives with a single employer to accrue more than one half of their retirement benefits during their last years of employment, when their wages are typically highest. For this reason . . . the conversion of defined benefit plans can reduce disproportionately the expected retirement benefits of participants with greater [years of] service unless affirmative measures are taken to prevent this outcome . . . [A]n individual whose coverage changes mid-career from defined benefit plans to cash balance plans may experience the worst of both worlds. (pp. 539, 540)

As one type of protective measure, some employers converting their defined benefit plans would allow older, longer-service workers simply to remain in the old plan until they retired. Effectively, these employees would be grandparented under the old plan, whereas their younger counterparts would see their old plan accounts frozen and be forced into the new cash balance plan. Another way to protect older employees would be to take what is known as an 'A + B' approach: the older employees' defined benefit accounts would be 'frozen' as of the date of plan conversion, meaning that the employer would no longer contribute to them. The employees would be allowed to keep the assets they had earned in the old accounts, as required by ERISA. In addition, a new account under the new cash balance plan would be opened with a zero balance, also as of the date of conversion, an account which would then begin to accrue in value under the cash balance formula. The older, longer-service employees would thus immediately begin earning pension benefits anew, albeit not at the rate they would have if the old plan had simply continued. At retirement, the employee's benefit would be based upon the sum of the frozen accrued benefit under the old plan and the benefit earned under the new cash balance plan—hence, the 'A + B' designation (U.S. General Accounting Office, 2000a, 2000b, 2005).

However, in most litigated cash balance conversions, instead of adopting either of these protective measures for their older, longer-service employees, employers take a much more aggressive cost-cutting approach, known as 'the greater of *either* A *or* B.' What this means is that, on the date of retirement, the employees will *not* receive the assets they earned under the their old plan on top of the benefits earned in following years under the new cash balance plan but instead will only receive the account which has the greater value. Under this approach, like A + B, the employer also freezes older employee's defined benefit account as of the date of plan conversion and also sets up a new cash balance account. But unlike the A + B approach to conversion, which opens the new cash balance at zero, the employer instead sharply reduces (discounts) the value of the employee's opening account in the cash balance plan relative to the total value of the assets the employee accrued in the old account. For example, if the annual benefit the employee had earned under the old plan as of the date of conversion was $12,000 ($1,000 per month), the new opening account balance under the new plan might be recalculated to be only $6,400 ($533 per month)—a discount of 47 percent. This discounted value then becomes the new opening balance. Thus, unlike what occurs when persons simply transfer their assets from one bank to another, this new balance would be worth significantly less than the benefits that the employees already accrued under the old plan.[1] At the time of the CIGNA and El Paso cash balance conversions, there was nothing in ERISA explicitly prohibiting this maneuver. But for reasons discussed later in the chapter and as will be illustrated in the disclosures contested in these cases, it is a maneuver that is very confusing to ordinary employees, and employers may use various discourse stratagems to try to conceal it.

At first glance, it might seem that an A + B approach yields a worse outcome for older employees. After all, their starting balance in the new cash balance plan is zero, whereas for employees whose companies convert by using the greater of *either* A *or* B approach, the opening balance may approach half of the value of their old plan assets. But this seemingly clear advantage proves to be illusory. The reason is that because the new cash balance account will grow in value at a much slower rate than the defined benefit account would have grown during the same years, it will take the new reduced opening account balance many months to many years to return to the value of the old, frozen account balance as of the date of conversion. When employees under this conversion approach reach their retirement date, ERISA requires that employees always have a right to the full amount of benefits they have earned up to the date of plan conversion. Under the greater of *either* A *or* B approach, the employees' old plan benefits may remain greater than what they earn under the new cash balance plan for many years. Effectively, there may be a lengthy period when the older, longer-service employees are earning no new pension benefits under the cash balance plan at all, stuck in what are known as 'wear-away' periods (U.S. General Accounting Office, 2000a, 2000b, 2005). That is, until the employee's cash balance account exceeds the amount of frozen benefit already earned, the pay and interest credits that the employer records in the new account remain merely hypothetical; the employee is actually earning *nothing*. The employer benefits by not having to pay any retirement during the wear-away period, which for a number of employees in the *Amara* and *Tomlinson* cases lasted ten or more years. When the number of converted employees is in the thousands or tens of thousands, it becomes apparent how enormous the savings to the employer can be, reaching hundreds of millions of dollars.

Among companies choosing to use the greater of *either* A *or* B approach to conversion, employers' disclosure documents may tell employees that at retirement "they will receive either the full balance of their old frozen account under their defined benefit plan *or* the balance of their new cash balance plan account, whichever is greater." But at the same time they may not be clearly told that their future pension accrual rates may be significantly lower than they enjoyed under the old plan, that their opening account balances in the new cash balance plan have been reduced relative to the benefits they have already earned, nor that this reduction will place them under wear-away periods. Without clear explanation of these things, they may be led mistakenly to believe that their retirement is steadily growing from the moment a new cash balance account is established for them or even that they are earning the same level of pension benefits that they would have earned had their old plan simply been continued.

Importantly, the legality of the greater of *either* A *or* B approach to conversion was uncertain when CIGNA Corporation (in *Amara*) and El Paso Corporation (in *Tomlinson*) decided to convert their employees' pension plans, and this is the approach that both companies adopted. It was also uncertain whether reducing employees' future pension accrual rates and their opening account balances under the new cash balance plan, and then imposing wear-away periods on employees' new accounts, violated age discrimination rules and anti-cutback protections. All three of these effects occurred in the *Amara* and *Tomlinson* cases. However, as of June 2005 the greater of *either* A *or* B method became illegal. In that year Congress amended ERISA to forbid this approach. For any conversion after June 2005 employees' post-conversion benefits cannot be less than those provided under the A + B approach, and any cash balance conversion that would cause wear-away periods is prohibited (Pension Protection Act of 2006, Public Law 109–280, § 701(a); 29 U.S.C. 1054(b)(5)(B)(iii)). Nonetheless, disclosure complaint cases filed under the older ERISA rules when the greater of *either* A *or* B approach was permitted are still coming forward and pending in federal district and circuit courts. In these, employees typically allege that the employer failed to disclose (and/or made affirmative misrepresentations about) some or all of the conversion's harmful effects and left employees to believe they were earning more post-conversion pension benefits than they actually were, indeed, only to discover when they retired that they had earned little or nothing since their plans were converted.

DISCLOSURE ISSUES AND EMPLOYER RELUCTANCE

Before the law changed, employers had strong incentives for misrepresenting, minimizing, or simply not disclosing the harmful effects of the greater of *either* A *or* B approach. They might try to suppress, as far as possible, any direct or substantive comparisons of employees' existing benefits with new cash balance plan benefits. Providing such comparisons in their required disclosure documents would make employers appear to be taking away future employee benefits to save expense and improve the company's bottom line—which, of course, usually are the key reasons companies undertake a cash balance pension plan conversion in the first place. As the U.S. General Accounting Office (2005) noted in an investigation of 133 companies' pension plans, cash balance conversions resulted in reductions in median monthly retirement income ranging from $59 for conversions at age 30 up to $238 for conversions at age 50 (p. 6). If revealed, such reductions would naturally generate ill will and unrest among employees at the same time that employers are eager to prevent employees from seeking employment and better pension benefits elsewhere. Employers are tempted to construct disclosures in ways that prevent employees from complaining to company officials or engaging in disruptive grievances or lawsuits that could hurt company morale and reduce productivity.

As will be further shown in Chapter 4, in *Amara* there was ample evidence that CIGNA leadership readily seized on the theory that ERISA's rules allowed for deception by both commission and omission in their conversion disclosures. As noted in the plaintiff's brief, in a July 1996 PowerPoint presentation, CIGNA's pension benefits consultant, Mercer, touted one of the advantages of a cash balance conversion as the ability to "mask a cut in pension plan benefits" from employees. Ellen Schultz, writing in the *Wall Street Journal* in May 1999, quoted an actuary from the consulting company credited with developing the cash balance plan design: "If you decide your plan's [sic] too rich, and you want to cut back . . . changing to a different type of plan will let you do that *without being obvious about it*" (Schultz, 1999, p. C1, italics added). Similarly, Schultz quoted actuarial consultants joking at a Society of Actuaries' meeting about how employees could be fooled. One stated, "You switch to a cash-balance plan where people are probably getting smaller benefits, at least the older-longer-service people; but they are really happy and they think you are great for doing it." Another explained that "[i]t is not until they [employees] are ready to retire that they understand how little they are actually getting," to which another replied, "Right, but they're happy while they're employed" (Schultz, 1999, p. C1).

Such evidence suggests that other employers pursuing cash balance plan conversions have been tempted to engage in discourse stratagems for 'disclosing without disclosing,' that is, stratagems that superficially may appear to satisfy ERISA's disclosure rules but that also prevent employees from a fully accurate or timely understanding concerning the reductions being made to their pension benefits. For instance, instead of comparing old plan benefits with new cash balance plan benefits in a way that clearly reveals their different financial impacts on employees, employers may vaguely assure employees that they are 'always entitled to receive' the full amount of benefit they already earned under the old plan up to the date it is frozen, or that they 'can never receive less' than they earned under the old plan, but without explaining that wear-away periods will occur and why. Employers might also engage in discourse stratagems that seem to affirm without affirming the 'equality' of benefits between the old and new plans or even vaguely affirm overall improvement in benefits under the new plan without issuing meaningful or understandable qualifications.

Ordinary employees, those without actuarial or pension plan expertise and knowledge and who are faced with such messages would likely remain unaware of the accrual rate reductions, reduced opening account balances, and wear-away periods resulting from cash balance plan conversions. As a result, they may fail to seek alternative retirement investments or increase their savings and thus may be caught quite short relative to the monthly pension income they reasonably expected to have. Although some employer communication stratagems for disclosing without disclosing have been analyzed and rejected by the courts, others have exposed unresolved interpretive uncertainties within ERISA's seemingly comprehensive disclosure framework.[2] In particular, the approach to the disclosures deployed by the defendants in *Amara* and *Tomlinson* can be seen as two similar but also subtly different experiments intended to satisfy ERISA while nonetheless preventing as little employee understanding as possible of the harmful consequences that cash balance conversions involve.

A closer look at ERISA's disclosure framework will help to reveal some of the interpretive uncertainties regarding disclosure that employers may have tried to exploit.

INTERPRETIVE CONFLICTS IN ERISA'S DISCLOSURE REQUIREMENTS FOR CASH BALANCE CONVERSIONS

Recent cash balance conversion lawsuits include employees' complaints that employers failed to tell employees about the existence, size, and nature of the reductions that the conversions trigger, including the wear-away effect (e.g., *Mezyk v. U.S. Bank*, 2009, 2012; *Osberg v. Foot Locker, Inc.*, 2012, 2014). The complaints typically allege that such failure violates ERISA's disclosure requirements for SPDs and SMMs, specifically 29 U.S.C. 1022(a) and (b) and 29 C.F.R. 2520.102(a) and 102(b). Significantly, these older ERISA provisions emphasize the employer's obligation to communicate unambiguously, understandably, and comprehensively about conditions under which employees' future pension benefits might be reduced, restricted, suspended, or terminated. ERISA requires, for instance, that an SPD

> shall be written in a manner calculated to be understood by the average plan participant, and shall be sufficiently accurate and comprehensive to reasonably apprise such participants and beneficiaries of their rights and obligations under the plan . . . [It] shall contain . . . a description of the . . . circumstances which may result in disqualification, ineligibility, or denial or loss of benefits (29 U.S.C. § 1022 (a) and (b)).
>
> The format of the summary plan description shall not have the effect of misleading, misinforming, or failing to inform participants and beneficiaries. Any description of exceptions, limitations, reductions, and other restrictions of plan benefits shall not be minimized, rendered obscure, or otherwise made to appear unimportant. Such exceptions, limitations, reductions or restrictions of plan benefits shall be described or summarized in a manner not less prominent than the style, captions, printing type, and prominence used to describe or summarize plan benefits. The advantages and disadvantages of the plan shall be presented without either exaggerating the benefits or minimizing the limitations. The description or summary of restrictive plan provisions need

> not be disclosed in the summary plan description in close conjunction with the description or summary of benefits, provided that adjacent to the benefit description the page on which the restrictions are described is noted. (29 C.F.R. § 2520.102–2(b))

Regarding SMMs, ERISA 1022(a) similarly states, “A summary of any material modification in the terms of [a] plan . . . shall be written in a manner calculated to be understood by the average plan participant. ” (29 U.S.C. § 1022(a)).

In recent contested plan conversions, employers typically assert either that they have met these disclosure requirements in certain messages or, for reasons to be discussed shortly, that these requirements do not apply to cash balance plan conversions. In contrast, employees typically argue that cash balance plan conversions do not constitute any sort of exception to these rules. They often point to the following broadly framed Congressional testimony at the time these requirements were drafted:

> Descriptions of plans furnished to employees should be presented in a manner that an average and reasonable worker participant can understand . . . It is grossly unfair to hold an employee accountable for acts which disqualify him from benefits, if he had no knowledge of these acts, or if these conditions were stated in a misleading or incomprehensible manner in plan booklets. Subcommittee findings were abundant that an average plan participant, even where he has been furnished an explanation of his plan provisions, often cannot comprehend them because of the technicalities and complexities of the language used . . . Experience has . . . demonstrated a need for a more particularized form of reporting so that the individual participant knows exactly where he stands with respect to the plan—what benefits he may be entitled to, what circumstances may preclude him from obtaining benefits, [and] what procedures he must follow to obtain benefits. (H.R. Rep. No. 533, 93rd Cong., 1st Sess., 8 (1973); reprinted in 1974 U.S. Code Cong. & Admin. News 4639, 4649)

Along with provisions governing SPDs and SMMs, ERISA § 204(h), which was added in 1986 and amended in 2001, has also become a flashpoint in contested conversions (29 U.S.C. 1054(h)). Both the original and later versions of § 204(h) require employers to notify employees in advance if the employer is about to amend a pension plan so as to cause a reduction in employees’ future pension benefit accruals, that is, relative to the accruals that the existing pension plan would provide. Importantly, however, the two versions of § 204(h) differ in what they say about this ‘notice’ requirement.

The original version in effect from 1986 to 2001 was passed as part of the Consolidated Omnibus Budget Reconciliation Act of 1985 (Consolidated Omnibus Budget Reconciliation Act of 1985, Title XI, § 11006, 100 Stat. 82, 1986). It states that that a pension plan “may not be amended so as to provide for a significant reduction in the rate of future benefit accrual, unless after adoption of the plan amendment and not less than 15 days before the effective date of the plan amendment, the plan administrator provides a written notice, *setting forth the plan amendment and its effective date* . . . to each participant in the plan (p. 243, italics added)." Temporary implementing regulations issued by the Treasury Department for this original version became effective in 1996 and stated that regardless of how the plan amendment is "set forth" in the notice, it must be "written in a manner calculated to be understood by the average plan participant," just as is required for SPDs and SMMs under ERISA (26 C.F.R. § 1.411(d)-6T, Q&A-10, 1996).

Providing somewhat further clarification as to the content of the notice, the Treasury regulations did not require the notice to go so far as to "explain *how the individual benefit* of each [plan] participant . . . might be affected by the [plan] amendment" (26 C.F.R. § 1.411(d)-6T, Q&A-10, 1996, italics added). Notably, this addition to the regulations has sometimes been argued by employers to mean that disclosures about reductions need not be specific as to the amount of benefit reductions or the mechanism by which they are implemented, such as wear away. But the fact that disclosures need not be tailored *to individual* participants' specific circumstances does not necessarily mean that the range of reductions and the methods used to implement reductions for different *types* (or groups) of employees need not be disclosed. Indeed, long before plan conversions are implemented, most companies engaging in cash balance conversions have precisely calculated the amount of benefit reduction and length of wear-away periods for employees in terms of their age and years of service. As will be shown, both CIGNA and El Paso Natural Gas Corporation calculated how much the reduction to participants' future benefit accrual rate would be and what the length of the wear-away period would be for groups of employees of different ages and years of service. Thus they potentially could be much more clear and specific in their disclosures than they were about the scope and effects of reductions without going so far as drafting individualized disclosures for each employee.

The version of § 204(h) currently in effect was passed as part of the Economic Growth and Tax Relief Reconciliation Act (EGTRRA) in 2002 (Public Law 107–16, § 659, 115 Stat. 38, 2001). This version primarily came about due to the complaints about employers' disclosure documents in cash balance conversions. The current version states that

> [a] pension plan may not be amended so as to provide for a significant reduction in the rate of future benefit accrual unless the plan administrator provides [a] notice . . . to each applicable individual . . . [This] notice . . . shall be written in a manner calculated to be understood by the average plan participant and . . . shall provide *sufficient information . . . to allow applicable individuals to understand the effect of the plan amendment*. (p. 140, italics added)

The current corresponding Department of Treasury regulations provide extensive elaboration as to what this requirement means in cash balance plan conversions. For instance, a § 204(h) notice must "apprise the applicable individual of the significance of the notice [itself];" it must permit that individual "to determine the approximate magnitude of the reduction for that individual" and "to determine which reductions are expected to apply to that individual" (26 C.F.R. § 54.4980F-1, Q&A-11, 2009). Additionally, this same regulation states that "[i]llustrative examples are in any event required . . . for any change from a defined benefit formula to a cash balance formula or a change that results in a period of time during which there are no accruals (or minimal accruals) with regard to normal retirement benefits or an early retirement subsidy (a wear-away period)." Finally, despite what might seem to be already manifestly clear in ERISA's provisions for SPDs and SMMs, § 204(h) notices "may not include materially false or misleading information (or omit information so as to cause the information provided to be misleading)."

As can be seen, then, the difference between the earlier and later versions of § 204(h) appears to turn on the amount and kind of information about benefit reductions required of the employer. The latest version obligates the employer to provide a detailed view of the *effects* of a cash balance conversion on employees' future benefit accruals, including any suspension of employer pension contributions during wear-away periods. It also details a requirement to provide an explicit, fair comparison between old and new plan benefits.

By contrast, what kind of information about benefit reductions the earlier version requires appears less clear. In particular, what information does the earlier version require when it states that a § 204(h) notice must "set forth the plan amendment"? How should the latter phrase be interpreted, given that the original purpose of the § 204(h) requirement was to inform participants in advance of significant reductions to their pension benefit accrual rate if such was an effect of the plan amendment? Given this underlying purpose, on what basis can one say that the phrase "setting forth the plan amendment" allows an employer to omit any and all mention of benefit accrual rate reductions and wear-away periods during which employees receive no benefits?

At least a half dozen conversion cases arising under the original 1986 version have confronted this issue, and they exhibit striking disharmony over what it means to "set forth [a] plan amendment" (*Register v. PNC Financial Services Group, Inc.*, 2007; *Bilello v. JPMorgan Chase Ret. Plan*, 2009; *Custer v. Southern New England Telephone Company*, 2008; *In re Citigroup Pension Plan ERISA Litigation*, 2006; *Hirt v. Equitable Retirement Plan for Employees, Managers & Agents*, 2006; *Amara v. CIGNA Corp.*, 2008). In *Register* (2007), *Bilello* (2009), and *Custer* (2008), for instance, the courts appear to interpret the original version as having a narrow scope much at odds with ERISA's earlier disclosure rules (i.e., ERISA §102). These decisions construe the employer's requirement to "[set] forth the plan amendment" as merely requiring employers to describe how the new cash balance plans work. In particular, they presume that the complicated conversion methods (i.e., the greater of *either* A *or* B approach) and the reductions resulting from them will somehow be clear from mere descriptions of how cash balance accounts increase from the accumulation of pay and interest credits. These courts further concluded that under the original version of § 204(h), employers do not need to *directly* describe *any* effects of the conversion on employees' benefits, including reductions to employees' benefit accrual rate, despite the fact that § 204(h) notices must be "written in a manner calculated to be understood by the average plan participant."

In contrast, decisions in *Amara* (2008), *Hirt* (2006), and *In re Citigroup* (2006) clearly reject such a narrow interpretation of the employer's requirement to "[set] forth the plan amendment." These decisions exhibit an interpretive approach that looks to the larger history and context of ERISA's earlier disclosure rules for guidance. They variously interpret the employer's requirement to "[set] forth the plan amendment" as involving more than simply explaining how employees' new cash balance accounts grow in value. At the same time, these courts also recognize, in varying degrees, the importance of the Treasury Department requirement that § 204(h) notices be "written in a manner calculated to be understood by the average plan participant." And further, in view of this particular requirement, they imply that these notices must include specific messages clearly indicating future benefit reductions will result from plan conversion.

A closer look at the reasoning in the divergent decisions in *Bilello* and *Hirt* can bring this interpretive conflict over the earlier (1986) version of the § 204(h) requirement into sharper relief. In *Bilello*, the plaintiffs argued that defendant J. P. Morgan Chase's notices for plan amendments added in 1989 and 1997 failed to warn them of a significant reduction to their future benefit accrual. Citing the earlier *Register* decision from the third circuit, however, the court rejected the plaintiff's argument, reasoning that "[b]y its plain language, the version of ERISA § 204(h) in place at the time that the notices were issued, requires that the notice include only the 'amendment' and its 'effective date,' not its effect on benefit accrual" (p. 13). Without discussing in its opinion any of the discourse contained in the notices themselves, the *Bilello* court summarily concluded that the defendants' notices "satisfy this standard" (p. 13). The court then further faulted the plaintiffs for failing to "explain how a notice of an amendment and its effective date, when that amendment could reduce benefit accrual, is necessarily not a notice of reduction, as it notifies participants of new terms that could affect their accrual"(p. 14). Effectively, the court in its opinion undertook no analysis of the disclosure texts while at the same time presuming that "average plan participants" could somehow infer the existence of benefit reductions from them despite the lack of any explicit mention of such.

With respect to its interpretation of § 204(h) itself, this decision and its reasoning appear problematic in two ways. First, how the court determined the plain meaning of the phrase "set forth the plan amendment" is unclear. The court simply declares the phrase to be "clear on its face" and offers no exegesis regarding its meaning at all (p. 14). In particular, the court does not say why or how the statutory requirement to "set forth [a] plan amendment" necessarily excludes the requirement to report that benefit reductions will occur when the full wording of § 204(h) makes it clear that the section's purpose is to notify participants of reductions to their future pension benefits. Indeed, the full wording of § 204(h) indicates that it is precisely the occurrence of reductions stemming from a pension plan amendment—and nothing else—that triggers the employer's obligation to provide the notice:

> [A] plan may not be amended *so as to provide for a significant reduction in the rate of future benefit accrual*, unless, after the adoption and not less than 15 days before the effective date of the plan amendment, the plan administrator provides a written notice, setting forth the plan amendment and its effective date (Consolidated Omnibus Budget Reconciliation Act of 1985, Title XI, § 11006, 100 Stat. 82, 1986, p. 243, italics added)

When viewed in the context of the entire amendment, it can be readily seen how the *Bilello* court divorces its interpretation of the phrase "setting forth the plan amendment" from the explicitly stated purpose of § 204(h), appearing to stand that purpose on its head.

Second, the court also appears to ignore the fact that one of the two contested J. P. Morgan Chase plan amendments was added in 1997. Before that year, as already noted, the Treasury Department already required that, to satisfy § 204(h), the amendment notice must be "written in a manner calculated to be understood by the average plan participant." Yet the court makes no mention of this regulatory standard, does not evaluate the disclosure in light of it, and appears instead to evaluate the company's 1997 notice with the same restrictive standard that it used to evaluate the 1988 notice.

A much different approach to interpreting the 1986 version of § 204(h) is visible in *Hirt*. In *Hirt* the court rejected defendant Equitable's notice of a 1990 pension plan amendment that caused significant reductions in the future rate of employees' pension benefit accruals, again, through conversion to a cash balance plan. The reasoning that the *Hirt* court used in nullifying Equitable's 1990 plan amendment clashes sharply with that seen in *Bilello*. The court reasoned that the 1990 notice and a "Benefits Update" sent along with it "did not themselves provide . . . descriptive details of the Cash [Balance] Account or interest rate . . . [and] did not offer a comparison of benefits under the Cash Balance Plan to those under the former plan" nor did it notify participants that the Cash Balance Plan would "significantly reduce the rate of benefit accruals" (p. 62). In particular, the court in *Hirt* interprets the 1986 statutory phrase "setting forth a plan amendment" both in view of the stated purpose of § 204(h) and also in view of ERISA's other rules requiring disclosure of pension benefit reductions. Indeed, whereas the *Bilello* court implies that employees should be able to figure out on their own from a description of cash balance plan mechanics that their future benefits could be reduced, the *Hirt* court reasons instead that "[a] notice is intended to give fair warning and fails to do so if it is cryptic, or requires research beyond the document itself" (p. 64), adding, importantly, that a notice should not require employees to "[perform] sophisticated calculations and comparisons" to learn that reductions are being effected (p. 63). The *Hirt* court further reasons that the "§ 204(h) requirement of a 'written notice setting forth the plan amendment,' as it read in 1990, implies *that the material terms of the plan amendment must be in the notice itself* and not requiring [sic] piecing together from other written documents and oral statements" (p. 64, italics added).

The *Hirt* court then adds that the later, more elaborated 2001 version of § 204(h) simply makes "explicit that which was implicit in the earlier iteration" (p. 64). To bolster this interpretation, the court approvingly cites the *Davidson v. Canteen Corp.* (1992) decision in the seventh circuit, which had stressed "the obvious common sense behind [section] 204(h)" as it existed in 1990.

Significantly, embedded in this judicial conflict over the interpretation of the phrase "setting forth a plan amendment" is the linguistic question of what it means to deceive by omission. On its face, the question as to whether certain information has been omitted or not in a document may seem straightforward and dichotomous: required information is *either* in a disclosure *or* it is not, and making this determination should seemingly present no difficulty to judges. As noted, however, the *Billelo* decision makes this understanding problematic. Although acknowledging that J.P. Morgan's notices contained no direct or explicit references to benefit accrual reductions, the court proposes nevertheless that the company did not "omit" this information because notice readers should have been able to infer such reductions through the explanation of cash balance plan mechanics, specifically the accrual of pay credits and interest credits. At the same time, the court clearly felt it was not *their* task to explain through analysis of the disclosure texts how such inferences really could be drawn by average plan participants. Indeed, regardless of whether *Billelo* or *Hirt* is more legally sound, missing from both court opinions is a careful analysis of the allegedly deceptive disclosure statements that the defendant companies were making in relation to the larger discourse context and stream of company communication within which these statements appear. The temporal and locative context in which contested disclosure statements are presented to readers must be considered when evaluating their likely impact upon readers and how readers might realistically understand them. Neither decision tries to trace, even as hypotheses, the inferences that readers might be able to construct from disclosure statements regarding the impact of the plan amendments on their future benefits in comparison with their old (existing) benefits.

As the theoretical and empirical research literature investigating deceptive language and communication robustly demonstrates, the reality is that there are many ways that deception by omission can occur, and, crucially, the question of the effect of such omissions upon readers' comprehension can never be wholly separated from the effects of information that is presented (Carson, 2012; DeScioli, Christner, & Kurzban, 2011; Dynel, 2011; Hancock, Curry, Goorha, & Woodworth 2008; Galasinski, 2000; Sarangi & Slembrouck, 1992; Shuy, 1998; Spranca, Minsk, & Baron, 1991; Tiersma, 1990, 1995). In other words, the omission of information does not occur in a vacuum but rather always in relation to some surrounding discourse context that may condition the effect of the omitted information itself.

As a possible approach to this problem in analysis, the next chapter will examine the strengths and limitations of IMT and the Gricean maxims as a heuristic framework for identifying and distinguishing different types of deceptive communication and evaluating the effects of each. A particular focus of this review will be to suggest how IMT can help make sense of the dynamic contextual relationship between *deception by commission* and *deception by omission*, a relationship that, from the foregoing discussion, appears to be a recurring issue in ERISA cash balance plan disclosure cases.

NOTES

1 In many cases, this reduction in the employees' opening account balance occurs because this new value is not expressed as an annuity (i.e., an annual amount the employee receives once retired) but instead as a lump sum payment. ERISA section 203(e) provides guidelines for making this lump sum valuation, but some company opening account balance recalculation methods remain controversial among lawyers and actuaries because of varying interest rate assumptions (Sennott, 2001). Additionally, companies may also reduce the employee's opening cash balance account by eliminating early retirement subsidies that are often provided by defined-benefit plans. As Forman and Nixon (2000) explain, "[A] worker who has already earned an early retirement subsidy prior to the conversion will have an accrued benefit under the old plan that is higher than the opening balance of her cash balance account" (p. 404). Effectively, and counterintuitively from the standpoint of an average employee lacking a technical or expert understanding of plan conversions, the new pension benefit account balance may not equal the full value of the benefits the employees had already accrued as of the conversion date under the old plan.

2 For example, at an earlier point in ERISA disclosure litigation, the courts prohibited employers' use of reservation of rights disclaimers (RORs) in their required SPDs. Such RORs typically state that any conflict in pension benefit terms between the official plan documents and the SPD would be resolved by applying the terms in the official plan documents, even though employees rarely have ready access to the latter and the official documents are not "calculated to be understood by the average plan participant." In *Glocker v. W. R. Grace & Co.* (1992), for instance, the court held that "where the Plan [language] favors the employer [and the SPD language favors the employee], the employer cannot invoke the Plan by relying on a disclaimer in the [SPD] that, contrary to the intent of Congress, designates the Plan as the controlling document" (pp. 542–543). See also *Burstein v. Retirement Account Plan for Employees of Allegheny Health Education Research Fund* (2003).

REFERENCES

Amara v. CIGNA Corp., 559 F. Supp. 2d 192 (D. Conn. 2008).
Bilello v. JPMorgan Chase Ret. Plan, 649 F. Supp. 2d 142 (S.D.N.Y. 2009).
Burstein v. Retirement Account Plan for Employees of Allegheny Health Education Research Fund, 334 F.3d 365 (3rd Cir. 2003).
Carson, T. (2012). *Lying and deception: Theory and practice*. Oxford: University of Oxford Press.
In re Citigroup Pension Plan ERISA Litigation, 470 F. Supp. 2d 323 (S.D.N.Y. 2006).
Consolidated Omnibus Budget Reconciliation Act of 1985, Title XI, § 11006, 100 Stat. 82 (1986).

Custer v. Southern New England Telephone Company, 42 Employee Benefits Cas. (BNA) 2479 (D. Conn. 2008).
Davidson v. Canteen Corp., 957 F. 2d 1404, 1408 (7th Cir., 1992).
Department of Treasury, Internal Revenue Service, 26 C.F.R. § 1.411(d)-6T, Q&A-10 (Matthew Bender & Company, 1996).
Department of Treasury, Internal Revenue Service, 26 C.F.R. § 54.4980F-1, Q&A-11 (Matthew Bender & Company, 2009).
DeScioli, P., Christner, J., & Kurzban, R. (2011). The omission strategy. *Psychological Science, 22*, 442–446.
Dynel, M. (2011). A web of deceit: A neo-Gricean view on types of verbal deception. *International Review of Pragmatics, 3*, 139–167.
Economic Growth and Tax Relief Reconciliation Act, Public Law 107–16, § 659, 115 Stat. 38 (2001).
Employment Retirement Income Security Act of 1974, 29 U.S.C. 1054(h) (Matthew Bender & Company, 2009a).
Employment Retirement Income Security Act of 1974, 29 U.S.C. 1054(b)(5)(B)(iii)) (Mathew Bender & Company 2009b).
Employment Retirement Income Security Act of 1974, 29 U.S.C. § 1022 (a) and (b) (Mathew Bender & Company 2007).
Employment Retirement Income Security Act of 1974, 29 C.F.R. § 2520.102–1,102–2, 102–3 (Michie 1996).
Forman, B., & Nixon, A. (2000). Cash balance pension plan conversions. *Oklahoma City University Law Review, 25*, 379–434.
Galasinski, D. (2000). *The language of deception: A discourse analytic study*. Thousand Oaks, CA: Sage Publications.
Glocker v. W.R. Grace & Co., 974 F.2d 540 (4th Cir. 1992).
Hancock, J., Curry, L., Goorha, S., & Woodworth, M. (2008). On lying and being lied to: A linguistic analysis of deception in computer-mediated communication. *Discourse Processes, 45*, 1–23.
Hirt v. Equitable Retirement Plan for Employees, Managers & Agents, 441 F. Supp. 2d 516 (S.D.N.Y. 2006).
Jefferson, R. (2001). Striking a balance in the cash balance plan debate. *Buffalo Law Review, 49*, 513–575.
Mezyk v. U.S. Bank Pension Plan, 48 Employee Benefits Cas. (BNA) 1118 (S.D. Ill. 2009).
Mezyk v. U.S. Bank Pension Plan, 2012 U.S. Dist. LEXIS 97762 (S.D. Ill. 2012).
Osberg v. Foot Locker, Inc., 907 F. Supp. 2d 527 (S.D.N.Y. 2012).
Osberg v. Foot Locker, Inc., 57 Employee Benefits Cas. (BNA) 1921 (2d Cir. 2014).
Pension Protection Act of 2006, Public Law No. 109–280, § 701(a), 120 Stat. 981 (2006).
Register v. PNC Financial Services Group, Inc., 477 F.3d 56 (3rd Cir. 2007).
Sarangi, S. K., & Slembrouck, S. (1992). Non-cooperation in communication: A reassessment of Gricean pragmatics. *Journal of Pragmatics, 17*, 117–154.
Saxinger, D. (2000). Cash balance plans: They work for employers but do they work for employees? *The John Marshall Law Review, 34*, 345–377.
Schultz, E. (1999, May 5). Actuaries become red-faced over recorded pension talk. *Wall Street Journal*, C1.
Sennott, D. (2001). Finding the balance in cash balance pension plans. *University of Illinois Law Review, 4*, 1059–1084.
Shuy, R. (1998). *Bureaucratic language in government and business*. Washington, DC: Georgetown University Press.
Spranca, M., Minsk, E., & Baron, J. (1991). Omission and commission in judgment and choice. *Journal of Experimental Social Psychology, 27*, 76–105.
Tomlinson v. El Paso Corp. 43 Employee Benefits Cas. (BNA) 1932 (D. Colo. 2008).
Tiersma, P.M. (1995). The language of silence. *Rutgers Law Review, 48*, 1–99.
Tiersma, P. M. (1990). The language of perjury: 'Literal truth,' ambiguity, and the false statement requirement. *Southern California Law Review, 63*, 373–431.

U.S. General Accounting Office. (2005). *Private pensions: Information on cash balance plans*. (U.S. General Accounting Office, Health, Education and Human Services Division, 06–42). Washington, DC: Author

U.S. General Accounting Office. (2000a). *Cash balance plans: Implications for retirement income* (U.S. General Accounting Office, Health, Education and Human Services Division, 00–207). Washington, DC: Author.

U.S. General Accounting Office. (2000b). *Private pensions: Implications of conversions to cash balance plans* (U.S. General Accounting Office, Health, Education and Human Services Division, 00–185). Washington, DC: Author.

U.S. House of Representatives Report No. 93–533 (1973).

3 Strengths and Limitations of Information Manipulation Theory and Grice's Maxims for Explicating Deceptive Communication in ERISA Disclosures

Drawing upon the seminal work of language philosopher Paul Grice and his cooperative principle (CP) of conversation, IMT has evolved as a useful heuristic for identifying the fundamental ways communicators may manipulate information within their messages to deceive their receivers (Grice, 1975, 1989; McCornack, 1992, 2008). Grice's CP states that, as communicators, we should "make our conversational contribution[s] such as [are] required, at the stage at which [they] occur, by the accepted purpose or direction of the talk exchange in which [we] are engaged" (Grice, 1975, p. 45). To specify further what is meant by this normative principle, Grice formulated four maxims which, when observed, facilitate intelligible, efficient, and constructive understanding among communicating parties.[1] As presented in the introduction, these are the maxims of quantity, quality, relation (or relevance), and manner (or clarity). Importantly, there is no indication that Grice himself thought of these maxims as constituting a theory of deception; he did not hypothesize, for instance, that these four maxims exhaust the possible ways in which verbal deception can occur. Rather, constructing such a theory based upon the maxims has been the primary goal of IMT researchers. Indeed, the violation of one or more of these maxims is better viewed as a necessary—but not sufficient—condition for determining whether or not a message is deceptive. In ordinary conversation, communicators can and often do violate one or more of these maxims and still communicate cooperatively and truthfully. They may do so through the use of conversational implicatures, that is, through verbal, nonverbal, and contextual cues that signal to the receiver that the maxim violation literally or seemingly committed by the communicator is not to be construed as an attempt at noncooperation or deception (Thomas, 1985).

For example, suppose that you and I are longtime friends, and we both just attended a university graduation. After the ceremonies are concluded, you ask me what I thought of the president's speech to the assembled graduates, to which you observed me listening carefully. I might stare blankly at you and reply, "What speech?" On the surface, this response appears noncooperative, seeming to deny that I witnessed the president speaking or that I paid any attention to it. My literal response thus violates the maxims of both quality and clarity. But you nevertheless recognize immediately that, despite the noncooperative character of my literal reply, I am expressing my complete disdain for the speech we heard. As McCornack, Levine, Solowczuk, Torres, and Campbell (1992) explain, "When the surface form of a received message deviates from [receiver] expectations, listeners assume that, contrary to appearances, the principles [of cooperative conversation] are being adhered to at some deeper level" (p. 18). Of course, conversational implicatures may be more or less obvious to receivers, and when they are obvious, they are termed 'flouts,' which as in the preceding example, often project humor or irony (or both) on the part of the communicator. However, when communicators' statements violate one or more of the maxims but do not generate readily apparent or understandable implicatures, the communicator's violation of a maxim is said to become masked or covert, and noncooperation or deception may result. As McCornack et al. (1992) summarize, "Deceptive messages are 'deceptive' in that, although they deviate from the [Gricean] principles underlying conversational understanding, the departures remain veiled. Listeners are misled by their belief that speakers are behaving in a cooperative fashion" (p 18).

In developing IMT, McCornack (1992, 2008) theorizes that the maxims constitute four recurrent dimensions along which information can be manipulated, separately or in combination, to produce deceptive messages. Although IMT and its reliance on these maxims is not without its critics, including McCornack himself (e.g., Buller & Burgoon, 1996a, 1996b; Galasinski, 2000;McCornack, 1997, 2008; Yeung, Levine, & Nishiyama, 1999), its chief promise has been to provide a comprehensive heuristic framework for identifying fundamentally different kinds of deceptive information manipulation in communicators' messages, particularly during conversation. McCornack (1992) argues that these four dimensions can account more parsimoniously for the wide range of deceptive information manipulation types described by earlier researchers (see also Galasinski, 2000, pp. 17–33). In particular, McCornack asserts that IMT "provides an account of how exactly deceptive messages deceive" (2008, p. 219). In a series of carefully reported experiments, McCornack and his colleagues as well as some others have provided interesting initial empirical support for his central thesis that violation of one or more of the maxims is inevitable in deceptive messages and also for the thesis, discussed in the introduction, that the nature and degree of deceptiveness (or dishonesty) of the violations can be reliably distinguished by observers (Carson, 2012; DeScioli, Christner, & Kurzban, 2011; Green, 2001; Hancock, Curry, Goorha, & Woodworth, 2008; Hubbell, Chory-Assad, & Medved, 2005; McCornack, Levine, Morrison, & Lapinski, 1996; McCornack et al., 1992; Spranca, Minsk, & Baron, 1991; cf., Jacobs, Brasher, & Dawson, 1996; Yeung et al., 1999).

The potential usefulness of the four maxims in explicating the workings of allegedly deceptive pension disclosure messages can be made apparent by more carefully examining each maxim in turn.

First, when deceptively violating the maxim of quantity, a communicator fails to provide all of the information pertinent to a receiver's request or reasonable expectation and, of critical importance, provides no signal suggesting that such information may be being withheld. For either receivers or third-party observers to establish that a violation of this maxim has occurred, we would need empirically verifiable evidence that the allegedly deceptive communicator possessed the withheld information *and* understood its pertinence to the receiver. Such covert violations of the quantity maxim are what are ordinarily considered to be deceit by omission. McCornack (2008) illustrates covert violation of the quantity maxim with an interpersonal example:

> [Suppose your] romantic partner spends the evening with a rival. When you ask your partner what she did or he did [that] evening, your partner tells you that, 'I watched a movie' (true) 'at home' (true) and 'went to bed early' (true). What your partner does not tell you is that she or he watched the movie with a romantic rival, after which they both went to bed early. This deceptive message is a quantity violation, in that while the information it presents is truthful, it leaves out information most of us would consider essential. (p. 219)

Notice that although this example appears straightforward, it masks a problem quite relevant to an analysis of contested pension reduction disclosures: how does the inclusion of particular "truthful" details affect the impact of the omitted information on receivers? What McCornack does not discuss in much detail is how the covertness (and thus the potential deceptiveness) of quantity violations might be enhanced rhetorically, for instance, by surrounding them with increasing amounts of truthful, plausible, pertinent (i.e., receiver expected) information. That is, the degree to which such omissions are deceptive is likely to be sensitive to the discourse context in which they occur, a context that can subtly condition the nature and strength of the effect that an omission has upon receivers' beliefs (Perelman & Olbrechts-Tyteca, 1969, pp. 115–133). For instance, continuing with McCornack's example, the deceiver might further include a statement like the following, either just before or just after the example statement:

> "It would have been more fun to watch the movie with you—I made way more popcorn than I could eat."

In this way a communicator may not only carefully avoid providing any signs that information has been omitted but strategically vary the amount and kind of accurate details provided to inconspicuously promote the seeming credibility and cooperativeness of the communicators' response. The impacts of such contextual 'framing' effects have been studied extensively in experimental cognitive investigations of message receivers' decision making, person perception, and judgmental processes (Berry, Scheffler, & Goldstein, 1993; Eagly & Chaiken, 1993; Entman, 1993; Fiske & Taylor, 1991; Iyengar & Simon, 1994; Price, Tewksbury, & Powers, 1997).

Importantly, McCornack's example makes it clear how the information manipulation involved in quantity violations may function independently of, and differently than, quality violations. In many legal contexts the latter violations are commonly referred to as either 'lies of commission' or as 'affirmatively misleading statements.' In these violations the communicator knowingly offers the receiver a verifiably (positively) false assertion:

S1: Well, are you sure that you were alone the whole evening?
S2: Yes, I was alone.

Although it is clear S2's reply is a lie, whether it also violates the quantity maxim is debatable. On the one hand, it omits the semantic information that S2 slept with another person just as certainly as the previously shown example of a quantity violation omitted this same information. On the other, however, it provides, at least pragmatically, the kind of information that S1 would expect: the topic of 'being alone' is preserved and no off-topic elaborative information is added.

Again, an issue not fully discussed by McCornack is that a deceiver may not only avoid providing any sign of unreliability concerning the false statement but in addition include otherwise truthful, pertinent details to promote unostentatiously the credibility of the false statement and boost its acceptance, as suggested by the popcorn example in the preceding paragraph (Galasinski, 2000, pp. 71–85). Thus, like the effects of omissions on receivers, effects of direct falsifications are also potentially sensitive to the surrounding discourse context.

The third type of deceptive information manipulation posited by IMT is known as a 'relevance violation.' In conversational settings these violations often may take the form of 'evasions.' However, as theorists such as Galasinski (2000) point out, it is important to understand that evasions may range from being *overt* (meaning that the communicator openly signals that he or she intends to be evasive and to not provide a relevant response) to *covert* (meaning that the communicator signals no such intention but, on the contrary, provides cues signaling the opposite, viz., that his or her message is intended to be and indeed must be taken as relevant) (pp. 55–60).[2] Consider these two conversational examples that extend McCornack's hypothetical example:

S1: Well, are you sure you were alone the whole evening?
S2: You know, that's not a question I feel I should have to answer because I really need for you to trust me more than you seem to do.
versus
S1: Well, are you sure you were alone the whole evening?
S2: I never feel alone when I am watching a movie. But right now I am starting to feel that not only should I not be alone, but I should have a psychologist or a lawyer with me.

The first of these pairs is an example of overt evasion, inasmuch as S2 openly and directly challenges the validity or fairness of the question on the table. S2 signals explicitly that S2 intends to ignore the question and also provides a reason why. In the second pair, the evasion is more covert because S2's objection to the question is, at best, only indirectly implied. Indeed, S2's intention to ignore the question is masked by a covert revision of the focus of S1's question, that is, as if S1 had asked, "Do you ever feel alone when watching a movie?" At the same time, S2's second statement appears to be a further attempt to distract S1 from S2's initial response with some wry, sarcastic humor. As Galasinski (2000, pp. 60–67) elaborates, communicators who wish to covertly violate the relevance maxim nearly always offer semantically irrelevant information while seeming to make more or less pragmatically relevant responses. Such communicators do so covertly in one or more of several ways: (a) by preserving the topical focus expected by the questioner while simultaneously altering *the relationship of that topic to the situational context* in a way that is different than what the questioner reasonably expected (e.g., S2's statement preserves S1's topic "alone" while expanding that topic to "feeling alone" and shifting it to a different context, viz., from "the whole evening" to "while watching a movie"); (b) by shifting the *topical focus* of a message away from the focus anticipated by a questioner's explicit request or contextually probable expectation (e.g., as in S2's second remark above, where S2 shifts away from S1's topic "alone the whole evening" to needing "a lawyer or psychologist with me"); or (c) by combining both of these approaches.

IMT theorists also note that violations of relevance are often part of, and help to effectuate, covert quantity violations (McCornack, 1992, p. 12). As is evident in the second pair, clearly the amount of information that S1 expects S2 to deliver is not forthcoming in S2's message, nor is that deficit overtly signaled or acknowledged textually by S2 in any way. It thus would seem that many relevance violations in ordinary conversation serve as rhetorical frames intended to help mask quantity violations in the response offered.

Finally, the fourth type of deceptive information manipulation is a manner (or clarity) violation; that is, the communicator provides a message that may be judged to be both semantically and pragmatically relevant to the receiver's question or expectation, but the message nevertheless offers the receiver divergent possible interpretations and no means for decisively choosing among them. In common parlance, these messages are often referred to as equivocations (and sometimes as obfuscations), but their key feature is that they involve semantic ambiguity or vagueness or both. Consider this example:

S1: Well, are you sure you were alone the whole evening?
S2: Yeah, pretty much.

S2's reply here may at first appear cooperative and responsive. However, the response creates an interpretive problem for the receiver: what does the phrase "pretty much" refer to? On the one hand, it could refer to whether S2 was "alone the whole evening," allowing S1 to infer that for some part of the evening, S2 was *not* alone. With this expression, S2 uses what linguists define as vague quantification: how much of the "whole evening" is "pretty much" (Channel, 1985, 1990)? On the other hand, "pretty much" could be taken to indicate quantitatively how "sure" S2 is. In this way S1 is confronted with different choices as to how to interpret S2's response. "Yeah" seems to provide a straightforward confirmation, but "pretty much" immediately and incongruously adds an unknown degree of uncertainty. Notice that if S2 also adds the partially irrelevant statement—"I never feel alone when I am watching a movie"—the unsatisfactory vagueness of the initial statement may be somewhat diluted through reframing of the "alone" topic. Indeed, even without this addition, and like relevance violations, violations of manner (clarity) might also be conceptualized as rhetorical means for helping to mask more fundamental quantity violations. Clearly, as with this relevance violation example, the amount of information that S1 reasonably expects S2 to deliver in this last example is not forthcoming in S2's message, nor is this deficit textually signaled by S2.

Looking back at the problem of assigning decreasing degrees of deceptiveness (and wrongfulness) to these maxims, which was introduced in Chapter 1, these examples would not seem to support such a hierarchical view any more clearly or decisively than the crosswalk case introduced there. For instance, is the romantic partner who omits stating to his significant other that he slept with another woman any less deceptive than the partner who declares outright that he was alone the entire evening? None of the rationales for differentiating degrees of deceptiveness readily supports such a conclusion. The omission, taken at face value and with no other contextual information, hardly looks to be more detectable by the partner receiving the message than was the direct lie. Similarly, it would be hard to attribute any less causal responsibility for the deception to the partner omitting the information that he slept with someone else. In the case of both the omission and the declaration, the significant other is given responses that encourage her to believe that her partner is faithful. And the effect of the omission upon her belief also appears to be no less predictable by the partner than the direct lie as well. Of course, we can easily imagine all sorts of ways in which the prior experiential context of the two persons with each other would condition the particular interpretation of these responses, such that the degree of deceptiveness accordingly might be increased or decreased in any of them. All of the respondent's answers arguably involve concealment and thus violate the quantity maxim through omission; all of them challenge, albeit with different nuances, the assumption that the expectation of disclosure of infidelity is a reasonable one.

Perhaps the most thorough review to date of the strengths and limitations of IMT's reliance upon these maxims as a conceptual theory of deceptive language has been provided by Galasinski (2000). As he points out, and as the discussion of these examples should suggest, there is some inherent fuzziness in the definition of each violation, and their possible interaction with each other in a given communication situation can make the reliability of their application uncertain. For instance, both relevance and clarity violations appear tied to underlying quantity violations and, through contextual and rhetorical dynamics, may be theorized to help effect such violations in the ways previously illustrated. This apparent dependency makes questionable whether relevance and clarity violations are simply different means to committing quantity violations or whether they are truly independent forms of deceptive information manipulation in the same way that violations of quantity and quality are conceptually distinct and independent. At the same time, critics of IMT, including McCornack (1997) himself, point out that IMT can scarcely be considered a theory that describes or predicts the cognitive processes of deceivers in constructing their messages.

It does not attempt such a description and thus ought not to be critiqued as if it did. Rather, it is more a linguistic theory that attempts to account for the semantic and pragmatic conditions and functioning of deceptive expressions, or as Galasinski (2000) puts it, the workings of deceptive messages. In this respect, Galasinski (2000) agrees with McCornack's claims concerning the comprehensiveness of IMT's maxims and argues that attempts by other researchers to add to these four basic types of deceptive information manipulation (or attempts to replace them with others) have generally lacked parsimony and consistency and have thus led to greater problems of definitional clarity without adding any apparent advantages (pp. 26–33).

READER–AUTHOR "CONVERSATION" IN DISCLOSURE DOCUMENTS: FAQS AND FRAMING

For purposes of the present inquiry, an important issue is whether or not IMT's maxims can be usefully applied to the extended "conversation" that is often theorized to take place between authors and readers of documents. Despite frequent calls for utilizing formal documents for investigating deceptive communication (e.g., Miller & Stiff, 1993), nearly all of the theoretical and empirical work elaborating and critiquing IMT has utilized real or hypothetical oral conversational exchanges like those presented in the preceding section. This predominant focus notwithstanding, application of IMT to analysis of written legal disclosures for their alleged deceptiveness certainly seems possible.[3] Legal researchers have already drawn upon IMT's maxims to investigate allegedly deceptive disclosures in written contracts (Craswell, 2006; Tiersma, 1986) and in print advertising (Craswell, 1985, 1991) as well as to critically evaluate courts' conclusions concerning allegedly deceptive practices in these texts. In these studies readers are analogized to conversational participants who are seen as bringing questions to, and thus conversing with, document authors. As Tiersma (1990) points out, the Gricean use of the term "conversational maxims" is perhaps "somewhat unfortunate because it suggests that implicature does not operate in more formal contexts;" he suggests instead that "a better appellation would [be] contextual or interactional implicature" (p. 381, note 22), thus allowing for expanding the application of Gricean maxims to reader–author interactions.[4]

The different ways that ERISA pension disclosure documents constitute author–reader interactions nonetheless raise interesting complexities. One way that a written disclosure may constitute a conversation is through the explicit simulation of employees' questions, for instance, when a disclosure places such questions within quote marks or highlights them with a contrastive typeface. Such simulation occurs in the now widespread practice of posing frequently asked questions (FAQs) in the voice of the employee; for example, "How will this new cash balance plan help me?" Such questions are often used as topical heads or subheads with the organizational author responding to them conversationally; for example, "It can help you in many ways. For instance, it can . . ."

Through such apparently reader-friendly means, however, disclosure authors may attempt preemptively to control conversation with their employees by projecting only those questions they want their employees to ask and that they are willing to answer. Although there is little published empirical research investigating how readers of disclosure documents interpret or make use of purported reader FAQs, their use is commonly recommended in technical, financial, and health risk communication disclosures (Morgan, Fischhoff, Bostrom, & Atman, 2002; Schriver, 1997). On the one hand, one might surmise that, given the prevalence of the FAQ device in all sorts of institutional documents, readers generally appreciate the device rather than see it as inherently involving a presumptuous usurpation of their right to pose questions for themselves. In other words, use of the device is itself likely presumed to represent an organizational author's intention to be cooperative in the ensuing author–reader conversation. On the other hand, use of the device does not *necessarily* either signify complete author cooperation or ensure reader comprehension. In particular, the use of putative FAQs can raise issues with the maxim of relevance, either because the FAQs are simply not those that employees would reasonably be most concerned about or because they are framed only partially or superficially to resemble readers' most important concerns while actually evading them.

For instance, notice that the hypothetical FAQ in the earlier paragraph is framed positively rather than negatively: it asks how the new cash balance plan can *help* the employees, not how or whether it might *harm* them. If the latter question about harm is not explicitly posed in the disclosure and the employees assume cooperativeness on the part of the disclosure authors, then the positive framing in the FAQ may lead employees to believe there are no harms. If in fact the harms exist and are not elsewhere identified or explained, the positively framed question can also be seen as helping to mask a violation of the maxim of quantity. Indeed, as the next two chapters explore in part, use of FAQs in pension disclosures has the rhetorical potential merely to seem cooperative and attuned to employees' concerns while masking authors' strategic goal to mute or morph employee concerns and thus to mislead them. Effectively, FAQs can be a tool for engaging in what Galasinski (2000, pp. 60–70) calls "metadiscursive" deception, that is, making a pragmatically relevant response to employees' need for information about their pension plan conversion while simultaneously masking a semantically irrelevant one.

CONTEXTUAL EFFECTS IN PENSION DISCLOSURE DOCUMENTS: INFORMATION SEQUENCE AND DETECTION OF CONTRADICTORY IMPLICATURES

What is also very important when examining pension disclosures through the lens of IMT and Gricean maxims is the role that the temporal and local context of given statements and implicatures may play in employee readers' understanding (van Dijk, 1999; Graesser, 1981). In many cash balance conversion cases, the employer sends out a series of precursor brochures to employees announcing and providing information about the plan transition.[5] Such brochures often begin to be distributed a year or more in advance of the official date of plan conversion and also in advance of any SPD. Sometimes employers will use one or more of these precursors to serve as §204(h) notices or as SMMs rather than create separate, explicitly self-identifying versions of these latter documents.[6] Within this complex stream of information, the temporal context of employer statements matters because statements on a particular topic presented in an earlier disclosure document may generate an implicature that either reinforces or conflicts with an implicature arising from a later statement addressing the same or a seemingly related topic. Consider some possible hypothetical sequences of messages about positive versus negative effects of a plan conversion shown in Table 3.1:

Table 3.1 Temporal Stream of Precursor Cash Balance Transition Documents

Possible Sequences	1st doc	2nd doc	3rd doc	4th doc	5th doc
A	Positive info	Positive info	Positive info	Positive info	Positive info
B	Positive info (about topic a)	Positive info	Positive info	Negative, contradictory info (about topic a)	Positive info
C	Negative info (about topic a)	Positive info	Positive info	Positive, contradictory info (about topic a)	Positive info

Concerning Sequence A, there is well-developed empirical communication research showing that sheer repetition of statements and implicatures has a powerful persuasive effect on readers. The more often receivers read a message, the more they are disposed to believe it (Hasher & Chromiak, 1977; Hasher, Goldstein, & Toppino, 1977; Kassin & Keichel, 1996; O'Keefe, 2002; Petty & Cacioppo, 1979). Through the psychological phenomenon known as 'expectancy,' consistently positive, repeated messages about various advantages of a cash balance plan made in earlier company documents may inoculate employees against perceiving or registering the importance of a lone discordant or even contradictory message presented in a later document, as illustrated in Sequence B (Eagly & Chaiken, 1993; Haugtvedt & Wegener, 1994; McGuire, 1964). Unless it is somehow flagged or discursively cued for readers, any contradiction arising from the negative information in Sequence B may be misconstrued or not even be noticeable to readers.

Similarly, in Sequence C, the converse problem may occur: a lone early message about a negative effect of a cash balance plan conversion may be overwhelmed and forgotten if the documents later in the precursor stream repeat and amplify the advantages of the new plan without again commenting upon or even mentioning the negative message offered earlier. Readers are naturally conditioned to make the most temporally and spatially proximate parts of texts fit together as they construct meaning, and they try to conserve their cognitive resources by combining only the nearest, most recent information with the next bit of information they read (Baker, 1989; Just & Carpenter, 1987; van Dijk & Kintsch, 1983; Kintsch & van Dijk, 1978; van Oostendorp & Goldman, 1999; Otero, 1998; Pressley & Afflerbach, 1995).

In addition to their temporal and spatial separation, statements that generate contradictory or ambiguous implicatures in readers may also appear in different information contexts, such that any relationship or topical connection between the two statements can be difficult to perceive or even detect (Johnson & Seifert, 1994; Walker & Meyer, 1980). Indeed, employee readers may have difficulty recalling and then integrating *unrepeated information* that was presented in a different context in an earlier document with later contradictory information they are currently processing *unless* they are given some explicit cue directing them to remember the much earlier contradictory information (Mannes & Hoyes, 1996; Otero & Kintsch, 1992; Perfetti, Rouet, & Britt, 1999). Subjecting ordinary employee readers who are lacking in knowledge about cash balance pension plan transitions to contradictory assertions or implicatures without discursively assisting such readers to see these contradictions and resolve them violates not only the maxim of clarity but potentially also the maxims of quality and quantity as well.

Interestingly, although it does prohibit "obfuscation," ERISA does not explicitly prohibit contradictory messages in pension disclosures *per se* (29 C.F.R. § 2520.102–2(b)). Other disclosure laws, however, do prohibit contradictory statements that may reasonably cause reader uncertainty, including those that are separated by one or more pages or that reach readers at different points in time in different documents. Consistent with the perspective of IMT, such contradictions have been held to constitute deception as a matter of law (e.g., see Griffith, 2012, 2008). For instance, under the Fair Debt Collection Practices Act (FDCPA) of 1977, consumer debt collection agencies are required to inform consumers that they have 30 days in which to request proof of the debt from the creditor and also to indicate that the collection agency may not further act against the consumer if such proof is requested or until the 30-day period has expired (Public Law No. 95–109, 91 Stat. 874 (1977)). However, defendant debt collection agencies that follow the law and place this required notice on one page, but then also state or imply that the debt must be paid *sooner than* 30 days on another page, have been determined to have violated the act's proscription against deceptive statements.

In the FDCPA case of *Russell v. Equifax* (74 F.3d 30, 2d Cir.1996), for example, the court determined that

> a collection notice is deceptive when it can be reasonably read to have two or more different meanings, one of which is inaccurate . . . No

> consumer—much less the least sophisticated one—is expected to know that the language on the back of the first [collection] notice takes precedence over the second notice when the instructions contained in the two notices are read in combination. We think it plain [that the] plaintiff would not realize she had a statutory right to dispute the debt within 30 days in the face of a second notice from the debt collector giving her only 25 days . . . Like the first notice, [the second] advances a message that is open to an inaccurate yet reasonable interpretation by the consumer, and is therefore deceptive as a matter of law. (pp. 13–15)

Importantly, the impact of contrary implicatures upon employee readers' understanding of cash balance plan transition disclosures may depend upon more than the local context, time, or space between and amount of repetition of each of the two contradictory messages, that is, as schematized in Sequences B and C. The impact may also vary with the amount of trust that employers encourage employees to place in the documents themselves through various 'goodwill' messages the employer sets forth; for example, "The company seeks to protect employees' pension benefits long after they leave the company." To the degree that employee readers do notice seemingly contradictory statements or implicatures, they are likely to feel some affective as well as cognitive dissonance. That is, contradictory messages or implicatures may not only affect readers' understanding about what the text means regarding their pension benefits but also how much trust they feel they can place in the documents and in the employer overall. They may react to apparent contradictions by looking for (or trying to recall) messages that seem to reassure them of employer cooperativeness in the conversation.

This reader response would seem especially likely if the contradictory messages involve unfamiliar or complex technical concepts about future pension benefit accrual. If disclosures repeatedly offer employee readers broadly worded 'goodwill' messages, these readers may experience some reduction in their concerns about employer cooperativeness and trustworthiness. But, in addition, and to readers' detriment, such affective dissonance reduction may also lead these readers to abandon further attempts to resolve the substantive ambiguity or contradiction that they originally thought they detected. In effect, readers may trade away accurate understanding for feelings of greater trust. Such a dissonance reduction process is quite plausible because some precursor brochures in cash balance plan transitions resemble marketing promotions in which the goal is both to tout and 'sell' employees on the new cash balance plan's 'overall' advantages to employees while also increasing employees' trust in the employer and in the accuracy of the disclosures themselves.[7] Building employee trust reduces fear, which in turn potentially lessens employee readers' diligence in asking questions about contradictory implicatures that may have surfaced during their reading comprehension process.

To illustrate how employees' reliance on apparent cues of employer cooperativeness and trustworthiness might work when cash balance plan disclosures contain contradictory implicatures, suppose that an early precursor document states:

> Employees' pension benefit growth under the new cash balance plan will be lower, but not all details of the plan transition are complete, and more information will be made available soon.

But then suppose another document, distributed months later, exclusively shows illustrative hypothetical examples of retiring employees whose benefits under the new cash balance plan equal or exceed those they would have earned had the old plan continued, whereas none even hint at a lower future rate of accrual.[8] This scenario is like that shown in Sequence C in Table 3.1. A lone, and *subsequently unrepeated* statement about a negative feature of the plan transition appears very early in the precursor stream. By the time employees read the later, consistently positive hypothetical examples, they may have all but forgotten the earlier statement. Alternatively, they may remember that statement and see that none of the hypothetical examples affirm or support it. Despite any cognitive uncertainty that this apparent inconsistency creates, these readers may simply infer that they are not, after all, likely to experience a reduction in future benefits given that none of the illustrative examples show that outcome.

This reader inference may be further strengthened through other signals in the brochures that encourage a general presumption of cooperativeness on the part of the employer. Employee readers may understandably but mistakenly surmise: "Wouldn't the employer hypothetically illustrate a negative, lower benefit case if that case could occur?" The uniformly positive hypothetical examples themselves, because they also represent *an increase in the specificity of information relative to the earlier lone hint of trouble*, may seem to employees to be convincing evidence that no reduction of future benefits is likely to occur. This erroneous employee resolution of the contradictory implicature becomes more likely owing to a reasonable default belief that documents distributed later in time are likely to represent more accurate and more authoritative information than those encountered earlier. This default belief may be reinforced by earlier cooperative employer remarks that accompanied the original negative statement, such as, "More detailed information about the plan transition will be sent to you over the next few months," or more simply, "Details of the plan transition have not all been worked out." These types of comments accompanying early precursor documents may well encourage employees to view the earlier documents as less reliable than later ones, and as a result the presentation of exclusively positive hypothetical examples may well lead employee readers to dismiss the earlier negative message altogether.

Other discourse features that accompany the presentation of hypothetical future benefit illustrations can further involve Gricean maxim violations. The employer may also try to disclose without disclosing by providing a disclaimer of reliability along with its uniformly positive hypothetical illustrations of future pension benefits. As with the employer's presentation of FAQs, the precise framing and focus of the disclaimer matters. Consider a simple disclaimer that states: "Your individual case may differ from these hypothetical examples." Does such a disclaimer resolve for the ordinary employee reader the contradictory implicature arising from the earlier warning about reduced future benefits and the uniformly positive hypothetical examples? The disclaimer may well state what is true and accurate. Indeed, it may be empirically demonstrable that no employee's situation is or will be exactly like *any* of the hypothetical examples offered. Nevertheless, this disclaimer fails to address the employees' question as to whether there *are any* cases in which employees will see a reduction in future benefits. Nor does it help them see what those reductions may look like. The disclaimer is, in effect, silent on these questions, and like the presentation of purely neutral or positive hypothetical employee examples themselves, it violates both the maxims of clarity and relevance while seeming to comply with them.

Specifically in terms of IMT and the Gricean maxims, this disclaimer is pragmatically relevant in that it responds to a question about the reliability or predictive accuracy of the positive examples that an employee reasonably would have. The reader's question is recognized; it is not ignored. But, at the same time, notice how the disclaimer effectively recapitulates the same failure of candor involved in the presentation of exclusively positive hypothetical scenarios themselves. It fails to provide semantically relevant information that an employee reader might reasonably expect; namely, could *any* employees' future benefit accruals be lower under the cash balance plan than under the old plan? If so, what types of employees might be affected and to what extent? In this instance, the disclaimer appears calculated to avoid providing a clear, explicit response.

Put another way, such a disclaimer makes the employer seem cooperative while simultaneously masking uncooperativeness: no hypothetical employee examples or illustrations confirming the occurrence of reduced future pension benefit accruals are provided even though the employer may well know that many employees will suffer such reductions. From the standpoint of IMT and the Gricean maxims, then, such a disclaimer could not be said to 'cure' the misleading effect of exclusively positive illustrations of employees' future benefits. It does not constitute such a cure because, in part, it does not provide any semantic cues that would remind readers of the statement in the earlier document apparently indicating lower future benefit growth for *most* employees.

Objecting to this Gricean analysis, a defendant employer might ask: "What would a fully cooperative disclaimer accompanying the hypothetical examples look like?" The answer may not be welcome to some employer ears. Beyond merely stating, "Your individual case may differ from these hypothetical examples," and to correct specifically the false implicature generated by only showing exclusively positive examples, a more cooperative and candid disclaimer would state something like this: "Contrary to what these particular examples show and in line with our earlier brochure's statement about 'lower benefit growth in the future,' some/many/all employees will experience future benefit reductions under the new plan." This expanded disclaimer would help serve to inoculate employees against the positive but misleading implicature about their future benefits that the exclusively positive hypothetical examples collectively generate. It acknowledges and thus helps the reader to resolve the apparent contradiction between an employer's earlier warning concerning lower future benefit growth and the harmless future that the exclusively positive hypothetical examples collectively paint. And consequently, in doing so, it arguably removes the violations of the Gricean relevance and clarity maxims that the more 'minimalist' disclaimer commits.

Alternatively, and more to the point, the employer could opt *not* to include any disclaimer but instead include hypothetical examples that realistically represent both employees who do *and* do not suffer reductions to their future benefit accruals under the new plan. Even with this change, however, employee readers might still better understand what they read in the examples if they are reminded explicitly about the warning offered in an earlier precursor document.[9]

THE PROBLEM OF EXPERT HINDSIGHT BIAS IN JUDGMENTS OF TEXTUAL ADEQUACY AND CLARITY

Finally, there is a much-studied cognitive phenomenon, known as 'expert hindsight bias,' which potentially interferes with courts' appreciation of the impacts that these complex contextual and discursive features of disclosures can have upon ordinary employee readers (Hoffrage, 2011; Knoll, 2010; Morgan, Fischhoff, Bostrom, & Atman, 2002; Schriver, 1989, 1997). Indeed, expert hindsight bias may lead some courts to draw erroneous conclusions about what disclosure texts actually communicate to 'average plan participants'—participants who have little or no prior knowledge about transitions to cash balance pension plans and the characteristics of the plans themselves. A growing empirical literature suggests that, partly as a result of this bias, expert writers and designers of technical documents rarely are able to predict accurately more than 50 to 60 percent of the comprehension difficulties and missteps that nontechnical readers of those same documents encounter (Dumas & Redish, 1999; Lentz & De Jong, 1997; Nielsen & Mack, 1994). It will be helpful to discuss briefly the manifestation of expert hindsight bias in relation to some of the contextual features of disclosure documents detailed in the preceding section.[10]

First, expert hindsight bias potentially leads judicial interpreters both to *de*contextualize and *re*contextualize disputed statements and in doing so give them a salience and meaning they would not necessarily have for a nonlegally trained reader or average plan participant. For example, as shown in information Sequences B and C in the preceding section, expert hindsight bias could lead courts to put undue emphasis upon the negative information appearing in these sequences without carefully analyzing and weighing how the negative statements would appear to average plan participants *in the context of both the statements that precede them and that follow them*. Instead, judges and other expert interpreters, because of their greater prior knowledge about cash balance transitions, could be led to perceive the negative albeit accurate statements by themselves as clearly 'trumping' any other contradictory statements that appear elsewhere in the disclosure document stream. It can also lead them even to overlook or ignore that the negative statements might appear in documents where average plan participant readers would not expect them to appear (Bransford & Johnson, 1973, 2004; Walker & Meyer, 1980). Effectively, expert hindsight bias can lead court interpreters to presume that inferences about the import and significance of certain statements *they themselves* derive could be just as easily derived by less knowledgeable readers, *regardless* of when and where the statements appear (Afflerbach, 1990). For instance, the hypothetical statement appearing in an early precursor document that I discussed above asserted:

> Employees' pension benefit growth under the new cash balance plan will be lower . . .

Expert hindsight bias may prevent a judicial interpreter from analyzing and weighing this statement in context with other statements made in the same document or in subsequent disclosure documents. Instead, expert hindsight bias could lead such an interpreter to treat this statement *ipso facto* as decisive evidence that employee readers were 'clearly informed' that their future pension benefits were being reduced. In this way, court interpreters may see little or no difference between themselves as readers and the employee readers for whom the documents were putatively written (Latin, 1994; Otero & Kintsch, 1992; Walker & Meyer, 1980). Unlike such expert interpreters, however, average plan participants may have processed and then dismissed or even forgotten the precursor statement in view of other, later statements that the employer makes in subsequently distributed documents. As will be discussed in Chapter 5, this type of expert hindsight bias problem appears to have impacted the court's reading of the complex disclosure documents in the *Tomlinson* case.

Second, expert hindsight bias can lead court readers to see as clearly 'obvious' connections between parts of texts that are temporally and spatially distant from each other, quite as if these parts were immediately adjacent to each other on the same page and encountered in the same moment. Expert hindsight bias leads the interpreter to collapse both time and space between widely separated statements when examining textual evidence, distorting the way nonexpert readers would encounter and deal with such separation. Typically, expert readers search legal disclosures knowing all or at least many of the things they are looking for and what questions they should ask, whereas ordinary readers simply may not (Baker, 1989; Davey & McBride, 1986; Graesser & McMahon, 1993; Graesser, Langston & Baggett, 1993; Hacker, Dunlosky, & Graesser, 1998; Magliano, Trabasso, & Graesser, 1999; McNamara, 2007; Otero, 1998). Prior knowledge of ERISA and actuarial intricacies involved in pension plans serve experts the way a powerful flashlight serves a person in the dark. This knowledge not only amplifies the significance of certain statements while discounting the discourse context in which they are embedded (as already discussed); it also enables expert readers to connect, integrate, and then draw complex inferences from widely separated statements within and across documents while *ignoring* intervening technical detail and terminology in a way that average plan participant readers could not.

On the other hand, precisely because they do not have much or any *a priori* knowledge of cash balance plans, average plan participants may be less able to connect statements separated by time and space, that is, as if they formed a single, continuous text. Conversely, they may also sometimes attempt to construct inferences from different parts of a text that actually are not connected to each other, while missing ostensibly 'obvious' connections that pension experts see (Afflerbach, 1990; Otero, 1998; Otero & Kintsch, 1992). Given the length of time and diversity of circumstance in which pension law experts have used their 'flashlights' to read legal disclosures, it can become almost second nature for them to assume that ordinary readers should be able to combine and construct inferences from widely separated pieces of information in the same way experts do (Latin, 1994; Steinberg, 1991; Tiersma, 1993a, 2000).

Indeed, empirical research investigating expert–novice differences in reading comprehension and decision making in cognitive psychology have shown time and again how distorting expert hindsight bias can be when experts try to estimate the inferential abilities of nonexperts. This distortion has been shown to occur even in experts who have been explicitly trained to recognize the unconscious influence of expert hindsight bias on their thinking (Hoffrage, 2011; Knoll, 2010).[11] As I will also discuss in Chapter 5, oversimplification of the inferences necessary to connect certain widely separated disclosure statements appears to have blinded the *Tomlinson* court to a number of contradictory and unexplained remarks made in defendant El Paso Corporation's disclosures—literally, almost as if these contradictory remarks were not there at all. However, once examined in their spatial and temporal context and in view of the inferior knowledge that average plan participants are likely to possess about cash balance plans, these remarks can be seen to seriously interfere with accurate inferences about the effects of the El Paso cash balance conversion.

IMT'S MAXIMS AND ERISA DISCLOSURE RULES: ARE THEY CONGRUENT?

ERISA's original language in §102 concerning disclosures, although not specifically mentioning the kinds of contextual violations of the Gricean maxims previously discussed, nonetheless clearly seems aimed at prohibiting them:

> The format of the summary plan description shall not have the effect of misleading, misinforming, or failing to inform participants and beneficiaries. Any description of exceptions, limitations, reductions, and other restrictions of plan benefits *shall not be minimized, rendered obscure, or otherwise made to appear unimportant.* Such exceptions, limitations, reductions or restrictions of plan benefits shall be described or summarized in a manner not less

> prominent than the style, captions, printing type, and prominence used to describe or summarize plan benefits. *The advantages and disadvantages of the plan shall be presented without either exaggerating the benefits or minimizing the limitations*. (29 C.F.R. § 2520.102–2(b), italics added)

With respect to IMT and the Gricean maxims, what is noteworthy is that the statute separately identifies "misleading," "misinforming," and "failing to inform." The first two of these terms each could reference either violations of quality or quantity. However, the third reflects only the maxim of quantity. When the statute prohibits "obscure" descriptions of benefit reductions, it reflects the maxim of clarity, and when it prohibits "exaggerating benefits or minimizing limitations," it could be argued to reflect the maxims of quantity and relevance. Moreover, ERISA §102's further requirement that disclosures must be "written in a manner calculated to be understood by the average plan participant" may also be seen as expressing the latter two maxims in broader terms. Implicitly, then, the very language of the statute seems to encompass the maxims that underlie the Gricean cooperative principle. Saying this, of course, scarcely means that judicial interpreters of contested disclosures may thus have no need or use for the perspective that IMT and the Gricean maxims bring to bear, that is, as if the statutory language provided an exhaustive and sufficiently precise framework for detecting and explicating instances of deceptive versus nondeceptive discourse practices. If that were really the case, the enormous gulf that can be seen between the application of this language in the *Amara* and *Tomlinson* decisions would likely not exist. On the contrary, the goal of the next two chapters is to show in detail how the analyses of the judiciary might change if the perspective underlying IMT and the Gricean maxims were brought to bear.

Further, consistent with basic principles of contract interpretation, we can also see from the foregoing discussion of contextual effects that applying IMT and the Gricean maxims obviously cannot be helpful if merely focused on employer disclosure statements in isolation from one another (Henderson, 1990). Rather, such application requires careful attention to the larger temporal, locative, topical, and pragmatic discourse context linking one disclosure document and statement with another and with employees' reasonable expectations. Some violations of a particular maxim may only become apparent if two or more written disclosure statements or text segments are considered together, including statements that are widely separated in time and location. In particular, the nature and impact of violations of quantity (i.e., omissions) in disclosure documents are likely to be highly sensitive to contextual considerations, including the prior knowledge and expectations of average plan participants. Omissions may have deceptive impacts on employees' understanding of their benefits even if the omissions are not accompanied by violations of quality, that is, by affirmatively misleading or positively false statements. A reductive analysis of disclosure documents, one that assumes that an omission must be accompanied by some affirmatively misleading statement to be considered deceptive, will not do. Rather, as illustrated in the use of conventional disclaimer statements, violations of relevance and of clarity can influence the nature and degree of deceptive impact that omissions (quantity violations) ultimately may have on employees' understanding.

ASSUMPTIONS AND METHODS GUIDING TEXTUAL ANALYSIS OF *AMARA* AND *TOMLINSON* DISCLOSURES

What is critically important in analyzing pension disclosures with the use of IMT's Gricean maxims is specification of the effects of cash balance conversions that readers would reasonably expect to be informed about. In my analysis of the contested benefit disclosure discourse in the *Amara* and *Tomlinson* cases that I present in the following chapters, these effects can essentially be boiled down to the following three:

1. Compared to employees' existing plan benefits, the accrual rate under the new plan is reduced such that their overall cash balance plan benefits will be less than those they would have earned if they were allowed to remain under the existing plan.
2. 'Wear-away' periods, lasting from months to many years, occur during which many employees will not earn any new pension benefits at all (zero accrual) starting from the date of plan transition.
3. Employees' opening account balances under the new cash balance plan are significantly discounted so that these balances are less than the total value of benefits already earned under the old plan as of the date of conversion.

As explained earlier, all three of these effects occur in the cash balance transitions undertaken by the defendants CIGNA Corporation and El Paso Corporation in the *Amara* and *Tomlinson* cases, respectively. Concerning the latter two effects, as also previously explained, transitions to cash balance pension plans cause reductions in employees' future benefit accrual rate through two related mechanisms. First, employers set the value of the employees' new opening cash balance accounts *lower than* the value of all of the benefits that employees have earned up to the date of the transition to the new plan. For instance, an employee's new cash account balance may only represent 60 percent of the value of their old plan benefit as of the date of transition. Second, partially as a result of these lowered opening balances, employers impose wear-away periods during which employees will earn *no* additional benefits at all until employees' new cash account balances catch up to the value of their old plan benefits, that is, at the time the latter were frozen.

Significantly, these latter two effects are ones that were not considered illegal under ERISA at the time both defendant CIGNA Corporation (in *Amara*) and El Paso Corporation (in *Tomlinson*) converted their old defined benefit plans. However, many if not most average plan participants working for these companies would be largely or completely unaware of these possible effects when they first encountered their employers' stream of disclosure documents. As discussed in Chapter 1 and 2, this lack of awareness would likely exist if employees had no prior experience with or knowledge of cash balance plans. And, obviously, regarding mechanisms that employees do not know about, employees cannot specifically or reasonably be expected to query the disclosure documents about or even know what to look for in them. Instead what is likely is that, in the absence of any explanation to the contrary, employees would expect their opening cash account balances under the new plan to *equal* the total value of the benefits they had earned so far under the old plan, that is, just as if the employees themselves were transferring dollars from one bank or equity investment account to another.[12] Without any clear notice that the total value of their old plan benefits is *not* represented in their new plan opening balance, employees would have no idea that they might suffer lengthy wear-away periods during which they would not earn a penny more in retirement. Or, stated a bit differently, they would not anticipate that as of the date of plan conversion, they would be 'marching in place,' simply re-earning their old plan benefit. Such, at least, was the impact of the cash balance plan conversions effected in both the *Amara* and *Tomlinson* cases analyzed in the next two chapters. Similarly, even if employees assumed or were told that it was possible that their new benefit plan might provide a lower rate of accrual than their old one, they would still naturally want to know that their opening account balances were being reduced, and whether wear-away periods would occur and for how long, so as to facilitate their forward financial planning and make investment adjustments for themselves and their dependents.

Given these assumptions, my basic analytic method is to identify all parts of the disclosures that appear to relate in any way to these three 'reduction' topics. I then describe and assess the extent to which statements about the same topic, both within and across documents, are consistent or inconsistent with each other. This method closely resembles the basic method of topic analysis used by the discourse analyst Dr. Roger Shuy in his forensic linguistic work (Shuy, 1993; 1998a, 1998b; see also Coulthard & Johnson, 2007; Gibbons, 2003; Howald, 2006; Solan, 1999). Specifically, this method requires that I search the employer's disclosures for any statement directly or indirectly referencing the topics of pension benefit increases, improvements, reductions, suspensions, or differences in benefits obtainable under the old versus the new cash balance plan, including any descriptions, warnings, illustrations, or assurances about such reductions or differences. Crucially, I did not simply examine relevant statements in isolation but also analyzed how these statements would likely be understood by average plan participants given the particular temporal sequence and spatial contexts in which the statements appear.

To provide as much insight into the context of various passages as possible, while at the same time not overwhelming the reader, I have arranged the disclosure discourse data to be discussed in two tables, presented in Appendix 5. Table A contains the *Amara* disclosure discourse data, and Table B contains the *Tomlinson* discourse data. In both tables, I organize the data according to which of the three effects of cash balance conversions it corresponds. Thus, in the left column of each table, I identify each distinct conversion effect as if it was a question posed by the employee reader; for example, "Compared to the old plan, will my future benefit accrual rate under the new plan be reduced?" Posing such questions explicitly enables one to begin to assess whether and to what extent the disclosure documents involve violations of IMT maxims and also to examine the manner in which different violations may interact. Then, to the right of each of these three questions, the data from each different disclosure document potentially or arguably corresponding to that question is shown. In Table A the *Amara* disclosure discourse data are presented in the chronological order in which they were distributed to employees, from left to right, so that disclosure documents that employees received earlier in time appear toward the left side and later ones to the right.

In Table B, the *Tomlinson* data are organized a bit differently. Instead of the chronological order of disclosure distribution being shown left to right (as in Table A), in Table B the chronological distribution order appears vertically, so that the earliest disclosure discourse appears in the first pages and the later discourse on succeeding pages. To save the reader inconvenience, as much as possible I quote specimen discourse from both tables within the flow of my analysis. Sometimes, however, the reader may wish to refer to the tables themselves to keep better in mind the temporal and locative contexts in which each discussed textual segment appears.

NOTES

1 Important questions continue to be raised concerning the meaning of Grice's CP and the extent to which the CP actually describes and regulates conversation in different social contexts and communicative exchanges. See the following: Brown & Levinson, 1987; Danziger, 2010; Davies, 2007; Dynel, 2011; Fairclough, 1985; Leech & Thomas, 1988; Levinson, 1983; Lindblom, 2001; Mey, 1987; Sarangi & Slembrouck, 1992; Thomas, 1995. A full examination of these critiques of the CP, however, is beyond the scope of this book and will not be pursued here.

2 Tiersma (1990) provides an excellent illustration and discussion of covert evasion in his analysis of an alleged act of perjury in *Bronston v. United States* (409 U.S. 352, 1973). A different analysis of evasion is also presented in Bavelas et al. (1990).

3 Numerous researchers and scholars of deceptive communication have also long called for investigations that focus actual, 'real-world' cases of misrepresentation as opposed to those that analyze messages generated by experimental participants (Galasinski, 2000, pp. 35–37; Miller & Stiff, 1993).

4 Miller (1990) similarly views the extension of Grice's maxims of conversational implicature to formal legal documents as appropriate, noting, "When a legislature expressly provides a particular bit of information, it creates a 'conversational' setting between the legislature and its audience—courts and citizens—in which other information of the same type is expected to be conveyed" by virtue of the maxims of relevance and quantity (p. 1196). Also see Green (1990) who points out generally that "despite [Grice's] ubiquitous references to talk exchanges, there is no reason to assume that [he] meant for his analysis to be an account of oral discourse to the exclusion of written communication . . . Grice's use of written language examples . . . indicates that it is a mistake to assume that he did not intend his analysis to apply to non-interactive discourse (such as narrative, exposition and persuasive speech) on the grounds that they are not literally exchanges of talk.

Written language and monologues would be artifacts of irrational behavior if they did not presuppose the existence of some intended addressee or class of addressees" (p. 714).

5 Here and throughout the remainder of the book I use the term 'precursor' to refer to all those documents that the employer sends to employees prior to the date that such employees are transitioned into the new cash balance plan. Typically, but not always, this is also the date on which accruals under the employees' old plan stop or are 'frozen.' I refer to all documents (such as personal pension benefit reports) that an employee receives after the date of transition as 'post-transition' documents.

6 An explicitly self-identifying disclosure document is one that, for example, explicitly states it constitutes and is intended to satisfy a §204(h) notice requirement or serves as a required SMM. In both the *Amara* and *Tomlinson* cases, the employers distributed precursor documents to employees without such explicit self-identification but instead, after litigation commenced, referred to some of these documents as serving as these statutorily required notices or summaries.

7 O'Keefe (2002) provides an excellent summary of cognitive dissonance theory and research as it applies to receivers' processing of both persuasive and contradictory messages.

8 As noted in Chapter 2, under the current version of ERISA §204(h) employers are prohibited from deploying exclusively positive or neutral hypothetical examples of the effects of cash balance transitions on pension benefits if a sizeable number of employees will experience negative outcomes (e.g., reduction in accrual rates or wear away) as a result. However, the use of such exclusively positive examples remains an issue in cases still pending under the 1986 version of §204(h). See Amoroso, Flagg, Polisner, Rietz, & Segal (2001, 2002).

9 Interestingly, under the disclosure rules set forth in the Fair Debt Collection Practices Act (1977), courts have not been tolerant of collector notices to consumers that deploy contradictions in the hope that notice readers will draw the wrong conclusions about their rights. As a matter of law, courts have found such a practice to be deceptive. In particular, courts in these cases sometimes intervene to show explicitly how the collector could have written a notice to prevent any reader error arising from two or more separate statements with contradictory implications that, when read together, produce ambiguity. In *Savino v. Computer Credit Incorporated* (CCI) (164 F.3d 81, 2d Cir. 1998), for instance, the defendant CCI included on the back of its collection letter the statutorily required notice that the consumer could request proof of the debt within 30 days and that the collector (CCI) could take no further action against the consumer until such proof was provided. However, on the front of its letter CCI also included statements that the hospital creditor "demands immediate payment or a valid reason for your failure to make payment" (p. 85). The court found these statements potentially to contradict what the statutorily required notice indicates and discussed how they could prompt the reader mistakenly to believe, despite the statutory notice on the reverse side of the letter, that he or she did not have 30 days to request validation of the debt. In a manner similar to the disclaimer revisions I suggested, the court offered two alternative revisions to illustrate how the defendant CCI could explicitly resolve the apparent contradiction for the consumer, as follows:

> Although we have requested that you make immediate payment or provide a valid reason for nonpayment, you still have right to make a written request, within thirty days of your receipt of this notice for more information about the debt. Your rights are described on the reverse side of this notice.
> OR
> Our demand for immediate payment does not eliminate your right to dispute this debt within thirty days of receipt of this notice. If you choose to do so, we

> are required by law to cease our collection efforts until we have mailed that information to you. Your rights are described on the reverse side of this notice. (pp. 85–86)

As I will discuss in both Chapters 4 and 5, the temporal and spatial distance between apparently contradictory statements in the ERISA disclosures examined in *Amara* and *Tomlinson* are much greater than seen in the typical debt collection notice case and thus pose even greater potential difficulties for ordinary readers.

10 Expert hindsight bias shares some features of the more general cognitive phenomena of confirmation bias, which is the tendency of observers (who may be experimental researchers, expert and lay witnesses, courtroom advocates, jurors, and even judges) to perceive in certain data or events what they hope to perceive or, more subtly, what they unconsciously expect to perceive (e.g., Stratman, 1994). Coulthard (2010) and Solan (2010) provide important perspectives on the susceptibility of forensic linguists to confirmation bias. Such linguists, as I have done in the present study, offer opinions and interpretations about disputed discourse, and consequently they must always be mindful of the likely influence of the attorneys who retain them in producing their analyses and drawing their conclusions.

11 Expert hindsight bias is a problem that lies at the center of a great many disputes over the meaning and comprehensibility of legal texts, from instructions to juries to real estate contracts to temporary restraining orders. Lawyers are highly prone to presuming that what they understand by a legal text is or should also be understood by ordinary readers. A vivid, extended illustration of the difficulties that linguists, discourse analysts, and reading comprehension researchers have in discussing this problem with law professionals is on full display in the renowned 1995 symposium jointly sponsored by Northwestern and Washington Universities, in which six experts from each community (linguistics and law) came together for a weekend to exchange views. Although the full transcript of those discussions is more than 200 pages, discussion of ordinary readers' comprehension of legal texts versus the comprehension of the same texts by lawyers occurs on pages 921 through 940. See Proceedings (1995).

12 That is, before a person transfers money from one bank or investment to another, that person would reasonably expect to have been informed whether or not some fee or deduction for making that transfer would occur and how much that fee or deduction would be.

REFERENCES

Afflerbach, P. (1990). The influence of prior knowledge on expert readers' main idea construction strategies. *Reading Research Quarterly, 25*(1), 31–46.

Amoroso, V., Flagg, D., Polisner, D., Rietz, R., & Segal, D. (2002). ABCD cash balance letter: Rephrasing the question. *Enrolled Actuaries Report, 27*(3), 1–7.

Amoroso, V., Flagg, D., Polisner, D., Rietz, R., & Segal, D. (2001) Pension professionalism, *Enrolled Actuaries Report, 26*(3), 4–6.

Baker, L. (1989). Metacognition, comprehension monitoring, and the adult reader. *Educational Psychology Review, 1*, 3–38.

Bavelas, J., Black, A., Chovil, N., and Mullett, J. (1990). *Equivocal communication*. Newbury Park, CA: Sage Publications.

Berry, C., Scheffler, A., & Goldstein, C. (1993). Effects of text structure on the impact of heard News. *Applied Cognitive Psychology, 7*, 381–395.

Bransford, J., & Johnson, M. (2004). Contextual prerequisites for understanding: Some investigations of comprehension and recall. In D. Balota & E. Marsh (Eds.), *Cognitive psychology: Key readings* (pp. 431–439). New York, NY: Psychology Press.

Bransford, J., & Johnson, M. (1973). Consideration of some problems in comprehension. In W. G. Chase (Ed.), *Visual information processing* (pp. xiv, 555). New York, NY: Academic Press.
Bronston v. U.S., 409 U.S. 352 (1973).
Brown, P., & Levinson, S. (1987). *Politeness*. Cambridge, UK: Cambridge University Press.
Buller, D., & Burgoon, J. (1996a). Another look at information management: A rejoinder to McCornack, Levine, Morrison, and Lapinski. *Communication Monographs, 63*, 92–98.
Buller, D., & Burgoon, J. (1996b). Reflections on the nature of theory building and the theoretical status of interpersonal deception theory. *Communication Theory, 6*, 311–328.
Carson, T. (2012). *Lying and deception: Theory and practice*. Oxford: University of Oxford Press.
Channel, J. (1985). Vagueness as a conversational strategy. *Nottingham Linguistic Circular, 14*, 3–24.
Channel, J. (1990). Precise and vague quantities in writing on economics. In C. Cooper & S. Greenbaum (Eds.), *The writing scholar: Studies in academic discourse* (pp. 9–117). London: Sage Publications.
Coulthard, M. (2010). Experts and opinions: "In my opinion . . . ". In M. Coulthard & A. Jamison (Eds.), *Routledge handbook of forensic linguistics* (pp. 473–486). New York, NY: Routledge.
Coulthard, M., & Johnson, A. (2007). *An introduction to forensic linguistics: Language in evidence*. New York NY: Routledge.
Craswell, R. (2006). Taking information seriously: Misrepresentation and nondisclosure in contract law and elsewhere. *Virginia Law Review, 92*, 565–632.
Craswell, R. (1991). Regulating deceptive advertising: The role of cost-benefit analysis. *Southern California Law Review, 64*(3), 549–604.
Craswell, R. (1985). Interpreting deceptive advertising. *Boston University Law Review, 65*(4), 657–732.
Danziger, E. (2010). On trying and lying: Cultural configurations of Grice's Maxim of Quality. *Intercultutral Pragmatics, 7*(2), 199–219.
Davies, B.L. (2007). Grice's cooperative principle: Meaning and rationality. *Journal of Pragmatics, 39*, 2308–2331.
Davey, B., & McBride, S. (1986). Effects of question generation on reading comprehension. *Journal of Educational Psychology, 78*, 256–262.
DeScioli, P., Christner, J., & Kurzban, R. (2011). The omission strategy. *Psychological Science, 22*, 442–446.
Dumas, J., & Redish, J.C. (1999). *A practical guide to usability testing*. Exeter, UK: Intellect Books Ltd.
Dynel, M. (2011). A web of deceit: A neo-Gricean view on types of verbal deception. *International Review of Pragmatics, 3*, 139–167.
Eagly, A., & Chaiken, S. (1993). *The psychology of attitudes*. Fort Worth, TX: Harcourt Brace Jovanovich.
Entman, R. (1993). Framing: Toward a clarification of a fractured paradigm. *Journal of Communication, 43*, 51–58.
Employment Retirement Income Security Act of 1974, 29 C.F.R. § 2520.102–2(b) (Michie 1996).
Fair Debt Collection Practices Act, Public Law No. 95–109, 91 Stat.874 (1977).
Fairclough, N. (1985). Critical and descriptive goals in discourse analysis. *Journal of Pragmatics 9*, 739–793.
Fiske, S., & Taylor, S. (1991). *Social cognition*. New York, NY: McGraw-Hill.
Galasinski, D. (2000). *The language of deception: A discourse analytic study*. Thousand Oaks, CA: Sage Publications.
Gibbons, J. (2003). *Forensic linguistics: An introduction to language in the justice system*. London, UK: Blackwell Publishing Ltd.

Graesser, A. (1981). *Prose comprehension beyond the word.* New York, NY: Springer.

Graesser, A., Langston, M., & Baggett, W. (1993). Exploring information about concepts by asking questions. In G.V. Nakamura, R.M. Taraban, & D. Medin (Eds.), *The psychology of learning and motivation: Vol. 29. Categorization by humans and machines* (pp. 411–436). Orlando, FL: Academic Press.

Graesser, A., & McMahon, C. (1993). Anomalous information triggers questions when adults solve problems and comprehend stories. *Journal of Educational Psychology, 85*(1), 136–151.

Grice, P. (1989). *Studies in the way of words.* Cambridge, MA: Harvard University Press.

Grice, P. (1975). Logic and conversation. In P. Cole and J. Morgan (Eds.), *Syntax and semantics*(Vol. 3, pp. 41–58). New York, NY: Academic Press.

Griffith, E. (2012). The search for better communication between the debt collector and the consumer under the Fair Debt Collection Practices Act. *Kansas Law Review 61*, 179–228.

Griffith, E. (2008). The peculiarity of language in the debt collection process: The impact of the Fair Debt Collection Practices Act. *Wayne Law Review*, 54, 673–734.

Green, S. (2001). Lying, misleading, and falsely denying: How moral concepts inform the law of perjury, fraud, and false statements. *Hastings Law Journal, 53*, 157–212.

Green, G. (1990). The universality of Gricean interpretation. *Proceedings of the Sixteenth Annual Meeting of the Berkeley Linguistics Society*, 411–428.

Hacker, D., Dunlosky, J., & Graesser, A. (Eds.) (1998). *Metacognition in educational theory and practice.* Mahwah, NJ: Lawrence Erlbaum Associates.

Hancock, J., Curry, L., Goorha, S., & Woodworth, M. (2008). On lying and being lied to: A linguistic analysis of deception in computer-mediated communication. *Discourse Processes, 45*, 1–23.

Hasher, L., & Chromiak, W. (1977). The processing of frequency information: An automatic mechanism? *Journal of Verbal Learning and Verbal Behavior, 16*, 173–184.

Hasher, L., Goldstein, D., & Toppino, T. (1977). Frequency and the conference of referential validity. *Journal of Verbal Learning and Verbal Behavior, 16*, 107–112.

Haugtvedt, C., & Wegener, D. (1994). Message order effects in persuasion: An attitude strength perspective. *Journal of Consumer Research, 21*, 205–218.

Henderson, R. (1990). The doctrine of reasonable expectations in insurance law after two decades. *Ohio State Law Journal, 51*, 823–853.

Hoffrage, U. (2011). Hindsight bias: A by-product of knowledge updating? In R. Hertwig, G. Gigerenzer, & T. Pachur (Eds.), *Heuristics: The foundations of adaptive behavior* (pp. 223–241). New York, NY: Oxford University Press.

Howald, B. (2006). Comparative and non-comparative forensic linguistic analysis techniques: Methodologies for negotiating the interface of linguistics and evidentiary jurisprudence in the American judiciary. *University of Detroit Mercy Law Review, 83*, 285–327.

Hubbell, A., Chory-Assad, R., & Medved, C. (2005). A new approach to the study of deception in organizations. *North American Journal of Psychology, 7*(2), 171–180.

Iyengar, S., & Simon, A. (1994). News coverage of the Gulf crisis and public opinion: A study of agenda-setting, priming, and framing. In W. Bennett & D. Paletz (Eds.), *Taken by storm* (pp. 167–185). Chicago: University of Chicago Press.

Jacobs, S., Brashers, D., & Dawson, E. (1996). Information manipulation theory: A replication and assessment. *Communication Monographs, 63*, 70–82.

Johnson, H., & Seifert, C. (1994). Sources of the continued influence effect: When misinformation in memory affects later inferences. *Journal of Experimental Psychology: Learning, Memory and Cognition, 20*(6), 1420–1436.

Just, M., & Carpenter, P. (1987). *The psychology of reading and language comprehension.* Newton, MA: Allyn and Bacon.

Kassin, S., & Keichel, K. (1996). The social psychology of false confessions: Compliance, internalization, and confabulation. *Psychological Science, 7*, 125–128.

Kintsch, W., & van Dijk, T. A. (1978). Toward a model of text comprehension and production. *Psychological Review, 85*, 363–394.

Knoll, M. (2010). *The effects of expertise on the hindsight bias*. Doctoral Dissertation. Ohio State University, Department of Psychology. Retrieved from ProQuest Information and Learning (AAI3368433).

Latin, H. (1994). Good warnings, bad products, and cognitive limitations. *UCLA Law Review, 41*, 1193–1295.

Leech, G., & Thomas, J. (1988). Pragmatics: The state of the art. *Lancaster papers in linguistics, 48*. Lancaster, UK: University of Lancaster.

Lentz, L., & DeJong, M. (1997). The evaluation of text quality: Expert-focused and reader-focused methods compared. *IEEE Transactions on Professional Communication, 40*(3), 224–233.

Levinson, S. (1983). *Pragmatics*. Cambridge, UK: Cambridge University Press.

Lindblom, K. (2001). Cooperating with Grice: A cross-disciplinary metaperspective on uses of Grice's cooperative principle. *Journal of Pragmatics, 33*, 1601–1623.

Magliano, J. P., Trabasso, T., & Graesser, A. P. (1999). Strategic processing during comprehension. *Journal of Educational Psychology, 91*, 615–629.

Mannes, S., & Hoyes, S. (1996). Reinstating knowledge during reading: A strategic process. *Discourse Processes, 21*, 105–130.

McCornack, S. (2008). Information manipulation theory. In L. A. Baxter & D. O. Braithewaite (Eds.), *Engaging theories in interpersonal communication: Multiple perspectives* (pp. 215–226). Thousand Oaks, CA: Sage Publications.

McCornack, S. (1997). The generation of deceptive messages: Laying groundwork for a viable theory of interpersonal deception. In J. O. Greene (Ed.), *Message production: Advances in communication theory* (pp. 91–126). Hillsdale, NJ: Lawrence Erlbaum.

McCornack, S. A. (1992). Information manipulation theory. *Communication Monographs, 59*, 1–16.

McCornack, S., Levine, T., Morrison, K., & Lapinski, K. (1996). Speaking of information manipulation: A critical rejoinder. *Communication Monographs, 63*, 83–92.

McCornack, S. A., Levine, T. R., Solowczuk, K. A., Torres, H. I., & Campbell, D. M. (1992). When the alteration of information is viewed as deception: An empirical test of information manipulation theory. *Communication Monographs, 59*, 17–29.

McGuire, W. (1964). *Inducing resistance to persuasion: Some contemporary approaches*. New York, NY: Academic Press.

McNamara, D. (Ed). (2007). *Reading comprehension strategies: Theories, interventions and technologies*. New York, NY: Lawrence Erlbaum Associates.

Mey, J. (1987). Poet and peasant: A pragmatic comedy in five acts. *Journal of Pragmatics, 11*, 281–297.

Miller, G. (1990, September–October). Pragmatics and the maxims of interpretation. *Wisconsin Law Review*, 1179–1226.

Miller, G., & Stiff, J. (1993). *Deceptive communication*. Newbury Park, CA: Sage.

Morgan, M., Fischhoff, B., Bostrom, A., & Atman, C. (2002). *Risk communication: A mental models approach*. Cambridge, UK: Cambridge University Press.

Nielsen, J., & Mack, R. (Eds.). (1994). *Usability inspection methods*. New York, NY: John Wiley & Sons.

O'Keefe, D. (2002). *Persuasion: Theory and research*. Thousand Oaks, CA: Sage Publications.

Otero, J. (1998). Influence of knowledge activation and context of comprehension monitoring of science texts. In D. Hacker, J. Dunlosky, & A. Graesser (Eds.), *Metacognition in educational theory and practice* (pp. 145–164). Mahwah, NJ: Lawrence Erlbaum Associates.

Otero, J., & Kintsch, W. (1992). Failures to detect contradictions in a text: What readers believe versus what they read. *Psychological Science, 3*(4), 229–235.

Perfetti, C., Rouet, J., & Britt, M. (1999). Toward a theory of documents representation. In H. van Oostendorp & S. Goldman (Eds.), *The construction of mental representations during reading* (pp. 99–123). Mahwah, NJ: Lawrence Erlbaum Associates.

Perelman, C., & Olbrechts-Tyteca, L. (1969). *The new rhetoric: A treatise on argumentation.* Notre Dame, Indiana: University of Notre Dame Press.
Petty, R., & Caccioppo, J. (1979). Issue involvement can increase or decrease persuasion by enhancing message relevant cognitive responses. *Journal of Personality and Social Psychology, 37*, 1915–1926.
Pressley, M., & Afflerbach, P. (1995). Verbal protocols of reading: The nature of constructively responsive reading. Hillsdale, NJ: Lawrence Erlbaum Associates.
Price, V., Tewksbury, D., & Powers, E. (1997). Switching trains of thought: The impact of news frames on readers' cognitive responses. *Communication Research, 24*, 481–501.
Proceedings. (1995). Northwestern University/Washington University Law and Linguistics Conference. *Washington University Law Quarterly, 73*(3), 769–970.
Sarangi, S.K., & Slembrouck, S. (1992). Non-cooperation in communication: A reassessment of Gricean pragmatics. *Journal of Pragmatics, 17*, 117–154.
Schriver, K. (1997). *Dynamics in document design.* New York, NY: John Wiley and Sons.
Schriver, K. (1989). Evaluating text quality: The continuum from text-focused to reader-focused methods. *IEEE Transactions in Professional Communication, 32*(4), 238–255.
Shuy, R. (1993). *Language crimes: The use and abuse of language evidence in the courtroom.* Cambridge, MA: Blackwell Publishers Inc.
Shuy, R. (1998a). *Bureaucratic language in government and business.* Washington, DC: Georgetown University Press.
Shuy, R. (1998b). *The language of confession, interrogation, and deception.* Thousand Oaks, CA: Sage Publications.
Solan, L. (2010). The forensic linguist: The expert linguist meets the adversarial system. In M. Coulthard & A. Jamison (Eds.), *Routledge handbook of forensic linguistics* (pp. 395–410). New York, NY: Routledge.
Solan, L. (1999). Can the legal system use experts on meaning? *Tennessee Law Review, 66*, 1167–1199.
Spranca, M., Minsk, E., & Baron, J. (1991). Omission and commission in judgment and choice. *Journal of Experimental Social Psychology, 27*, 76–105.
Steinberg, E. (Ed.). (1991). *Plain language: Principles and practice.* Detroit, MI: Wayne State University Press.
Stratman, J. (1994). Investigating persuasive processes in legal discourse in real-time: Cognitive biases and rhetorical choices in briefs. *Discourse Processes, 17*(1), 1994, 1–57.
Tiersma, P. M. (2000). *Legal language.* Chicago: University of Chicago Press.
Tiersma, P. M. (1993). The judge as linguist. *Loyola of Los Angeles Law Review, 27*, 69–283.
Tiersma, P. M. (1990). The language of perjury: 'Literal truth,' ambiguity, and the false statement requirement. *Southern California Law Review, 63*, 373–431.
Tiersma, P. M. (1986). The language of offer and acceptance: Speech acts and the question of intent. *University of California Law Review, 74*(1), 89–232.
Thomas, J. (1995). *Meaning in interaction.* London: Longman.
van Dijk, T. (1999). Context models in discourse processing. In H. van Oostendorp & S.R. Goldman (Eds.), *The construction of mental representations during reading* (pp. 123–148). Mahwah, NJ: Lawrence Erlbaum Associates.
van Dijk, T.A., & Kintsch, W. (1983). *Strategies for discourse comprehension.* New York, NY: Academic Press.
van Oostendorp, H., & Goldman, S. (Eds.). (1999). *The construction of mental representations during reading.* Mahwah, NJ: Lawrence Erlbaum Associates.
Walker, C., & Meyer, B.J. (1980). Integrating different types of information in text. *Journal of Verbal Learning and Verbal Behavior, 19*, 263–275.
Yeung, L., Levine, T., & Nishiyama, K. (1999). Information manipulation theory and perceptions of deception in Hong Kong. *Communication Reports, 12*(1), 1–11.

4 *Amara v. CIGNA*

The district court in *Amara v. CIGNA* (2008) decided numerous other ERISA issues besides the adequacy or deceptiveness of CIGNA's benefit reduction disclosures. Nevertheless, the court devoted almost 30 pages of its 122-page opinion to the question of whether CIGNA satisfied ERISA's disclosure rules, providing an unusually detailed consideration of the documents that CIGNA employees received. In the 30-page disclosure section, the court divides its discussion into two main parts, first addressing whether CIGNA violated § 204(h) of ERISA and then addressing whether CIGNA violated ERISA's requirements for SMMs and SPDs. To support my discussion of the court's analysis, which follows, Table A (in Appendix 5) provides a breakdown of CIGNA's disclosure statements in relation to the three topics indicated at the end of the preceding chapter. The table also shows (from left to right) the basic chronological sequence in which these statements were issued.

As noted, the plan transitions in both *Amara* and *Tomlinson* fall under the earlier version of ERISA § 204(h) in effect from 1986 to 2001 (Consolidated Omnibus Budget Reconciliation Act of 1985, Title XI, § 11006, 100 Stat. 82, 1986). This version requires employers to "[set] forth the plan amendment and its effective date" if the amendment results in a "significant reduction in the future rate of benefit accrual." And thus, just as in the *Bilello* and *Hirt* decisions discussed earlier, one issue facing the *Amara* court was what § 204(h) means by these phrases. The court initially states, "As for the content of the notice itself, § 204(h)—as it existed prior to 2001 required only the text of the amendment and its effective date" (p. 73). However, the court also carefully summarizes the opposing contentions of the defendants and plaintiffs concerning these very phrases:

> CIGNA argues that . . . [it] was required at most to provide a summary of the [cash balance plan] amendment and its effective date [and that] no explanation of the nature or extent of the reductions themselves, or even an indication that [its disclosure document] was intended to comply with § 204(h), was necessary. Plaintiffs, on the other hand, assert that not only was a statement needed to the effect that "your benefits may be reduced," but in order to comply with the [§ 204(h)] requirement that the [amendment summary] be 'written in a manner calculated to be understood by the average plan participant,' some explanation of wear away and the other means by which benefits would be

> reduced was required" [citing Treasury Regulation 1.411(d)-6, Q&A-10] . . . Plaintiffs further argue that it was unrealistic of CIGNA to believe that a summary of [the cash balance plan amendment], without explicitly acknowledging the potential for reductions and how they might occur, could be comprehensible to the average plan participant. (p.78)

Ultimately, the court rejected CIGNA's claims that it satisfied § 204(h). But it does so by declining to address the question as to whether or not § 204(h) notices must include statements indicating that employees' future benefits are being reduced by wear away and other mechanisms, such as reducing employees' new opening cash account balances relative to the total value of their benefits they had already earned under the old plan. Referring to the litigants' opposing claims in the excerpt, the court reasoned that "[we] need not resolve this issue [about omissions] today, for even if § 204(h) did not require the additional information regarding reductions that Plaintiffs request, the statute certainly does not permit CIGNA to avoid providing information [about reductions] and to offer material misrepresentations suggesting benefit increases instead" (p. 78).

Interestingly, the court's hesitancy here to view § 204(h) as requiring employers to provide reduction information *per se* is belied by both its construction of the purpose behind § 204(h) and by its careful analysis of the effects of CIGNA's omissions in its disclosure documents. As for the purpose of § 204(h), the court adopts a similar view to the court in *Hirt*, stating that "the purpose underlying ERISA's notice requirements . . . is to protect employees' interests and their reasonable expectations [and] a primary purpose of notice under § 204(h) is to provide employees the opportunity to learn about changes to their retirement plan and perhaps to complain or otherwise seek to modify those if they are unacceptable" (p. 75). Clearly, even in the absence of affirmatively misleading statements, omissions of information indicating accrual rate reductions and wear-away periods following from a cash balance conversion would thwart the purpose that the court ascribes here to § 204(h). Assuming employees possess little knowledge about cash balance transitions before they encounter an employer's § 204(h) notice, such omissions will almost certainly violate employees' "reasonable expectations" and deprive them of "the opportunity to learn about changes to their retirement plan."

Indeed, as will be shown, the court itself goes on to catalogue the problems separately posed for employees by CIGNA's omissions as distinct from CIGNA's affirmatively misleading assertions, implying that many of these omissions *by themselves* would result in materially misleading inferences on the part of employee readers. Nonetheless, in concluding its analysis of CIGNA's § 204(h) notice, the court discounts the effect of CIGNA's omissions *per se* and rests its judgment instead upon CIGNA's affirmatively misleading language, that is, what in IMT would be termed violations of the quality maxim. As the court states:

> Taking all of this information into consideration, the Court concludes that CIGNA was aware of the significant reduction in the rate of future benefit

> accrual that would affect at least a substantial proportion of its employees as a result of the transition . . . CIGNA wished to avoid the employee backlash likely to result from a thorough discussion of [the transition], and . . . CIGNA sought to negate the risk of backlash *by producing affirmatively misleading notices*." (p. 87, italics added).

Without question, the court is correct to stress the debilitating effects that CIGNA's particular combination of affirmatively misleading statements and omissions would have on employee understanding. Yet, although basically congruent with this analysis, IMT suggests that even in the absence of affirmatively misleading statements of the sort that CIGNA made, the potentially deceptive impact of omissions could be enhanced by other *facially truthful* statements made by CIGNA as well as by violations of the clarity and relevance maxims, which can be demonstrated to help mask the omissions themselves. By closely examining CIGNA's disclosure statements in Table A together with important features of their context, I will attempt here to articulate this potentially problematic aspect of the court's analysis of the § 204(h) issue.

COMPARED TO THE OLD PLAN, WILL MY ACCRUAL BENEFIT RATES UNDER THE NEW PLAN BE REDUCED?

To begin, CIGNA stipulated that a precursor document titled "Signature Benefits Newsletter," which included a letter addressed to employees from CIGNA CEO Bill Taylor, was meant to serve as its § 204(h) notice. Chronologically this document was the first one that employees received regarding CIGNA's transition to the cash balance plan. As Table A shows, several statements in this document appear to respond directly to the employee's first question about possible reductions in their future benefit accrual rate (shown in the leftmost column), and all of them struck the court as affirmatively misleading responses:

> CIGNA will significantly enhance its retirement program.
> [Employees] will see an overall improvement in their retirement benefits.
> [The] new plan is designed to work well for both longer- and shorter- service employees.

Undoubtedly, the court is correct to reproach CIGNA for deceiving employees with these statements. All three statements are affirmatively misleading (violating the maxim of quality) because they imply that no benefit reductions would occur under the new plan when in fact the trial evidence indicated that the defendant knew a large number of older, longer-service employees would see significant reductions. The second and third statements also arguably violate the maxim of clarity: what, exactly, do the phrases "work well" and "overall improvement" mean? When these two phrases are combined with the first statement, CIGNA appears to deny that any significant reductions in the future rate of benefit accrual will occur.

The potential relevance of IMT in assessing deceptiveness, however, becomes more apparent when we hypothetically remove these statements from the newsletter and consider the likely impact upon employees of what remains (see Appendix 1 for the text of the newsletter). The entire tone of the altered letter is still relatively upbeat, and one must question whether the simple removal of these statements would somehow lead employees to discover that their future benefits were being reduced by the plan transition. The court seems to take the position that § 204(h) prohibits employers from deceiving employees about the existence of reductions, but it does not seem to appreciate that violations of quality are not always necessary for potently deceptive communication to occur. Other cues besides these statements in the newsletter also disingenuously encourage employees to trust the employer's message and to assume no reductions to their future accrual rate will occur.

For instance, in the altered version shown in Appendix 1, consider the possible impacts on employees' understanding resulting from these two statements:

> These changes will make our retirement program highly competitive with those offered by other companies in our industry.
>
> While the new Retirement Plan continues to provide a secure, company-funded benefit, the improved SIP plan gives employees another opportunity to share in the company's success.

Although these two statements cannot be said to be affirmatively misleading and therefore violate the quality maxim (it would be difficult to establish, at least, that they are positively false statements), the general 'news' about the company's new plan seems positive, the more so because no negatives are mentioned or even hinted.

Appropriately, the court shows that it will extend the benefit of the doubt to the employer by examining other precursor documents as well as the SMMs and SPDs that were sent along with and after this newsletter, that is, to see if the employer offered statements that would reverse the implications arising from the affirmatively misleading statements in the § 204(h) notice itself. These documents were put together in a packet titled "Information Kit on Your Retirement Program" and sent to employees about a month later. Here, the court found that CIGNA offered still more affirmatively misleading (positively false) statements concerning the existence of reductions (see the far right column of Table A), carefully noting that some of these affirmatively misleading statements were repeated in two or more places or documents (sentence numbers added for reference):

(1) [CIGNA] is not reducing the overall amount it contributes for retirement benefits, nor has the new program been designed to save money.

[FAQ Section]

(2) Q: I was hired in 1989. Why wasn't I allowed to stay in the [old] Pension Plan?

(3) A: Our analysis showed that, in comparison to people with a higher age and service combination, you have plenty of time to take full advantage of the many attractive features of the [new] Retirement Plan.

(4) Q: Will my benefit be better under the new retirement plan?

(5) A: The new retirement plan is different from the current pension plan, so exact comparisons of benefits that cover all possible outcomes are difficult. **(6)** Generally speaking, the new retirement plan, in comparison with the current pension plan, tends to provide larger benefits for shorter-term employees and comparable benefits for longer service employees.

The *Amara* court is surely correct to rebuke CIGNA for making the first statement (1), given that it was demonstrated at trial that CIGNA was saving the company millions of dollars through plan conversion. The court further appears correct to rebuke CIGNA for making the response portions of the two FAQ segments shown in the excerpt (*Amara v. CIGNA Corp.*, 2008, pp. 80–82). Importantly, however, the court did not quote the FAQ question portions in its opinion, and it otherwise overlooked in its discussion the subtle role that these questions might play in employees' understanding of the responses themselves. Let us look more closely at the first question-and-answer pair.

The answer (3) to the first question is certainly misleading. But, in IMT terms, it appears incorrect to say, as the court does, that this first response is *affirmatively* misleading (i.e., a violation of the quality maxim). The reason the statement is not affirmatively misleading is that the statement is not positively or literally false: those employees not grandparented under the old plan would indeed be able to "take full advantage" of certain aspects of the new cash balance plan not available to those who were grandparented. Rather, the response is deceptive because it violates the maxim of quantity; it *omits* crucial information that employees hired in 1989 reasonably would have wanted to know.

Specifically, the reason employees would ask why they were not allowed to continue under the old plan is their underlying concern about possible loss or reduction of benefits under the new plan. CIGNA's response, although literally true, is semantically irrelevant to employees' underlying question—it is an example of what Galasinski (2000, pp. 71–85) identifies as "metadiscursive" deception. On the one hand, the response is pragmatically relevant to the question in that it appropriately offers some comparison of and differentiation between the two employee groups. It recognizes that the employee questioner seeks an explanation for the difference in treatment between those hired in 1989 and those hired earlier. On the other hand, however, CIGNA's response covertly evades the employee's underlying concern as to whether any benefit reduction occurs for those who are not grandparented and who are forced instead into the new cash balance plan.

The response also violates the maxim of clarity by vaguely referring to "plenty of time" and the "many attractive features" of the new plan. In response, employees may well ask, what does CIGNA mean by "plenty of time" and "many attractive features"? These vague references may invite some employees to believe that they may be better off or at least no worse off under the new plan because CIGNA notes explicitly that it allowed certain "higher age and service" employees who *would be hurt* by the transition to stay in the old plan. That is, the fact that CIGNA grandparented certain older employees to prevent harm to them can be seen as an inducement to the other employees to believe that they also will not be harmed but rather protected from future accrual reductions. The response as a whole, then, seems reassuring and forthcoming while encouraging employee readers to believe that CIGNA is protecting them. Instead, CIGNA knew that these employees "hired in 1989" would indeed be harmed by the conversion and yet does not tell them that. Thus, this response is like that of the bystander in the crossing light case (case 3) discussed in the introduction. Recall in that case the bystander says, "I think it's safe to cross [the street] now," rather than telling the blind person that the light is red—this, despite the blind person's direct question about the color of the light. The bystander thereby omits information crucial to the blind person's safety while seemingly encouraging her to cross. Similarly, the fundamental problem with the first FAQ response portion is that it omits materially significant information (thus violating the maxim of quantity) while masking this omission with a pragmatically relevant but semantically irrelevant answer.

In contrast, the second FAQ pair does appear to violate the quality maxim by making an affirmatively misleading (positively false) statement. The term "comparable," which is a type of vague quantifier (see Channel, 1990) might be taken to mean either "exactly equal" or "the same,"—or, perhaps, "nearly equal" or "nearly the same." It is thus not a term that one can plausibly use to characterize benefit accrual rate reductions of 30 to 45 percent as occurred for a substantial number of CIGNA employees. At the same time, notice that by posing this question, the employer appears genuinely cooperative in the simulated conversation, seeming to tackle head-on and acknowledge what the employee is most worried about. However, as illustrated in the preceding chapter, this seemingly cooperative question involves a potentially biasing frame. The question imputed to the employees asks if their benefits will be "better"—as opposed to "worse" or "the same"—under the new plan.[1] This positive frame, when combined with the impression of candor generated by the directness of the question, potentially impacts the way employees would take the response offered, nudging them toward a false belief. In other words, the positive frame and the seeming directness of the question may subtly invite employees to trust that the company is not abusing the limits of the term "comparable" nor trying to use it as a veiled, vague warning that benefits could be lower to any significant degree. But that misleading discourse strategy appears to be exactly what CIGNA was trying to accomplish with this second FAQ, as further analysis of the response portion will now show.

In particular, other hedges included in the response ("Generally speaking" and "tends to") serve as a type of negative politeness known as "association cues" (see Brown & Levinson, 1987). Such cues ambiguously hint at a communicator's unwillingness to take responsibility for speaking categorically, precisely, or decisively. In addition to the uncertainty produced by the term "comparable," these hedges would likely generate some additional cognitive dissonance and uncertainty in employees along with some reasonable expectation that more information would be provided. When a communicator uses the qualifying phrase "Generally speaking" in beginning to answer such a clear and direct question, the phrase implies that the speaker knows about some exceptions or situations in which benefits will *not* be "better" or not "comparable." Similarly, the hedge "tends to" suggests that the employer is speaking in probabilistic terms and is aware of some undisclosed percentage of conditions or circumstances in which benefits may not be "comparable" (Crismore & Vande Kopple, 1988).

To avoid violating the maxim of quantity, the cooperativeness principle underlying IMT calls for the employer to communicate something about the exceptions implied by such hedges, or, at least, to issue a disclaimer with specific directions as to where the employee could find more information.[2] Strategically, the hedges that CIGNA uses here may be included precisely to allow deniability, that is, to support a subsequent claim that the employer did not violate the maxim of quantity and omit a material truth. The employer might claim that the hedges warn the employee that the employer knows it is not speaking completely or categorically in response to the question. But, at the same time, the specific distinction in statement (6) made between "shorter-term" and "longer service employees" blunts the warning conveyed by the hedges and leaves employees to lean mistakenly toward the more positive understanding of the term "comparable" as meaning "nearly the same." In particular, by making the distinction between shorter- and longer-service employees salient in statement (6), the employer is also implicitly suggesting that it is addressing the underlying concerns of "longer service" employees and implying that they can trust the employer to look out for their interests in the absence of more specific information. In the end, it is not only the affirmatively misleading term "comparable" that masks the deceptive material omission here but also these other 'truth-neutral' discourse features.

Of course, the *Amara* court is undoubtedly correct to rebuke the defendant for stating that employees' future benefit growth will be "comparable." The court is also correct to note how the earlier newsletter statements that it examined initially and considers to be affirmatively misleading interact with these *later* omissions in the Information Kit to reinforce materially misleading inferences in employees' understanding (*Amara v. CIGNA Corp.*, 2008, pp. 80–82).

As noted, the court's express hesitation to conclude that § 204(h) requires the employer to disclose lower future accrual rates seems to conflict with its broad view of the purpose underlying § 204(h) and the considerable weight that the court places on CIGNA's omissions *per se*. For instance, the court sharply observes that even CIGNA's key disclosure witness could not point to *any* employee document, let alone the "Newsletter," its purported § 204(h) notice, where CIGNA indicated the reductions in accrual rates resulting from the new plan (p. 79). The court then further stresses that

> nothing in the Newsletter indicated to plan participants that their rate of benefit accrual might decrease, much less by a significant margin. And yet that is exactly what happened. Even looking outside the purported § 204(h) notice to the other publications provided by CIGNA, information regarding possible reductions in the rate of future benefit accrual is equally non-existent . . . [T]he problem lies not with the volume of information CIGNA chose to provide, but rather with some of the statements made in CIGNA's disclosures, which the Court finds were not "written in a manner calculated to be understood by the average plan participant" and which failed to include important details regarding the transition . . . that reasonable employees would have wanted to know . . . Simply providing information about the [new plan] set up and content of opening account balances could not counteract the more favorable impression made by CIGNA's other statements about the positive features of the new plan and how employees benefits would grow under [it] . . . [G]iven the substantial amount of misinformation on the subject contained in the notices and disclosures CIGNA provided, the court refuses to accept that the information regarding opening account balances, while admittedly accurate, cured the defects in the previous disclosures . . . CIGNA employees suffered from the lack of accurate information in CIGNA's disclosures, and CIGNA was aware of this fact (pp. 80, 82, 83).

Interestingly, these statements show the court struggling to frame its major premise for finding CIGNA in violation of § 204(h) while simultaneously sticking to its initial interpretation that § 204(h) does *not necessarily* require disclosure of accrual rate reductions. The first two statements here stress omission of materially significant information in CIGNA's disclosures; in contrast, the third statement points to "statements made" rather than to omissions; and then the remainder again stresses the effect of CIGNA's omissions when combined with other "misinformation."

This shifting back and forth is telling. From the perspective of IMT and its cooperativeness principle, a key concern about the *Amara* court's analysis of the § 204(h) issue is that it does not appear to appreciate sufficiently the deceptiveness of omissions *per se* and, further, the way that omissions can be enhanced by accompanying truth-neutral statements and discursive means *other than* statements that can demonstrated to be affirmatively misleading. Expressed in a formalism the court seems to base its finding that CIGNA violated § 204(h) on the following three incompatible premises:

Affirmatively misleading statements = deception
Affirmatively misleading statements + omissions of information = *greater* deception

But,
Omissions without affirmatively misleading statements ≠ deception

Applying the more particularized focus of IMT maxims, however, might have helped the court to see that interpreting § 204(h) to forbid deception *by any means, including by omission of mention of reductions*, makes more sense in view of the court's own construction of the purpose of the statute, as quoted earlier. To the extent that the employee readership does not possess prior knowledge about cash balance plans and transitions to such plans, omissions by themselves can be a potent means of deception. As the comparison of newsletter statements in Appendix 1 should suggest, CIGNA's omissions could remain deceptive even without the affirmatively misleading statements in the initial newsletter to which the court took such immediate and strong exception. Indeed, as the analysis of other language in CIGNA's Information Kit shows, the deceptive effect of CIGNA's omissions *per se* was enhanced not only by affirmatively misleading statements but also by its violations of both IMT's relevance and clarity maxims, as shown. For these reasons, it is hard to square the court's analysis of CIGNA's disclosures with its express position that § 204(h) does not necessarily require any disclosure of future accrual rate reductions, wear-away periods, and reductions to employees' new account balances under the new plan.

WILL A WEAR-AWAY PERIOD OCCUR IMMEDIATELY FOLLOWING THE DATE OF TRANSITION DURING WHICH THE EMPLOYEE WILL NOT EARN ANY ADDITIONAL PENSION BENEFIT AT ALL?

Before looking at what the *Amara* court has to say about disclosure of wear-away periods, it is important to remember what causes them: they are the result of the employer setting employees' opening account balances in the new cash balance plan at a value significantly *below* the value of the employees' old plan benefits on the date of transition—by some 40 to 50 percent. Because of this lowered value, the employee will need to work for some years before the new account balance returns to the value of the old account on the date it was frozen. As the plaintiffs' actuarial witness explained,

> the values of initial account balances, which were already set artificially low by stripping out the values of protected early retirement and surviving spouse benefits, [were] further decreased as a result of a pre-retirement mortality discount and lower interest rates. Effectively, CIGNA's cash balance conversion . . . transformed the defined annual annuity benefits before the conversion into the stripped down variable annuities that are discounted for pre-retirement mortality, with no possibility of recapturing that discount, and that fall further below the previously earned level when interest rates decline. Additional benefit accruals under [the new cash balance plan were] conditioned on

> accepting these losses or discounts. (Declaration of Claude Poulin, F.S.A., Plaintiff's Actuarial Witness, April 25, 2003, para. 34–35)

In consequence of the discounts described here, the employee's old frozen benefits are *not* simply transferred unaltered into the employee's new cash balance account. As discussed in Chapter 2, it is highly unlikely that average plan participants would expect or anticipate such reductions to occur. They might expect, rather, that their old plan benefits would simply serve as the new plan opening balance, that is, much as if one transferred one's assets from one bank account to a new bank account. As will be seen in the third section of this chapter, CIGNA appears to engage in a three-pronged discourse strategy with respect to imposing and ostensibly communicating about opening account balance reductions: CIGNA omits any direct or explicit mention of their occurrence (i.e., quantity violations); it uses vague and ambiguous predicates to characterize how the old plan balance compares and relates to the new plan balance (clarity violations); and it also uses affirmatively misleading (patently or positively false) statements.

Similarly, and as will now be shown in this section, CIGNA uses this same combination of discourse strategies to prevent employees from learning about lengthy wear-away periods during which employees would not earn any new benefits at all—periods that actually reduce their future benefit accrual rate to 0 percent. Just like the reductions to their new opening account balances, employees would not be sufficiently aware even of the *possibility* of wear-away periods to ask about them. For instance, in relation to the crossing light hypothetical case discussed in the introduction, opening account balance reductions and wear-away periods are akin to a green crossing light that lasts no more than two to three seconds and not long enough to allow anyone except perhaps a world-class sprinter to make it across the intersection before the light changed back to red. Even blind users of an intersection would never think to ask someone if such a condition exists.

The *Amara* court does not discuss the disclosure of wear-away periods as part of its analysis of the then-existing § 204(h) notice requirements (pp. 72–87 of its opinion). It thus leaves unaddressed the question as to whether such notices must inform employees regarding these periods. Instead, the court indicates that the disclosure of such periods is required under ERISA §102, specifically the provisions dealing with SMMs and SPDs quoted earlier. Notwithstanding this jurisdictional placement, the court revisits statements pertinent to wear away that appeared in CIGNA's § 204(h) notice (i.e., the initial newsletter) as well as those appearing in CIGNA's putative SMM and SPDs. The court does so to give CIGNA the benefit of the doubt. As the court further notes, CIGNA stipulated that the entire document titled "Information Kit on Your Retirement Program" was intended to serve as its SMM (see Table A for CIGNA statements pertinent to wear-away periods contained in all of its documents).

Upon carefully considering the discourse evidence, the court found that CIGNA egregiously violated ERISA's §102 standards. After rejecting three different technical arguments that CIGNA advanced as to why no notice of wear-away periods was required at all, the court turns to the text of CIGNA's disclosure documents themselves. The court had no difficulty in locating what it considered to be "materially misleading" statements in CIGNA's disclosures (see the italicized text segments in Table A), stating: "Even assuming . . . that CIGNA did not have an affirmative duty to inform plan participants regarding wear away, it nonetheless could not provide, instead of no information, materially misleading statements. Yet that is just what CIGNA did" (pp. 95–96).

What is interesting about the court's statement here is that in distinguishing "materially misleading" statements from omissions, it appears to suggest that it equates "materially misleading" statements with "affirmatively misleading" statements. But, in fact, not all statements that are materially misleading are necessarily affirmatively misleading; conversely, not all affirmatively misleading statements may be materially misleading. At least, in IMT terms, an affirmatively misleading statement explicitly or expressly asserts something to be true when the very opposite is the case, regardless of whether or not the consequences of the statement are "material" in the legal, evidentiary sense. The problem in the court's use of terms can be seen by turning to the general legal definition of materially misleading statements. In the ERISA disclosure context, as Wiedenbeck (2008) explains, materially misleading statements are any misrepresentations that "would influence a reasonable participant's career or financial planning," and a test for such statements should be "whether known or reasonably foreseeable participants would attach importance to the information" as a basis for such planning and related decision making (pp. 100, 103). In contrast with the *Amara* court's apparent assumption that materially misleading statements and affirmatively misleading statements are the same thing, Wiedenbeck's definition would encompass discourse that leads plan participants to misunderstand actual plan transition consequences *either* through omission of information *or* through positively false statements, *or* from both in some combination.

Speaking precisely from the standpoint of IMT, and given the way cash balance conversions based upon on the greater of *either* A *or* B approach work, how we characterize the statements pertinent to wear-away periods in Table A that CIGNA made depends at least in part upon the employee readers' prior knowledge (if any) of cash balance conversions. As pointed out, readers who know little or nothing about these conversions when encountering CIGNA's stream of disclosure documents would not think *even to pose questions about* opening account balance reductions or wear-away periods. Given their prior experience with defined benefit plans, these features would likely be wholly unexpected by them. In this sense, employees 'do not know what they do not know.' Thus, these readers could not begin to pose a question like the one shown in the left-hand column of Table A: "Will a wear away period occur during which the employee will not earn any benefit at all?" As I will attempt to show here, for these low- or no-knowledge readers, the statements by CIGNA that the *Amara* court characterizes as affirmatively misleading (quality violations) may be somewhat more accurately characterized as misleading through omission (quantity violations).

Consider the following hypothetical statements that CIGNA might have made about wear-away periods, but did not:

> (0) No CIGNA employees will experience a wear-away period as a result of transition to the new cash balance plan. The payment to you of the dollar value of your new cash balance account credits can never be suspended.

In IMT terms, such a statement would be considered affirmatively misleading and constitute a clear violation of IMT's quality maxim because it explicitly or expressly asserts the *direct opposite* of the actual state of affairs. Now compare this hypothetical statement with each of those below that CIGNA actually made in its precursor documents (italics and sentence numbers have been added):

(1) *[The new plan] provides steadier benefit growth throughout [the employee's] career.*
(2) As of [January 1, 1998], the benefits you have earned under the Pension Plan will be converted to an opening account balance in the new plan. *At the same time, you will begin earning retirement benefits under the new plan.*
(3) You will earn no further benefit under the Pension Plan after December 31, 1997. *Starting in 1998, you will earn benefits under the new plan.*
(4) *[Y]our retirement benefit will continue to grow.*
(5) **How Your Account Grows**
Each dollar's worth of credit is a dollar of retirement after you are vested. Under the plan, your benefit will grow steadily throughout your career as credits are added to your account.
(6) [Your quarterly statement will show] the amount of accumulated credits in your [cash balance] account. *You'll see that amount continue to grow every year you are with CIGNA.*
(7) *Each dollar's worth of credit is a dollar of retirement after you are vested. Under the plan, your benefit will grow steadily throughout your career as credits are added to your account.*

Consider statement (1) that touts "steadier benefit growth" under the cash balance plan. As discussed earlier, compared to final pay-averaging plans, cash balance plans *do* in fact provide for "steadier benefit growth" over an employee's career in the sense that more retirement is earned earlier in the employee's career under a cash balance plan than would occur in a more 'back-loaded' defined benefit plan; that is one of their key differences. In addition, experts in cash balance plans will correctly point out that even employee cash balance accounts that are under a wear away are nevertheless "steadily" accumulating 'hypothetical' income and interest credits from the date of plan conversion. These accumulating credit totals are then regularly shown on quarterly reports that the employee receives, including the reports of employees under a wear-away period. Statement (1) above ostensibly reports no more than this fact and does not assert or necessarily imply that wear-away periods will not occur.

However, for employee readers who already know what wear-away periods are and what causes them, and who thus know enough to be looking for specific employer statements or assurances about them, this statement may be understood more like the explicit *denial* of such periods (in statement 0) that I posed previously. In particular, these knowledgeable readers might note that statement (1) does not refer to "steadier" growth in cash balance *income credits* but rather seems to assure them of *actual* (as opposed to hypothetical) "benefit growth." For instance, notice that statement (6) makes a more limited and accurate claim by referring to growth in "accumulated credits" rather than growth in retirement benefits. In effect, for knowledgeable readers, statement (6) would not be affirmatively misleading, whereas statement (1) is. For knowledgeable readers, then, statement (1) violates IMT's quality maxim because it falsely suggests that no wear away or suspension of benefit accruals will occur following the date of plan conversion. Conversely, for average plan participants with no prior knowledge of cash balance plan transitions, statement (1), taken by itself, would violate IMT's quantity maxim because it fails to provide the crucial caveat that while employees are under a wear-away period, the accumulating income credits in their accounts will *not* translate to any actual growth in their pension benefits. Thus, for both reader groups, statement (1) is both deceptive and materially misleading but in different ways depending upon these readers' different prior knowledge regarding the possibility and causes of wear-away periods.

The impact on employee readers of statements (2), (3), and (4) can be similarly analyzed. For naïve readers who do not know enough about cash balance plans even to ask about and look for information about wear-away periods, the deceptiveness of these statements chiefly arises from information about wear-away periods that they omit. In contrast, for knowledgeable readers who may be actively seeking specific reassurances about wear-away periods, these statements also are deceptive because they issue empirically false denials regarding the imposition of wear-away periods, albeit not as expressly or explicitly as the hypothetical statement (0) that I posed. In particular, note again that all three of these statements (2), (3), and (4) use the term "benefits" rather than the technically accurate and more precise term 'income credits,' a difference that makes them affirmatively misleading for knowledgeable readers.

Finally, compared with the rest of the statements, statements (5) and (7) are the most egregiously and affirmatively misleading. For those readers knowledgeable about wear-away periods, these two statements most nearly approximate the express, explicit denial of wear-away periods shown in statement (0). In these two statements, and contrary to the way its plan conversion actually worked, CIGNA appears to say that employees will always receive the accrued dollar value of the interest and income credits they have accumulated in their new cash balance accounts and that growth in these credits will never be merely hypothetical. In effect, these statements say that, as far as the new cash balance account goes, 'what you see is what you get;' this is patently false for CIGNA employees under wear-away periods, the overwhelming majority of the more than 25,000 employees in the lawsuit class. At the same time, for employee readers with no prior knowledge about wear-away periods, these statements, like all of the others, omit any hint of the existence of wear-away periods so that these employees continue 'not to know what they do not know.' In relation to the crossing light hypothetical described earlier, all of the statements CIGNA made can be analogized to case 3 in which, when the blind person asks if the light is green, the bystander replies, "I think it is safe to cross now," despite seeing that the light is red.

The possible strategic goal of the disclosure drafters in making the previous statements was to be able, if challenged later about disclosure, to tout their partial technical truth value relative to the actual mechanics of the plan transition while still preventing employees from detecting the existence of wear-away periods. Although CIGNA's disclosures included examples purportedly showing how hypothetical employees' new cash balance accounts would grow following plan conversion, none of these examples indicated that the employee's opening account balance had been lowered relative to the employee's old plan frozen benefit, nor did any show an employee suffering a wear-away period. The *Amara* court reviewed much direct oral and e-mail evidence from CIGNA officials strongly suggesting the deceptive intent behind these discourse strategies (*Amara v. CIGNA Corp.*, 2008, pp. 83–87).

Indeed, CIGNA had tried to argue that the following two additional statements, either singly or in combination, were enough to signal to employees that wear-away periods could occur:

> Keep in mind that this [hypothetical employee] benefit comparison is intended to provide you with general information about opening balances and benefit growth . . . *Your actual benefit will depend upon your age, future service, and salary history, and may differ from the benefits shown in the examples.*
>
> *Your final plan benefits cannot be less than your old plan benefits on December 31st, 1997* (italics added).

If readers already possessed knowledge of cash balance transitions, already knew what wear-away periods were, and that wear-away periods were a possible outcome of such transitions, this argument might have some slight plausibility. But CIGNA made no showing at trial that the employees were so equipped. The court tersely rejected CIGNA's argument about these putative 'signals' of wear away, stating that

> [n]owhere in any of the notices is the phenomenon of wear away, or any substantive equivalent, discussed or described. Further, in light of all the above-mentioned statements that unequivocally state that all plan participants will begin accruing benefits . . . on January 1, 1998, the Court finds that plan participants would reasonably believe that wear away was not a component of, or a likely result of [the conversion to a cash balance plan].

> As CIGNA's counsel admitted to the Court, he could point to no statement in the notices that told employees "they were actually earning no retirement benefits." The indirect reference to the protected minimum benefit to which CIGNA now points is simply inadequate.
>
> (*Amara v. CIGNA Corp.*, 2008, p. 97)

Thus the court, which began its analysis of the wear-away issue seeming to claim that CIGNA's approach to disclosing the wear-away effect was deceptive primarily because of affirmatively misleading statements (violations of quality), actually shifts its ground somewhat by the close and bases its finding of illegality more on the fact that CIGNA omitted all mention of wear-away periods, thus pointing to an equally egregious violation of quantity. As will become apparent in the next section, the lack of any mention of wear-away periods was made more powerfully deceptive in the context of CIGNA's statements concerning how employees' new opening cash account balances were set.

ARE OPENING ACCOUNT BALANCES IN THE NEW PLAN EQUAL TO THE TOTAL VALUE OF BENEFITS EARNED UNDER THE OLD PLAN?

As explained, CIGNA's reductions to employees' new opening account balances directly contributed to the length of wear-away periods that employees would suffer: the greater the reduction, the longer, in general, the resulting wear-away period. With respect to this question, the court also found CIGNA's statements about the setting of employees' opening account balances to be affirmatively misleading (see Table A). Rather than see the full value of all of their old, final average plan benefits simply transferred to the new opening cash balance account, many employees' new account balances were set significantly below the value of these old plan benefits. This reduction occurred chiefly as a result of the elimination of their early retirement benefit, an erasure that CIGNA never disclosed let alone explained in its documents (Declaration of Claude Poulin, F.S.A., Plaintiff's Actuarial Witness, April 25, 2003, para. 34–35). Even more disturbingly, and as will be shown, CIGNA went beyond omission of specific reduction information and included statements directly denying that any reductions in employees' new opening account balances could or would occur as a result of the pension plan transition.

CIGNA nonetheless contended that it warned employees about opening cash balance account reductions in its precursor document titled "Information Kit," sent to employees in December 1997. In a section headed, "Converting Your Final Pension Benefit to an Opening Balance," the company explained:

> Your normal pension benefit is an annual payment made to you for life, beginning when you turn age 65. To convert that annual pension benefit into an opening balance for the new plan, a calculation has to be made to determine

> how much that future stream of payments is worth today. This type of calculation is called a present value calculation.
>
> The method used to calculate the present value of a pension benefit is established by law.

The company argued that because it indicated here that a "present value calculation" must be used to "convert" employees' current old plan balances, employees should realize that old plan benefits could not be transferred like a simple cash asset to their opening balances under the new plan. Further, they argued that employees should have inferred from this language that the output of this calculation might not equal the total value of their old plan benefits. But, as the *Amara* court pointed out, and as CIGNA was forced to admit at trial, the company makes an affirmatively misleading statement when it claims that the calculation method it used is "established by law" (*Amara v. CIGNA Corp.*, 2008, p. 82). This false claim constitutes a quality violation. Further, the calculation that CIGNA presents in this document did not show all of the adjustments that CIGNA made to the value of the employees' final, old plan balances (Declaration of Claude Poulin, F.S.A., Plaintiff's Actuarial Witness, April 25, 2003, para. 34–35). Nor did CIGNA ever acknowledge what their effects would be. Instead, CIGNA encouraged employees to trust the 'fairness' of the calculation, not only by falsely imputing its basis to federal law but also by seeming to suggest that in cases where new balances did not equal the value of old plan balances, CIGNA would lower the interest rate it applied in its calculation to make up the difference. CIGNA stated the following:

> Because of the relatively low interest rate, the amount [of plan benefits] available to you today is relatively large. In fact, to increase your opening balance, CIGNA has selected a much lower interest rate than the 7% or 8% rate adopted by most companies making similar pension plan changes.

CIGNA's apparent discourse strategy regarding opening cash balance account reductions, however, also involved inconsistency and ambiguity. In particular, what is most notable across the statements concerning opening account balances shown in Table A is CIGNA's shifting use of different verbs used to characterize what is happening to employees' old plan benefits at the time of plan transition (see Table A). Consider these three key statements (numbering and italics added):

(1) [Benefits] are *fully* protected [and] their value will be reflected in the new plan balance.

(2) *Any* benefits that you have earned under the CIGNA Pension Plan will be converted to an opening account balance in the new plan.

(3) If you are eligible for the new CIGNA Plan, *all* of your benefits earned under the current pension plan through 12/31/97 will remain yours. As of 1/1/98, those benefits will be transferred to the new plan.

Why does CIGNA use these three different verbs rather than just one? The verbs "reflected" and "converted" may have been chosen to thwart an accusation of deception and ostensibly enable the company to later argue that it had signaled semantically to employees that the value of the opening cash account balance might not, after all, equal the value of their old plan benefits. But if that was CIGNA's goal, then the term "transferred" is obviously a fly in the ointment. A "transfer" of benefits does not suggest or imply benefits have been "converted;" the former term implies movement of an object from one place to another, whereas the latter implies some transformation will occur within the object itself beyond or in addition to its relocation. Also inconsistent with the implications of the verbs "convert" and "reflect" are the company's repeated use of categorical adjectives when referring to employees' old plan benefits. For instance, the company states that "*all* of your benefits earned under the current pension plan through 12/31/97 will remain yours" (italics added). When the company also states that "[Benefits] are *fully* protected [and] their value will be reflected in the new plan balance (italics added)," employee readers could hardly suspect that a "reflected" benefit is not, in fact, equal to the "protected" benefit, any more than one would suspect that an image of a person reflected in a mirror would be missing her nose and ears through some "conversion" process. CIGNA may have strategically deployed the term "reflected" with the mistaken notion that it somehow signaled that the value of new cash account balances could be less than the value of old plan benefits.

Employees unfamiliar with cash balance plans could thus only find the subsequently simulated questions-and-answer exchange shown in Table A to be confusing in light of the statements that unqualifiedly assure them their old plan benefits are "fully" protected:

> **Q:** How do I know that the lump sum conversion is fair and accurate?
> **A:** The conversion factors we are using to determine your opening account balance are based on guidelines established by the government to ensure a fair transition for employees.

If, as employees are being told, "all" of an employee's old plan benefits are being "transferred" to the new plan account balance, why would the company even project or anticipate the employee question, "How do I know that the lump sum conversion is fair and accurate?" The company adds to the confusion and uncertainty provoked by this question by cryptically referring to "conversion factors" putatively "based on guidelines established by the government to ensure a fair transition for employees." Again, however, as was made clear at trial, no such federal guidelines for setting the value of opening account balances during plan transitions existed at the time of CIGNA's conversion (see U.S. General Accounting Office, 2000a, 2000b, 2005).

Upon reviewing CIGNA's internally discordant statements about the value of employees' new opening account balances in relation to the value of their old plan benefits, the court had no trouble concluding that "the notices were not written in a manner calculated to be understood by the average plan participant" (p. 99). The court found that "in light of apparently contradictory statements within the [Information] Kit, to the effect that *any* benefits previously accrued would be protected, and the lack of any indication in the later, authoritative SPDs that early retirement benefits would not be included in the opening account balances," the "disclosures as a whole [were] statutorily inadequate" (pp. 99–100).

To summarize, overall it would probably be going too far to claim that the *Amara* court's factual and legal conclusions about CIGNA's disclosure documents would be greatly altered by consideration of IMT's maxims. Nonetheless, these maxims do help to focus some problematic aspects of the court's analysis in interpreting ERISA's complex statutory framework, particularly as regards what § 204(h) requires and prohibits in an amendment disclosure notice. Consideration of the maxims may help courts to appreciate that the deceptiveness of omissions (violations of quantity) can be enhanced by statements and textual elements *other than* those that are demonstrably shown to be affirmatively misleading. In particular, use of IMT's maxims reveals that contested statements that are judged to be "materially misleading" do not necessarily have to be *affirmatively* misleading and assert something that is positively false. Instead, statements judged to be materially misleading can, as discussed, effect deception either *entirely* through omission *or* through some combination of omission and violations of the clarity and relevance maxims. This possibility appears to be anticipated in the language of ERISA §102 when it proscribes "failing to inform participants and beneficiaries" while also requiring that disclosures must be "written in a manner calculated to be understood by the average plan participant." And it thus would seem incongruous for § 204(h) to forbid "materially misleading" statements that are based upon quality violations (affirmatively misleading statements) while possibly allowing "materially misleading" implications that arise from either quantity (omission), relevance, and or clarity violations. This is a statutory interpretation problem that the *Amara* court, for all of its care in examining CIGNA's disclosures, leaves unsatisfactorily addressed.

As will be explored in the next chapter, the potential value of IMT's maxims in analyzing cash balance transition disclosures can be seen more strikingly in *Tomlinson*. Not tested in *Amara* are questions regarding more contextually complex and inconsistent messages about the effects of a cash balance conversion. Indeed, when viewed on a continuum, *Amara* may well be an extreme case because of the occurrence not only of so many gross violations of IMT's quality maxim (seen in CIGNA's numerous affirmatively misleading statements) but also, as the court clearly discerned, because of the *consistent pattern of implications* formed by these violations across numerous documents disseminated at different points in time. This overall pattern, together with extrinsic evidence available in other internal company documents, pointed strongly toward a carefully calculated and coordinated high-level effort to deceive employees about future benefit reductions and wear-away periods. This effort even included an employee survey conducted by CIGNA corporate officials to assess *post hoc* the success of the deceptive discursive strategies the company constructed (see *Amara v. CIGNA Corp.*, 2008, p. 86). In comparison, El Paso Corporation's disclosures in *Tomlinson* exhibit numerous statements that give rise to contradictory implications about employees' future benefits—implications that, in turn, generate both a confused and deceptive picture of what the transition to its new cash balance plan would mean for employees.

NOTES

1 To see the difference in frame, compare CIGNA's question, for instance, with this one: "Will my benefits be better or worse under the new plan?"

2 Discussing the general problem of incompleteness of information in SPDs when compared to plan documents themselves, Wiedenbeck (2008) argues for an approach to determine employer liability that he terms the "material omissions approach" (see pp. 98–105). As he notes, "the proposed material omissions approach would permit the employer to avoid liability if the SPD contained a *particularized warning* that additional information should be consulted in special circumstances" (p. 100, italics added). In CIGNA's questions-and-answer segment discussed here, a warning is arguably conveyed by the hedges, but that warning could not be construed as "particularized" because no direction is offered either as to where a clear explanation can be found or to the specific employee factors or contexts where the warning applies. Whether or not a material omissions approach should also be applicable to § 204(h) notices is not discussed by Wiedenbeck, but his outline of this approach at least partially reflects IMT's cooperativeness principle.

REFERENCES

Amara v. CIGNA Corp., 559 F. Supp. 2d 192 (D. Conn. 2008).

Brown, P., & Levinson, S. (1987). *Politeness*. Cambridge, UK: Cambridge University Press.

Channel, J. (1990). Precise and vague quantities in writing on economics. In C. Cooper & S. Greenbaum (Eds.), *The writing scholar: Studies in academic discourse* (pp. 95–117). London: Sage Publications.

Consolidated Omnibus Budget Reconciliation Act of 1985, Public Law No. 99-272 § 11006, 100 Stat. 82 (1986).

Crismore, A., & Vande Kopple, W. (1988). Readers' learning from prose. In C. Cooper & S. Greenbaum (Eds.), *Studying writing: Linguistic approaches* (pp. 184–202). Beverly Hills, CA: Sage Publications.

Declaration of Claude Poulin, F.S.A., Plaintiff's Actuarial Witness, April 25, 2003 (in Amara v. CIGNA, 2008).

Galasinski, D. (2000). *The language of deception: A discourse analytic study*. Thousand Oaks, CA: Sage Publications.

U.S. General Accounting Office. (2005). *Private pensions: Information on cash balance plans* (U.S. General Accounting Office, Health, Education and Human Services Division, 06–42). Washington, DC: Author.

U.S. General Accounting Office. (2000a). *Cash balance plans: Implications for retirement income* (U.S. General Accounting Office, Health, Education and Human Services Division, 00–207). Washington, DC: Author.

U.S. General Accounting Office. (2000b). *Private pensions: Implications of conversions to cash balance plans* (U.S. General Accounting Office, Health, Education and Human Services Division, 00–185). Washington, DC: Author.

Wiedenbeck, P. (2008). *ERISA in the courts*. Washington, DC: Federal Judicial Center.

5 *Tomlinson v. El Paso Corporation*

The basic effects of the cash balance conversion in *Tomlinson* were the same as those in *Amara*. Both cases involved significant reductions in future benefit earnings compared to what the old plan would provide if it had been continued; both companies imposed lengthy wear-away periods on a substantial number of employees; and both companies reduced employees' opening cash balance accounts compared to the total value of the plan benefits to which employees were entitled under their old plans.

However, in contrast with *Amara*, the *Tomlinson* plaintiffs lost on all of their disclosure complaints. At the same time certain aspects of *Tomlinson* also make it a more complicated disclosure case than *Amara*. First, defendant El Paso Corporation had recently acquired two other companies, Sonat and Coastal, and thus there were actually three distinct sets of transition disclosure documents targeting three different groups of employees. Each group of employees was transitioned to the new cash balance plan in a different time frame. The conversion date for the El Paso employees of January 1, 1997, meant that the older version of § 204(h) was applicable to this group, whereas the transition date for the Sonat and Coastal employee groups was December 31, 2004, and March 31, 2007, respectively, so that the later version of § 204(h) would be applicable to disclosures that El Paso sent to them. However, the Tomlinson court never certified the Sonat and Coastal employee groups as a class, and instead only decided the complaint of the three named plaintiffs, all of whom were El Paso employees (Tomlinson, 2008, 2009).[1] Thus, my analysis in this chapter will focus on disclosures sent to the El Paso employees.

As a second difference when compared to *Amara*, El Paso touted in its documents that it was setting up a five-year "transition" period from the date of plan conversion. Such a period was not created by CIGNA. During this period, El Paso employees continued to earn benefits under both their old final average pay plan and the new cash balance plan. They were further told that during this transition period, they were entitled to receive the "greater of" either plan's benefits. This transition period was to begin on the date of plan conversion January 1, 1997, and continue until December 31, 2001, when accruals under their old plan would cease and benefits earned under it would be frozen. For reasons detailed in the next sections, however, certain statements that El Paso makes specifically about this transition period and its significance conflict with each other, resulting in contradictory implications regarding employees' future benefits that would be likely to thwart employees' understanding.

Third, as discussed previously, whereas CIGNA declared that the very first of its precursor documents (i.e., the "Newsletter" from CEO Bill Taylor) constituted its § 204(h) notice, El Paso created a separate, stand-alone § 204(h) notice and distributed it well *after* employees had received El Paso's precursor documents announcing the pension plan change. Thus, the temporal context in which El Paso employees would likely encounter these two types of documents was reversed compared to the *Amara* case.

As a fourth difference, unlike *Amara*, in *Tomlinson* no trial occurred. The district court in *Tomlinson* court initially found against the plaintiffs' disclosure claims on the defendant's motion for judgment on the pleadings and then, about nine months later, also found against the plaintiffs on their motion for reconsideration. In particular, the *Tomlinson* court did not hear expert testimony about El Paso's disclosure documents under direct and cross-examination. Although the court appears aware that an expert report concerning the adequacy of the disclosures was prepared, the court apparently dismissed it as irrelevant based upon conclusions it drew about an initial El Paso disclosure statement whose impact is analyzed and discussed further in the following sections.

Fifth, and perhaps most significantly, the different circuit court precedents underlying *Amara* and *Tomlinson* set forth conflicting standards for determining harm when employees complain about disclosure inadequacy and inaccuracy. Some circuit courts impose a *likely harm standard*, whereas others impose a *detrimental reliance* standard. In the initial district court decision in *Amara* (2008, pp. 100–105), the court relied on second circuit precedent, which had adopted the former, more liberal standard (*Burke v. Kodak Retirement Income Plan*, 2003). Under a likely harm standard, regardless of whether or not the plaintiffs ever read CIGNA's disclosures, the plaintiffs were only required as a class to demonstrate likely material harm resulting from these disclosures' deficiencies; they were *not* required to show in some measurable or documented way what degree of harm *each individual plaintiff suffered*. For instance, CIGNA had contended that the plaintiffs experienced no actual harm because they did not leave the company and because, even if CIGNA's disclosures completely informed employees about benefit reductions and wear-away periods, employees' benefits from the plan transition date would have remained exactly the same. But in *Amara* (2008) Judge Kravitz rejected these arguments as unavailing because of the consistently expansive interpretation of the likely harm standard in the underlying second circuit precedents (*Amara*, 2008, pp. 100–105). Judge Kravitz explained that, to obtain relief for inadequate disclosures, it was not necessary *for each plaintiff* to provide measurable evidence of harm. As noted in the preceding chapter, the *Amara* court found that the plaintiff employees had indeed been harmed because CIGNA's failure to notify them of the new plan's harmful effects deprived them of their right to protest these effects to management in a timely fashion. They were deprived of the chance to take timely self-protective actions, such as finding a new employer, demanding higher salaries, or changing their future savings and investment plans. Indeed, the court pointed to evidence showing that preventing these very employee responses was CIGNA's intention in producing the misleading disclosures in the first place (*Amara*, 2008, pp. 100–105).

In contrast, in *Tomlinson* (2009) Judge Miller relied on third circuit precedent, which had adopted the much more strict *detrimental reliance* standard set by *Register v. PNC Financial Services Group, Inc.* (2007). Under this standard, *individual employees* first must provide evidence showing *both* that they *actually read* the disclosure documents and second that as a result of the messages either contained or missing in them, they were *actually and verifiably (rather than merely likely) harmed.* In a particularly narrow interpretation of this standard, the court treated the question of whether El Paso employees ever read the disclosures as a dispositive threshold issue: unless employees could somehow demonstrate that they had read the disclosures, the court considered that it had no obligation even to examine the notices themselves for materially misleading messages. Judge Miller stated:

> Because I agree with the Defendants that Plaintiffs do not present evidence giving rise to a genuine issue of material fact regarding reliance or prejudice, I do not address whether additional information [about reduced future pension accrual rates and wear way periods] had to be contained in the SPD. Plaintiff's deposition testimony establishes that they did not consult the SPD, except for the limited purpose of finding specific information that was contained in the SPD. In response, Plaintiffs assert that it is not established that the Plaintiffs ever received the SPD and contend that Plaintiffs could have heard about the contents of the SPD from other employees. Plaintiffs miss the point. Regardless of the reason, if Plaintiffs did not ever read the SPD, they cannot have been injured by any reliance upon allegedly inadequate information contained therein. (*Tomlinson*, 2009, pp. 21–22) [2]

It is beyond the scope of this investigation to analyze the complex evolution and merits of these conflicting standards for showing harm or injury resulting from faulty ERISA disclosures that exist across the circuit courts. However, in May 2011 this conflict over standards finally reached the U.S. Supreme Court in *CIGNA v. Amara* (2011). In its appeal from Judge Kravitz's 2008 district court decision, CIGNA challenged that court's ruling that "likely harm" and not "detrimental reliance" was the correct standard to be applied before any remedy for disclosure violations could be determined. The Supreme Court agreed with CIGNA that the second circuit standard of mere "likely harm" was not sufficient, vacating the district court's judgment and remanding the case. At the same time, though, the court expressly disagreed with CIGNA that "detrimental reliance" was the appropriate standard, either. The Court stated:

> We believe that, to obtain relief by surcharge for [disclosure] violations of §102(a) and 104(b), a plan participant or beneficiary must show that the

> violation injured him or her. But to do so, he or she need only show harm and causation. Although it is not always necessary to meet the more rigorous standard implicit in the words "detrimental reliance," actual harm must be shown. (*CIGNA v. Amara*, 2011, p. 22)

Further, the Court added that under the law of equity "there is no general principle that 'detrimental reliance' must be proved *before* a remedy is decreed" (p. 22, italics added).The Court did allow that detrimental reliance might be appropriate in disclosure cases involving the remedy of estoppel, asserting that in such a situation "actual harm may sometimes consist of detrimental reliance, but it might also come from the loss of a right protected by ERISA or its trust-law antecedents" (p. 22). The Court in dicta further added that "[i]n [*Amara*], it is not difficult to imagine how the failure to provide proper summary information, in violation of the statute, injured employees even if they did not themselves act in reliance on summary documents—which they might not themselves have seen—for they may have thought fellow employees, or informal workplace discussion, would have let them know if, say, plan changes would likely prove harmful. We doubt that Congress would have wanted to bar those employees from relief" (p. 22). The Court thus disagrees that each individual plaintiff must demonstrate that he or she read any disclosures *before* they may claim that they were harmed as a result of omissions or misrepresentations in them. Finally, it is important to note that the Supreme Court did not address or disturb any of the District Court of Connecticut's factual findings regarding the misleading character of CIGNA's disclosures.

Subsequently, in the *Amara* (2012) decision on remand to the District Court of Connecticut, Judge Arterton essentially followed the Supreme Court's analysis. Examining the standards previously applied in equity law, Judge Arterton concluded that harm and causation, rather than strict detrimental reliance, was the appropriate standard that the CIGNA plaintiffs must satisfy. Interestingly, Judge Arterton also concluded that CIGNA had the burden of proof in showing that harm had *not* been caused to its employees once the plaintiff–employees had established that materially misleading omissions and misrepresentations were present in the disclosures. She found that CIGNA never met this burden. Further, she reasoned counterfactually that if these textual manipulations had not been made and the employees had been given accurate disclosures instead, then the employees could have protested the plan changes, demanded higher salaries, or otherwise protected themselves against harm in timely fashion, as had occurred in other companies where cash balance transitions had already been enacted and sometimes modified in response to employee backlash. Judge Arterton thus agreed with the initial district court decision in *Amara* (2008) that plaintiffs had indeed been harmed and that the cause of the harm lay in CIGNA's misleading disclosures (*Amara*, 2012, pp. 13–25).

These subsequent developments in the case law notwithstanding, nothing in ERISA itself states or suggests that the issue of whether or not the employees read the disclosures is to be treated as a dispositive threshold issue in the strict manner seen in the *Tomlinson* (2009) opinion. Moreover, in the passage quoted, the *Tomlinson* court's statements about whether the named plaintiffs did in fact read El Paso's disclosures appear contradictory. On the one hand, the court asserts that "testimony establishes that [plaintiffs] did not consult the SPD;" then, on the other hand, the court immediately but cryptically acknowledges that the plaintiffs *did* consult the SPD "for the limited purpose of finding specific information that was contained in [it]" (p. 22). The court offers no further explanation as to why or how "consulting" the SPD for the "purpose of finding specific information" is not the same as reading it.

As will be discussed, what is particularly interesting for the purpose of this study is how the *Tomlinson* court, although stating it was not required to examine the adequacy of El Paso's disclosures at all (given that it concluded that the plaintiff employees had not read them) nevertheless does so and determines them to be adequate under ERISA's standards.

Tomlinson can also be compared with *Amara* with respect to its interpretations of what the 1986 version of § 204(h) required in employers' notices. The *Tomlinson* court's interpretation of § 204(h) is the same narrow one seen in the *Bilello*, *Register*, and *Custer* decisions discussed in Chapter 2. The *Tomlinson* court concludes that El Paso's § 204(h) notices were satisfactory, reasoning that

> [i]n 1996, when notice of the plan changes was sent to the participants, then existing regulations required only that the notice be written, set forth the amendment (or summary thereof), and set forth the amendment's effective date. 26 C.F.R. §1.411(d)-6T (1996). Moreover, the regulation expressly did not require the [notice] to "explain how much the individual benefit of each participant . . . will be affected by the amendment." I [conclude] that the notice provided was adequate . . . Plaintiffs again argue that the notice expressly had to tell employees about benefit reductions and that evidence indicates that El Paso did not intend to notify its employees of a reduction in benefit accruals. Again, however, in light of the express requirements of the regulations, I see no basis to conclude that El Paso's conduct violated the law as it existed at the time. (*Tomlinson v. El Paso Corp.*, 2009, pp. 12–13)

As already shown, the *Amara* court took the same basic position on what § 204(h) requires. Yet when compared with the *Amara* court's overall approach to the § 204(h) issue, the *Tomlinson* court's comments above appear significantly different and problematic in at least two ways.

First, unlike *Amara* (2008), the *Tomlinson* (2009) court does not offer any construction of the policy and purpose behind § 204(h) notices. The *Amara* (2008) court repeatedly notes that, like SMMs and SPDs, § 204(h) notices must be "written in a manner calculated to be understood by the average plan participant" (citing Treasury Regulation 1.411(d)-6, Q&A-10). In contrast, the *Tomlinson* court takes no cognizance of this specific requirement in its opinion nor does it explain how this requirement relates to the underlying purpose of § 204(h). In particular, the court makes no effort to explain how El Paso's summary of the cash balance amendment as provided in its § 204(h) notice would or could be understood by an average plan participant. Apparently, the court felt that because § 204(h) in its view does not require any indication of benefit reductions on the part of the employer, there would be no point in even addressing whether the description of the plan amendment itself could be understood by an average plan participant—thereby illogically ignoring the fact that the reduction of employees' future benefit accruals caused by a plan amendment is exactly what triggers the § 204(h) notice requirement in the first place. In sharp contrast, the *Amara* court, in evaluating CIGNA's § 204(h) notice and commenting upon its various statements, repeatedly invokes the requirement that the notice must be "calculated to be understood by the average plan participant" and explains that the purpose of a § 204(h) notice "is to provide employees the opportunity to learn about changes to their retirement plan and perhaps complain or otherwise seek to modify those changes if they are unacceptable (p. 75)." In other words, the *Amara* court looked to both the plain language of § 204(h) *as well as* to its particular purpose and role among ERISA's disclosure protections and on this combined basis explained why CIGNA's disclosures were unacceptable. As will be detailed, the *Tomlinson* court applies only what it conceives to be the plain meaning of § 204(h) and thus does not consider whether or not El Paso's cash balance plan amendment would be understandable to "an average plan participant."

A second problem with the *Tomlinson* court's reasoning is that the court makes it appear that the plaintiffs had claimed (or believed) that § 204(h) requires *individually tailored* notices, that is, ones uniquely addressing each individual employee's circumstances. But the plaintiffs never advanced such a claim. As noted earlier, useful information about the size and extent of future accrual reductions and wear-away periods could instead be provided categorically in terms of age and years of service across employee groups. This was information that the company clearly analyzed and possessed. Contrary to what the court implies, the fact that the regulations did not require El Paso to "explain how much the individual benefit of each participant . . . will be affected by the amendment" does not necessarily mean that *no* indication of the existence and size of future reductions and wear-away periods is required (26 C.F.R. §1.411(d)-6T (1996)). There is a leap in the court's logic here. Notably, when quoting the same regulatory language, the *Amara* court's analysis of CIGNA's § 204(h) notice reflects that court's comparatively broader construction of the underlying purpose of such notice, that is, to "protect employees' interests and their reasonable expectations," a construction that recognizes employees' right to *some* notice of future benefit reductions (*Amara*, 2008, p. 75).

In addition to its "plain language" conclusion about the substance of the § 204(h) requirement quoted, the *Tomlinson* court elsewhere implies that even if § 204(h) did require El Paso to disclose future accrual rate reductions and wear-away periods, the company already satisfied this requirement in certain precursor documents sent to employees. The court concludes, *without any comparison of these precursor documents with statements made in El Paso's § 204(h) notices themselves*, that these precursors 'cure' any problem with the § 204(h) notices' language and implications. However, the precursor statements that the *Tomlinson* court views as adequate are themselves taken disturbingly out of context, with no regard for their possible meaning in view of other confusing statements that El Paso makes in these same documents. There is little judicial focus on how El Paso's disclosure messages would work dynamically and cumulatively, over time, to affect employee readers' comprehension.

Having thus outlined important differences between the *Tomlinson* and *Amara* decisions, it is time to turn to El Paso's disclosures themselves. As with those examined in *Amara*, here again we will use IMT maxims to analyze whether—and if so, how—El Paso addressed each of three distinct employee questions about cash balance conversions.

COMPARED TO THE OLD PLAN, WILL MY ACCRUAL BENEFIT RATES UNDER THE NEW PLAN BE REDUCED?

Precursor documents: Reduced future accrual rates? To begin, the statements that El Paso makes regarding reductions to employees' future benefit accrual rates in its precursor documents are shown in Appendix 5, Table B.1; relevant statements appearing in its § 204(h) notice are shown in Table B.2; and those in the SPD are shown in Table B.3. At first blush, it may seem that the *Tomlinson* (2009) court's conclusion that El Paso adequately disclosed reductions in the rate of employees' future benefit accrual is a slam dunk. Judge Miller in his opinion shines his flashlight on two sentences in the first segment shown in Table B.1. As will be discussed further, these statements appeared in January 1996 in an early precursor document whose simple title, "Employee Update," gave no clue that it contained federally required information about a change in the company's pension plan (italics added):

> *Under the cash balance plan, employees will earn future benefits at a lower rate than under the current plan.* Additional contributions related to Company profitability may be considered. Details of this new type of plan have not been finalized . . . *Under the cash balance plan, employees will earn future benefits at a lower rate than under the current plan* . . . Corporate Benefits will provide more details about this new program later in 1996.

Without question, such statements are nowhere hinted in CIGNA's disclosures, and in comparison with CIGNA's statements, they may seem to communicate exactly what CIGNA did not. But excising and decontextualizing statements in this manner is to overlook two crucial questions implied by ERISA's basic requirement that disclosures be "written in a manner calculated to be understood by the average plan participant." First, how would employee readers, with little prior knowledge of cash balance plans (and no familiarity with the *Amara* case) understand these statements and interpret their significance in their personal decision-making contexts? In other words, it is one thing to read the disclosure documents as lawyers and judges do, who like detectives pursuing a theory from the outset are *specifically seeking* such statements, and quite another to read them as employees would, who have no particular reason to suspect such statements would be present or of importance to them. And second, again looking at the temporal and locative context of these statements in the whole stream of El Paso's pension plan communications, are there other statements that conflict with these, such that the apparent meaning of the italicized statements shown here is either subsequently diluted, contradicted, or subject to doubt and uncertainty?

In turn, both of these questions require that we ask in what ways the *combination* of statements and omissions of information could be materially misleading. In the ERISA disclosure context, one respected scholar has argued that a proposed test for such statements should be "whether known or reasonably foreseeable participants would attach importance to the information" or its omission as a basis for "ex ante career and financial planning" and related decision making (Wiedenbeck, 2008, pp. 100–103). As illustrated in the *Amara* case and as the following analysis should make clear, IMT's four maxims can prove helpful when addressing this question of materiality.

Importantly, the italicized statements in the excerpt that the court seized upon appeared in a 45-page document titled "Employee Update." This document dealt with many other topics besides employees' pensions and included sections such as "Business Update," "Transformation and Reengineering Project Updates," and "Work Force Reduction," among others. A letter from El Paso CEO William Wise prefaced the entire document, and although he mentions a number of important challenges facing the company, he makes no mention of changes to the company's pension plan. As shown, the statement appeared twice on the same page in a section simply titled, "Employee Benefits Update," which began on page 23. This position deep inside the document and the lack of any earlier semantic cues in its table of contents (such as a heading or subheading) indicating a pending conversion of the pension plan raises a concern as to whether many employees would even notice it. Assuming that employees knew that ERISA explicitly requires disclosure of future benefit accrual rates in both the § 204(h) notice and in the employer's SPD, they might not expect or anticipate such disclosures would be presented in this document, which does not identify itself as a substitute for either of these. Alternatively, if they do notice these statements, some readers might look to El Paso's § 204(h) notice and SPD for confirmation. These documents were not distributed until months later. Significantly, however, and as will be shown, *no* statements disclosing future accrual rate reductions appear in either of these statutorily required notices (see Tables B.2 and B.3). Upon discovering the absence of these statements in these later disclosures, employees might simply conclude that El Paso's statements in the earlier "Employee Update" document were untrue and merely a false alarm.

Thus, even if this initial El Paso document was intended to serve as an SMM or as a proxy for disclosure intended to replace the company's SPD and its § 204(h) notice, then it would seem that ERISA §102 should still apply:

> The format of the summary plan description shall not have the effect of misleading, misinforming, or failing to inform participants and beneficiaries. *Any description of exceptions, limitations, reductions, and other restrictions of plan benefits shall not be minimized, rendered obscure, or otherwise made to appear unimportant*. (29 C.F.R. § 2520.102–2(b), italics added)

Given the relatively inconspicuous location of the warnings in this initial precursor document, what material significance employees would attach to them upon reading them is a real concern. It is true the statement that employees will "earn future benefits at a lower rate" appears twice on the page. But the perceived significance of these statements is potentially qualified by El Paso's additional comments that "[d]etails of this new type of plan have not been finalized" and that "Corporate Benefits will provide more details about this new program later in 1996" (see the first segment in Table B.1.1). That the plan conversion "details" have not been "finalized" might imply to employees that there is some possibility reductions may not after all occur or turn out to be insignificant. Second, and more importantly for the materiality test, there is no indication regarding *how much lower* the future rate of accrual under the cash balance plan will be, who will be affected, and when. In fact, El Paso's accrual rate reductions ranged from 35 to 50 percent of the value of the former plan's benefit accrual rate. And, for a large number of older, longer-service employees put under wear-way periods by the new plan, *the future accrual rate would be exactly 0 percent*. The lack of any information as to the size of the accrual rate reductions, together with the qualification that conversion details have not been finalized, might further imply that no action or decision making on the employees' part is needed. Another noted ERISA scholar, Stephen Bruce (1993) suggests that a disclosure that fails even to estimate (or to offer a range) in the size of future benefit reductions may fail to meet ERISA's standard regarding the "reasonable understanding" of employees (pp. 343–364)

No other communications regarding the new cash balance plan were sent to El Paso employees until eight months later, when they received a new cluster of documents about the conversion in October 1996. The first of these is an unsigned letter from the company announcing the pension plan change. The *Tomlinson* court in a footnote referenced a statement in the second paragraph of this letter as clearly indicating to employees that El Paso's future benefits would be "less generous" than those offered in the prior plan (*Tomlinson*, 2009, p. 23, footnote 7). But, when examined closely, the text of the letter does not in fact say or even imply that El Paso's future benefits would be "less generous" *than those under the old plan*; indeed, the phrase "less generous" is not used in the letter at all. Rather, the pertinent statement is shown together with its context in the second segment of Table B.1.1 (italics added):

> In the past, El Paso was able to provide employees with a very rich retirement benefits package. Our plans still provide excellent benefits, but *are no longer at the top of the range*.

The court's reading of these statements, that is, that in them El Paso implied its future benefits would be "less generous" than the old plan's benefits, appears open to question. The court's reading appears to reflect some degree of expert hindsight bias. Certainly the statement does not clearly or directly answer the employee's question, "Compared to the old plan, are accrual rates under the new plan reduced?" In IMT terms and in relation to this question, the statement involves a violation of the relevance maxim because it does not clearly or unambiguously imply that future accrual rates will be lower than those under the current plan. Rather, in the second statement the company compares its new plan benefits *not to its old plan benefits* but rather to the benefits offered *by other employers* who may now be "at the top of the range." In other words, this statement could be taken to mean that other employers in the industry have started offering better, more competitive benefit packages than El Paso and that El Paso has fallen behind *them*. Thus it is not possible to conclude with any certainty from this second statement that new plan benefits *will be* "less generous" than *old plan benefits*, as the court apparently believes, or that future accrual rates will be lower. This violation of the relevance maxim, combined with the lack of any further substantive elaboration of these statements, leaves it unclear what material significance readers could or should attach to them. Further, the company statements shown in Table B.1.1 that follow those earlier in this section, although urging employees to contribute "at least 10% of [their] pay to [the company's] Retirement Savings Plan," do nothing to clarify or estimate the size of the accrual rate reductions.

It might be contended that El Paso implied the possibility of a reduction in the future accrual rate when, at the close of this letter, employees could read the following (see Table B.1.1; sentence numbers added here for reference):

> **(1)** Active participants in the current pension plan as of December 31, 1996 will transition into the new plan over the next five years. **(2)** What this means is that the current pension plan formula will remain in effect for all those plan participants until December 31, 2001. **(3)** After that date the current pension plan formula will be frozen for those participants and they will not earn any additional benefits under the current plan of benefits. **(4)** An employee who retires after December 31, 1996 will always be entitled to the greater of their benefit figured under the current pension plan formula or a benefit based on the cash balance under CBP Select. **(5)** As a result, employees within five years of retirement are eligible to receive a pension benefit equal to what they would receive under the current plan.

IMT can help to explain why a claim of disclosure of future accrual rate reductions in this passage is not tenable. There are two types of IMT violations, clarity and quantity (i.e., omission of information). Both violations occur as the employee moves from the third to the fourth sentence, which seems to give rise to a contradiction and thus creates ambiguity. Let's look more closely at these.

After El Paso states in sentence (3) that employees "will not earn any additional benefits under the current plan formula" after December 31, 2001, sentence

(4) seems to offer a different, broader, and more unrestricted assurance about the value of the employee's future benefit to the effect that if the ultimate benefit under the new cash balance plan is lower than that offered under the old plan, the employee need not worry because the employee "will *always* be entitled" to the benefit that has the "greater" value (italics added). What sentence (4) states is truthful. But readers without prior knowledge of cash balance transitions will likely misunderstand how it relates to sentence (3) due to both misleading and missing semantic cues. The misleading cue is that the use of the term "always" in sentence (4) is likely in employee readers' minds to cancel out the statement in sentence (3) that future benefits from the current plan will be "frozen" after December 31, 2001. That is, employee readers may reason, "If the 'greater of' the two plans' benefits are 'always' available, then how can old benefits really be frozen"? Faced with this sort of seeming contradiction in a text, experimental reading comprehension research studies show that readers may often privilege the next or a later statement in the text sequence over the previous one, with the natural expectation that the later one would clarify the meaning of the previous one (Vande Kopple, 1986; Otero & Kintsch, 1992; Just, Carpenter, & Wooley, 1982). In this case, they might readily and erroneously believe that sentence (4) means that they will receive *either* "the greater of" what the old plan would earn *had it continued* ("*always* be entitled to the greater of their benefit figured under the current pension plan formula") *or* what the new cash balance plan earns starting on January 1, 1997.

In fact, a mistaken reader interpretation regarding "always" is made more likely because of crucial omissions in sentence (4). The effect of these omissions can be suggested in the following revision, one which would prevent the mistaken interpretation arising from readers' attempts to integrate sentence (4) with sentence (3) and make them consistent with each other:

> **(4)** (original) An employee who retires after December 31, 1996 will always be entitled to the greater of their benefit figured under the current pension plan formula or a benefit based on the cash balance under CBP Select.
>
> versus
>
> **(4)** (revised, new language is italicized) An employee who retires after December 31, 1996, will always be entitled to the greater of the *frozen* benefit figured under the current pension plan formula *as of December 31, 2001 (the date its accruals are frozen)* or a benefit based on the cash balance under CBP Select.

The pieces of information included in this revision of sentence (4) would help readers more easily and accurately integrate its meaning with sentence (3). Indeed, these pieces are crucial to grasping the full, combined import of sentences (3) and (4) together. By reinstating key pieces of information from sentence (3), the revised version would likely prevent readers from construing the assurance seemingly offered in sentence (4) to mean something it does not.

This revision would also likely make employee readers' interpretation of sentence (5) more accurate than it would be given El Paso's current version of sentence (4). After reading sentence (5), employees may well feel reinforced in their inaccurate interpretation of sentence (4): "Okay, from this last sentence I see that I can receive the same benefits that I would receive under the old plan during the five-year transition, until December 31, 2001, the date when the old plan benefits are frozen. But then what happens? Above, it just says I will 'always' get 'the greater of their benefit figured under the *current pension plan formula*' or the new cash plan benefit. So it looks like a situation where I cannot lose. I'll 'always' get the higher benefit." That the employee is only entitled to receive the *frozen* value of the old account *as of December 31, 2001*, is lost sight of, in effect 'overwritten' by sentence (4), which may seem to say something less restrictive and very different.[3]

The company might argue that the fifth sentence *implies* that after the five-year transition period expires, an employee's benefit *could be less* than the value of their old ('current') plan benefit. But, without the missing pieces of information shown in the revision of sentence (4), employee readers' ability to draw such an implication is doubtful, unless again, they happen to have substantial prior knowledge as to how cash balance transitions work. It would have been easy for the company to state, immediately following the last statement in the paragraph, that "after December 31, 2001, your future benefit accruals will no longer equal what the old plan would have provided were it continued." Indeed, this was the result for some 1,500 El Paso employees. Given that this letter is ostensibly intended as an 'overview' of changes, it would seem to be the appropriate place to repeat and *confirm* the unelaborated statement about reduced future accrual rates that was inconspicuously placed in the initial "Employee Update" months before, as already discussed. But instead, here the company speaks evasively, and readers are forced to try to infer a picture of what is happening from insufficient and disconnected cues.

Notably, CIGNA, using this same strategy of omission and evasion when announcing the freeze of employees' old plan benefits, argued that employees could only conclude that they are given this entitlement to the old, frozen benefits because their benefits under the new plan might be less. But nothing is said in the El Paso letter *about why* employees' benefits under the new plan might be less, and so it is unlikely that average plan participants could make this inferential leap. As shown in the preceding chapter, the court in *Amara* flatly rejected this 'disclosure' strategy as unrealistic and unacceptable.

Along with the letter, in October 1996 El Paso employees also received a brochure titled "Manager's Update." As will be shown in Table 5.1, this document provides similar, but even more prejudicial indications about employees' future benefit accrual rates compared to those in the company letter—indications that the *Tomlinson* court never mentions (and perhaps never even noticed). To see the differences, it is useful to place these segments side by side to show both their correspondences and alterations in context:

Table 5.1 Comparison of Earlier and Later El Paso Statements Regarding Participants' Future Benefits

1996 El Paso Letter	**1996 "Manager's Update"**
(1) [A]ctive participants in the current pension plan as of December 31, 1996 will transition into the new plan over the next five years.	**(6)** The Company feels very strongly that employees who are close to retirement should not be disadvantaged by this new plan.
(2) What this means is that the current pension plan formula will remain in effect for all those plan participants until December 31, 2001.	**(7)** As a way to protect those employees who have worked for the Company for most of their careers and are now near to their retirement, we will transition to CBP Select over a five-year period.
(3) After that date the current pension plan formula will be frozen for those participants and they will not earn any additional benefits under the current plan of benefits.	**(8)** Here is what this means: the current pension plan formula will continue for all active participants as of 12/31/96 for 5 years.
(4) An employee who retires after December 31, 1996 will always be entitled to the greater of their benefit figured under the current pension plan formula or a benefit based on the cash balance under CBP Select.	**(9)** After 12/31/01, the current pension plan benefit for all participants will be frozen and employees will not earn any further benefits under the current plan of benefits.
(5) As a result, employees within five years of retirement are eligible to receive a pension benefit equal to what they would receive under the current plan.	**(10)** An employee who retires in the future will be entitled to the greater of their benefit figured under the current pension plan formula or the value of their cash balance in CBP Select.
(Shading and sentence numbers added)	**(11)** As a result, older, longer service employees are assured of a pension benefit equal to what they would receive under the current plan.
	[Shading and sentence numbers added].

Here, in the "Manager's Update," the same information integration problem arises for employee readers between sentences (9) and (10) as occurs between sentences (3) and (4) in the letter paragraph, as described. Specifically, as with sentence (4) in the letter, sentence (10) in the "Manager's Update" does not clarify that the employee will only be entitled to the *frozen* current plan benefit *as of December 31, 2001*. And just as sentence (4) refers to an "employee who retires after December 31, 1996," the "Manager's Update" drops "always" and refers to an employee who retires "in the future." But the "Manager's Update" passage becomes more prejudicial to an accurate comprehension of what is happening in the plan conversion than even the letter passage when we examine other differences between them.

Consider the reassurances with which the "Manager's Update" passage begins and ends, that is, in sentences (6), (7), and (11). These do not appear in the letter passage, and they would almost certainly alter the employee's context for understanding the rhetorical the point of the passage taken as a whole. Indeed, in combination, these sentences can reasonably be taken by readers unfamiliar with cash balance plans to contradict the initial El Paso statement in the January 1996 "Employee Update" that "[u]nder the cash balance plan, employees will earn future benefits at a lower rate than under the current plan." Even more so than when reading the letter passage, older, longer-service employees could leave this passage believing that, unlike *other* employees, *they* will not suffer a reduction in their future benefit accrual rate because the company is going to protect them.

A closer look can show why such a misinterpretation could occur. Although the company states, "After 12/31/01, the current pension plan benefit for all participants will be frozen and employees will not earn any further benefits under the current plan of benefits," the last two statements, (10) and (11), seem to say nevertheless that older, longer-service employees "are assured" (not merely "entitled," as in the letter) to receive benefits equal to the old plan benefits. The problem, again, is that statement (11) violates IMT's quantity maxim. It omits a crucial piece of information, one with significant material consequences. Instead of saying that whenever they retire "in the future . . . older, longer service employees are assured of a pension benefit equal to *what they would receive under the current plan*," the last statement again should be qualified to say that "older, longer service employees are assured of a pension benefit equal to what they would receive under the current plan *as of 12/31/01, the date on which their old plan benefits are frozen*." Without this explicit caveat, older, longer-service employees could reasonably conclude that they have somehow been grandparented under the old plan. At the very least, the statements in this passage would be likely to create ambiguity in employees' minds about whether or not old plan benefits will be equaled by new cash balance benefits, thus violating IMT's clarity maxim.

This same crucial omission occurs in another contemporaneous El Paso document titled "Program Highlights," where the company purports to explain the "Special Transition Benefit" (see Table B.1.2). In addition, and significantly, here the company also makes two positively false statements (shown in italics). This passage thus violates both IMT quality and quantity maxims (sentence numbers added):

> **(12)** The employee's benefits under the old plan formula will continue to accrue from January 1, 1997 until December 31, 2001. **(13)** (*After this date, the employee earns pension benefits only under CBP Select*). **(14)** When the employee retires, his/her benefits under the old plan formula and CBP Select

> will be compared. **(15)** *The pension benefit paid will be the higher of the two formulas on the date of retirement.*

Sentence 13 is a false statement because *after* December 31, 2001, the employees' old plan benefits as of the date of plan conversion *will remain greater* than what the new CBP Select formula would provide. Instead of earning future benefits "only under CBP Select" after December 31, 2001, as sentence (13) declares, employees will earn no new benefits under CBP Select at all. That is, they will have a future accrual rate of *exactly 0 percent* under CBP Select for years going forward, in some cases even beyond a normal retirement age. Sentence (14) is false because it says both formulas will be compared "on the date of retirement," that is, inviting the employee reader to mistakenly believe that *both* formulas will be projected forward to that date. But the truth is that the old plan formula will be restricted to the employee's account as of December 31, 2001. As a result, what the company does not want to say, but what older, longer-service employees reasonably would need to know, is that employees will suffer wear-away periods.

As discussed in Chapter 2, what triggers wear-away periods are reductions to the employees' new opening CBP Select balances relative to the value of their old plan benefits as of December 31, 1996. El Paso omits any mention of these initial reductions in its precursor and post-transition documents as well as in the segments already examined. Without knowing about these up-front reductions and having some illustration showing their effects, it would be nearly impossible for average plan participants to understand that their old plan value *as of December 31, 2001*, would be *all* of the future pension benefit they could expect to receive.

To illustrate, if the employee had earned a future monthly benefit of $1,000 by the date of plan conversion on January 1, 1997, he or she might think that amount (or perhaps its lump sum equivalent) would also be the starting amount in the new CBP Select account. But that is not what El Paso did. Instead, as the plaintiff's actuarial witness testified, the starting balance in the new CBP Select plan did not equal the old plan frozen benefit but was significantly reduced by as much as 50 percent or even more (Declaration of Mr. Claude Poulin, F.S.A., April 15, 2008, paras 34–40). This up-front reduction to the new opening balance is the chief cause of lengthy wear-away periods. The employees must work long enough following the end of the five-year transition period to 're-earn' benefits that they already have earned and are entitled to under the old plan. Thus it is not only the lower future accrual rates *per se* under CBP Select that may make the old plan benefit as of December 31, 2001, more valuable, but in addition hugely reduced opening balances in employees' new CBP Select accounts.

Because the employee is nowhere told about this up-front reduction, the likely default employee assumption would be that the new plan *starting* benefit amount would *equal* the total value of benefits already earned under the old plan—much as if one were taking one's savings from one bank account and putting them into another bank account. In other words, the natural and reasonable expectation on the part of an average plan participant would be that, even if future growth rate in the new account might be lower, one would still be starting from the old plan balance.

Now let's return to the last passage sentences (12 through (15) taken from El Paso's "Program Highlights" precursor document. On the one hand, the company falsely states that after December 31, 2001, "the employee earns pension benefits only under CBP Select." Because of this falsehood, average plan participants simply could not understand how or why their future CBP Select benefits would be less than those earned under the old plan *as of December 31, 2001*. The confused employee might ask, "If my new CBP Select account continuously grows from December 31, 2001, then how can this new account balance be less than the old account balance as of December 31, 2001? It doesn't make sense." Indeed, the statements in this passage do not make sense because the company makes no mention that it is reducing employees' new CBP Select opening balances to values much lower than those of their old plan benefit as of December 31, 2001. Nor does it mention that these reductions will trigger wear-away periods during which employees will earn nothing from CBP Select at all and thus have a 0 percent future benefit accrual rate.

Employee readers' ability to detect and grasp this complex scheme is thwarted not only by El Paso's failure to indicate reductions to employees' opening account balances and resulting wear-away periods; as noted, it is further blocked by the way sentences (14) and (15) stress the comparison of old and new plan "formulas" as taking place "on the date of retirement." Experimental psycholinguistic research shows that readers' attention is heightened at the beginning and ends of sentences, with slightly greater attention placed on the information at the ends than at the beginnings (Vande Kopple, 1986; Williams & Colomb, 2010). The phrase "on the date of retirement" would thus be highly salient to employees. As a result, despite what sentence (13) says, the last two sentences, (14) and (15), may seem to imply that both old and new plans will continue to accrue beyond December 31, 2001, until the employee's retirement date. This mistake in reader comprehension could perhaps be partially ameliorated if crucial pieces of information were added to sentences (14) and (15), similar to what was shown in two earlier passages, as follows (italics show revisions):

> **(14)** When the employee retires, his/her *benefits in the new* CBP Select account and his/her *frozen* benefits under the old plan formula *as of December 31, 2001*, will be compared. **(15)** The pension benefit paid will be the *greater of these two benefits* on the date of retirement.

Of course, making this kind of revision, although it might clarify that the new CBP account could be less than the employees' old account balance as of December 31, 2001, does nothing to help employees understand *why* it could be less. They are still not told that their opening account balance is being significantly reduced. At best, then, average plan participants could only leave this paragraph in the "Program Highlights" precursor with the sense that it is contradictory. In the worst and more likely case, and given the other seemingly solicitous company messages employees contemporaneously received and that have already been discussed, they might reasonably think: "Even though this comparison of old and new plans is taking place for some employees, as an older, longer-service employee I have been assured that I will get the greater of what the two plans would earn by my retirement date."

It could perhaps be contended that any ambiguity provoked by El Paso's reassurances about older, longer-service employees' benefits is rectified by subsequent statements in yet another precursor brochure, in a short section titled "Advantages and Drawbacks" (see Table B.1.2). Here the company states the following (italics added):

> On the plus side . . . [e]mployees cannot lose any value in their accounts—accounts can only go up in value. Employees may see some drawbacks too. Benefits will accrue at a slower rate in the future than under the current plan . . . This change in our pension plan may not be an easy one for *some* employees to accept. We have tried to balance employees' concerns with the Company's need to preserve financial resources. This led us to reduce the overall future benefits for employees and *some* employees will feel negatively about this . . . [T]he bottom line is that the Company needs to make changes to our benefits if we are to survive and prosper in the future.

Again, it can be argued that such statements as these appear nowhere in CIGNA's disclosures in the *Amara* case. Nevertheless, IMT maxims can help to show serious problems with this passage when viewed in context with the other problematic messages we have already examined.

When the employer here states, "Benefits will accrue at a slower rate in the future than under the current plan," it may seem that the employer is simply repeating, and thus reinforcing, the disclosure putatively made in the earlier 1996 "Employee Update" document. However, even if older, longer-service employees noticed the earlier statements despite their inconspicuous location and, further, managed to remember them (a feat that seems questionable, given that they were sent eight months before), without some additional explanation they would not likely be able to determine if these later statements pertain *to them*. These older employees, after all, are the focus of *later*, *repeated* assurances that their old plan benefits are being protected. Notice that, in this passage, precisely which employees may suffer the reductions is left vague, with the passage twice referring to "some employees." The passage thus creates a puzzle to be solved and consequently violates IMT's clarity maxim.

Still another contemporaneous document titled "Introducing CBP Select" also asserts that "El Paso created the new CBP Select" plan because it "wanted to . . . [p]rovide for long term service and older employees [and] [p]rovide adequate retirement benefits at age 60 and older" (see Table B.1.2). In particular, the El Paso claim, "Employees cannot lose any value in their accounts—accounts can only go up in value," may seem to assure older, longer-service employees that the company is going to spare them any significant reductions. In reality, this statement is simply false for all older longer-service employees who, due to the undisclosed opening balance reductions and wear-away periods, will see a future pension benefit accrual rate of 0 percent after December 31, 2001.

Let me now summarize what has been shown in this section so far. El Paso employees received, at best, three putative warnings about the reduction of the future benefit accrual rate: one appears in the January 1996 "Employee Update," and two others appear in a subsequent precursor document provided in October 1996. But it would be a serious mistake to conclude that these add up to an unambiguous, understandable disclosure. As shown in the preceding analyses with IMT maxims, the three putative 'warnings' that El Paso employees received were *contextually diluted*, if not dissolved altogether, by repeated and contradictory employer assurances that it was seeking to "protect" older, longer-service employees. In addition, the checkerboard pattern of quality, quantity, relevance, and clarity violations make consistent, accurate conclusions about the future benefit accrual rate almost impossible for employee readers.

Indeed, consistency among statements and concrete, accurate illustrations using clear examples are equally crucial features of understandable warnings and disclosures (Amoroso, Flagg, Polisner, Rietz, & Segal, 2001, 2002; Latin, 1994; Morgan, Fischhoff, Bostrom, & Atman, 2002; Schriver, 1991, 1997). And, as will be detailed later in this chapter, none of the hypothetical employee examples presented in El Paso's disclosure documents provide what is called a 'side-by-side' comparison, one that accurately illustrates *how much* the accrual rate could drop compared to the rate under employees' old final average pay plan, that is, had the latter plan continued. Such side-by-side comparisons would be what employees would reasonably expect to see to gauge financial impact (Amoroso et al., 2001, 2002). Instead of such comparisons, the hypothetical examples that El Paso provided in its disclosures *only* show how much a fictional employee would earn after a specified time *under the cash balance plan*. The absence of comparisons thus could serve to reinforce that the accrual rate reduction would not significantly affect older, longer-service employees, particularly given the company's statement that it seeks to protect these workers from "disadvantage." These readers would still have no idea that as a result of reduced opening account balances and consequent wear-away periods, their future accrual rate would not only be lower but actually equal *0 percent*. The *Tomlinson* court seems not to have noticed the one-sided nature of El Paso's hypothetical examples, or if it did, it makes no mention of their possible impact on employee understanding in context. In sharp contrast, the *Amara* court was highly critical of CIGNA's refusal to provide any side-by-side comparisons (*Amara*, 2008, pp. 82–87).

The SPD and § 204(h) notice: Reduced future accrual rates? If the Tomlinson court's specific claim that El Paso's precursor documents satisfied ERISA's disclosure requirements concerning benefit accrual rate reductions is doubtful, what, then, do El Paso's SPD and § 204(h) notice communicate about these reductions? Do they cure the ambiguities and omissions in El Paso's precursor documents already identified in a way that average plan participants could understand? As will be discussed next, the answer is no.

With respect to El Paso's SPD, the *Tomlinson* court notes that El Paso acknowledged that the SPD sent to its employees failed to mention accrual rate reductions. However, the court specifically notes that El Paso defended this omission by arguing that "the changes to a plan need only be described in a § 204(h) notice, not necessarily the SPD" (*Tomlinson*, 2009, p. 21). The court then stated that it would not address this particular argument because, again, it felt that the initial "Employee Update" document in January 1996 and CEO William Wise's cover letter provided all of the disclosure necessary concerning future accrual rate reductions.

This reasoning is quite troubling. If El Paso intended its precursor documents to serve the same statutory function as served by its SPD, that is, as proxies, there is no communication of that intent in any of the precursor documents or within the SPD. Average plan participants who knew that an SPD is a statutorily required disclosure may have deliberately bypassed the precursor documents as likely to be less reliable sources of information. Alternatively, even if they did read all of the precursors, they may reasonably have taken them less seriously or opted to look for answers to their questions about future benefit reductions in the more 'official' SPD. But as Table B.3 shows, the SPD says nothing at all about reduced future accrual rates under the new cash balance plan. Participants would find nothing within it to suggest that their future benefit accrual under the new CBP Select plan would be significantly less, by as much as 35 to 50 percent (Declaration of Mr. Claude Poulin, F.S.A., April 15, 2008, para. 25–33). The company's strategy therefore appears to be to disclose without disclosing, by placing key disclosure information in a document (i.e., the 1996 "Employee Update") where employees are less likely to anticipate it while *omitting* that same language and information from the statutorily required SPD. The *Tomlinson* court fails to see the gross unfairness of this strategy.

Similarly, with respect to El Paso's § 204(h) notice, the court did not offer an analysis of the notice's language because of its underlying interpretation that the version of § 204(h) in effect at the time did not require disclosure of future benefit reductions. Specifically, the court interpreted the 1986 language that a § 204(h) notice must "set forth the plan amendment" as expressly not requiring any notice of reductions. Yet, again, in lieu of any disclosure provided in the § 204(h) notice itself, the court took the position that El Paso's precursors adequately communicated that future benefit accrual rate reductions would occur.

The problems with this stance, especially in comparison with the *Amara* court's view of the purpose of § 204(h), were outlined at the start of this chapter. The legal question of what is required in a § 204(h) notice notwithstanding, it is important to examine just what El Paso's § 204(h) notice does and does not say and how it communicates relative to ERISA's requirement that it must be "written in a manner calculated to be understood by the average plan participant." As detailed earlier, the *Amara* court explicitly based its analysis of CIGNA's § 204(h) notice on this standard, and El Paso's § 204(h) notice is an important piece in the complex picture puzzle that the company gave to its employees to try to assemble. (The complete text of El Paso's § 204(h) notice is shown in Appendix 2.) Further, how employee readers would comprehend the § 204(h) notice *in the context of the precursor documents they already received* is a materially significant and relevant question.

As Appendix 2 shows, and just as is the case with El Paso's SPD, there are no statements in the § 204(h) notice indicating that reductions in employees' future benefit accrual rates will occur. Nor is there any indication that for employees under wear-away periods, the future benefit accrual rate will not only be lower but exactly 0 percent. To a person with expert prior knowledge concerning cash balance conversions, it might seem the second paragraph implies that future accrual rates were going to be reduced. However, as explained here with the help of IMT maxims, any claim that average plan participants could reach such an implication is highly implausible.

First, consider the statements in the two initial paragraphs of the notice (sentence numbers added for reference):

> **(1)** Effective December 31, 2001, all participants described below in item 1 will cease accruing a minimum benefit under the El Paso Corporation Pension Plan (the "Plan"). **(2)** You have received a variety of communications describing this change since 1997 when the Plan was amended to provide a cash account benefit. **(3)** This notice is simply a reminder of how the Plan was changed in 1997. **(4)** During a five year transition period that will end December 31, 2001, you have received benefit accruals under the Plan equal to the greater of the new cash account benefit and the existing minimum benefit formula.
>
> **(5)** This notice is intended to satisfy the requirements of Section 204(h) of the Employee Retirement Income Security Act of 1974. **(6)** Section 204(h) requires that all retirement plan participants be notified of plan amendments that freeze or reduce future benefit accruals. **(7)** The following again summarizes how your benefit will be affected.

Sentence (1) violates the IMT clarity maxim when it refers to participants' "minimum benefit" under the "Plan." The term "minimum benefit" has not yet been defined within the notice, and it is extremely unrealistic for the company to expect average plan participants to remember how this term was defined and used in prior precursor documents that were sent to them almost a year before. And when in sentence (3) the company states, "This notice is simply a reminder of how the plan was changed," it is encouraging these participants not to read further and to believe that no new information about the conversion is being imparted.

However, this is not exactly true. To the extent that employees believed from the precursor documents or from any other source that their future benefits might be lower as a result of plan conversion, the *omission* of any mention or repeated declaration concerning such reductions in this more formal, more legally authoritative document would itself constitute new information. That is, by omitting any mention of future benefit reductions, the notice may well seem to be *confirming* that no reductions in rate, as compared to the rate under the old plan, are going to occur. Readers may think, "Well, given that this notice is statutorily required, and there is no mention of reductions in the future accrual rate, it looks like I do not have to be concerned about that outcome after all."

Turning to sentence (6), the specific reference here to ERISA's notice requirement might reasonably be taken to imply that El Paso's conversion will entail either reducing *or* freezing employees' future benefit accruals *or* possibly both things. Yet, importantly, "freezing" and "reducing" are not the same. A freeze on employees' old plan benefits does not automatically mean that future benefit accruals will be reduced. It just means the old benefit plan no longer grows. Average plan participant readers would thus naturally anticipate some clarification as to whether one or the other or both things is going to occur.

Sentence (7) seems to promise just such clarification. However, as can be seen in the full text of the § 204(h) notice (see Appendix 2), the remainder fails this promise. It makes statements only clarifying *when* old plan benefits will be *frozen*. Nothing is stated concerning a lower future rate of accrual under the new plan. In particular, there is no statement about lower future accrual rates even remotely comparable to the qualified statement that El Paso made in its 1996 "Employee Update." So, contrary to what the § 204(h) notice states in the first paragraph, it is *not* providing employee readers "simply a reminder." For employee readers who may already be aware that the § 204(h) notice is statutorily required and who, for that reason, paid little or no attention to the 1996 "Employee Update" and other precursors which are *not* statutorily required, the § 204(h) notice cannot function as a "reminder." One cannot be reminded of what one never learned or read before. Based on the § 204(h) notice language alone, such readers would therefore have no basis for inferring that El Paso's new plan will involve significant reductions to their future benefit accrual rates. Thus, the notice violates the IMT maxim of clarity because it leaves the question of future accrual rate reductions ambiguous.

It also arguably violates the maxim of quantity, given that record evidence clearly indicated that El Paso knew what the *range* of the accrual rate reductions would be in percentage terms and chose not to disclose that range in this notice. Indeed, with nothing directly or explicitly stated regarding reductions, it would be reasonable and understandable for average plan participants to assume they are receiving the notice *only* because of the freezing (and termination) of their old final average pay plans, an event they would have learned about in El Paso's other precursor communications. Yet, nothing in the notice helps to disconfirm the notion *suggested repeatedly* in the precursor documents we have examined so far that older, longer-service employees could still receive benefits equal to what they would receive had the old plan continued.

From the standpoint of IMT, then, this pattern of inconsistencies across multiple documents makes for a materially deceptive disclosure. It is true that El Paso, unlike the defendant CIGNA in *Amara*, repeats in its precursors that future benefit accruals will be "lower." Yet we have also seen that El Paso repeats contradictory and misleading assurances to employees about receiving the "greater of" their old or new plan benefits—assurances that could be easily misunderstood given the two most serious IMT maxim violations explained above: (a) El Paso omits any explanation or mention that employees new opening balances in CBP Select accounts are being significantly reduced relative to the value of employees' benefits under the old plan as of December 31, 2001; and (b) El Paso claims, without any qualification, and therefore falsely, that after December 31, 2001, employees' pension benefits in their new cash balance accounts "can only go up" when in fact the wear-away periods caused by the opening balance reductions will mean many older, longer-service employees will see zero growth in these accounts, in some cases even until their normal retirement age. Again, the company's apparent disclosure strategy strongly suggests a calculated effort to disclose without disclosing by deploying textual cues that it might later use to argue revealed reductions. But as previously shown, the disclosures present a fractured and contradictory picture of what is actually happening to employees' pension benefits, a picture that hides entirely the most materially damaging consequences of plan conversion.

The strategy appears to have been quite successful, given that the *Tomlinson* court seizes on the first evidence it finds in the January 1996 "Employee Update" document and never examines either the full context of El Paso's statements there or the problematic aspects of the § 204(h) notice just discussed. And, although stating that it was not deciding the question of the adequacy of El Paso's SPDs and § 204(h) notice, it nevertheless concluded that employees "were informed of the reduction in the benefit accrual rate . . . through other sources," specifically in various precursor documents (*Tomlinson*, 2009, pp. 22–23). The court states:

> Defendants point to numerous sources of information that disclosed to Plaintiffs that accrual rates would be lower, including a January 11, 1996 document entitled "Employee Update," which contains the following [statement] . . . "Effective January 1, 1997, the current pension plan will be converted to a new type of plan called a cash balance plan . . . Under the cash balance plan, employees will earn future benefits at a lower rate than under the current plan." (*Tomlinson*, 2009, pp. 22–23)

The court here implies that this single early statement should preemptively make irrelevant El Paso's other subsequent precursor assertions as well as the omissions and ambiguities in the § 204(h) notice and SPD that confound it. As suggested, however, these latter documents form important parts of the employee readers' context in understanding the effects of the plan conversion. They cannot simply ignore the messages that they seem to find in them the way the court does. In this way, the court's reading of El Paso's disclosures is manifestly decontextualized relative to how average plan participants would be able to read the disclosures and make sense of them.

In particular, the problems with the court's view of the SPD and § 204(h) notice here are comparable to the problems discussed in Chapter 3 concerning the effects of information sequence and context on readers. The statements in the January 1996 "Employee Update" constitute initial negative information about the effect of the cash balance transition. But, as demonstrated in the foregoing discussion, in subsequent El Paso documents there are some messages that appear to confirm the initial message, whereas there are others that dilute or contradict it. The *Tomlinson* court takes no account of this confusing pattern. This, despite the fact that even the initial "Employee Update" cautions employees that the transition plan is not yet finalized and that more information about it would be forthcoming, thus explicitly inviting employees to weigh later information more heavily than earlier information.

A plausible explanation for the court's decontextualized analysis is the psychological phenomena of expert hindsight bias: like El Paso itself, the court knows what cash balance transition plans involve *before* reading these disclosures. This is knowledge that average plan participants do not possess and thus cannot use as a guide when reading and trying to integrate the complex information they are provided. Expert prior knowledge confers salience on the initial statement in the "Employee Update," making it stand out. In this regard the court is very much like a person assembling a jigsaw puzzle with a large, clear photograph of the completed puzzle in front of it to check its interpretation in progress (Bransford & Johnson, 1973; Mannes & Hoyes, 1996; Magliano, Trabasso, & Graesser, 1999; van Dijk, 1999). Given this photograph, the court can quickly seize on the telling, significant pieces and know where they fit in. In contrast, the average plan participant has no photograph or 'big-picture' view but instead has only a collection of disassembled pieces, a collection from which some pieces have been strategically removed via omissions—in IMT terms, quantity violations. Those pieces that remain have been carefully shaped to make connecting them difficult, requiring unexpected inferential leaps and inviting mistaken assumptions and thus making the whole conversion scheme extremely difficult if not impossible to see.

Thus, as far as the reduction of employees' future accrual rate is concerned, it is hard to conclude that El Paso's disclosures do satisfy ERISA's unqualified standard that notices of reductions "must be written in a manner calculated to be understood by the average plan participant." In sharp contrast with the court in *Amara*, the *Tomlinson* court takes no notice of this particular standard in its review of any of El Paso's disclosures.

WILL A WEAR-AWAY PERIOD OCCUR IMMEDIATELY FOLLOWING THE DATE OF TRANSITION DURING WHICH THE EMPLOYEE WILL NOT EARN ANY BENEFIT AT ALL?

As with reduced future accrual rates, the *Tomlinson* court also found that El Paso adequately disclosed the existence of wear-away periods. The court did so, not by examining statements in El Paso's SPD or § 204(h) notice but rather, for reasons already noted, based upon information provided in both the precursor and post-transition documents that El Paso provided. As will be discussed here with the help of IMT's maxims, the soundness the court's conclusion is open to serious challenge.

Precursor documents: Wear-away periods? To begin, internal, undisclosed analyses that the company prepared prior to the change of pension plans showed that for some El Paso employees, wear-away periods could last in excess of 10 years and therefore extend well beyond the end of the 5-year transition period that the company touts as protecting its older, longer-service employees (Declaration of Mr. Claude Poulin, F.S.A., April 15, 2008, para. 43). The precursor documents that El Paso employees received contained no mention of the wear-away effect but, instead, repeatedly suggested that transitioned employees would earn benefits *continuously* in their new cash balance account from the date of conversion (see Table B.1.3). One such document, titled "Introducing CBP Select," stated:

> **You can't lose.** Your account will be credited with interest quarterly, so your account can only go up, never down.
>
> [and]
>
> **You have your own personal account.** It's easy to watch your account grow; you'll always know how much your account is at any time.

Further, in the "Program Highlights" precursor discussed in the preceding section, El Paso stated:

> **(12)** The employee's benefits under the old plan formula will continue to accrue from January 1, 1997 until December 31, 2001. **(13)** (*After this date, the employee earns pension benefits only under CBP Select*). **(14)** When the employee retires, his/her benefits under the old plan formula and CBP Select will be compared. **(15)** *The pension benefit paid will be the higher of the two formulas on the date of retirement*. (Sentence numbers and italics added.)

With respect to wear-away periods, these assertions in El Paso's disclosures are very similar to those of CIGNA in *Amara*, assertions that the latter court found to be materially misleading. The problem with these El Paso statements is rooted both in what they omit (violations of quantity) and in what they falsely affirm (violations of quality). To be sure, none of these statements directly asserts that "wear-away periods will *not* occur as a result of plan conversion." At the same time, it is true that for purely bookkeeping purposes, pay and interest credits are being recorded in the employee's new cash balance account after January 1, 2002. However, sentence (13) is nonetheless materially misleading. Because of the undisclosed opening balance reductions that El Paso made to the new CBP Select accounts, the dollar value of those credits will be less than what the employee already had earned under the old plan as December 31, 2001. Starting on this date the employee will be under a wear-away period and *not* be earning any new pension benefits at all. Therefore, it cannot be truthfully said that after December 31,

2001, employees will "[earn] pension benefits only under CBP Select." The failure to qualify statement (13) with this additional information results in simultaneous violations of the IMT maxims of quantity and quality.

Moreover, consistent with the unqualified assurance of continuous CBP Select benefit growth from the time their old plan is frozen, no illustrative hypothetical examples in El Paso's precursor documents show employees who might suffer a wear-away period. Instead, all of the examples show employees who do *not* suffer a wear-away period.[4] This absence of any examples showing these periods, when combined with the company's unqualified assurances about the continuous growth of employees' cash balance accounts after December 31, 2001, would in context prevent employees from suspecting their occurrence.

Consider the example of hypothetical employee "Bob" shown in Appendix 3. As can be seen, this example focuses entirely on what Bob will earn under CBP Select from the date of transition. It does not clarify whether or not his opening account balance of $12,000 represents a significant reduction compared to what his old plan ending balance might be. Nor, if that were the case, does the accompanying bar chart show whether he is actually earning no benefit at all (0 percent benefit growth) because his old plan frozen balance remains higher than the benefit value shown, say, at 3, 5, and 10 years. Indeed, in this as in all of the hypothetical examples provided in El Paso's precursors, neither opening account balance reductions nor wear-away periods are ever illustrated.

Just like defendant CIGNA, and prior to presenting Bob's example, El Paso does offer a general disclaimer:

> Of course, your personal situation and calculations may be different [than in the examples shown].

As discussed in Chapter 3, however, in IMT terms this disclaimer fails to address directly the employees' question as to whether there are *any* circumstances in which, as a result of plan transition, employees will suffer a wear-away period. Thus, although not asserting anything positively false, the disclaimer nonetheless hides crucial information. To fully qualify the implication generated by El Paso's consistently positive hypothetical examples, the disclaimer should include more specific information, stating something to this effect:

> Contrary to what these particular examples show, opening account balances may be reduced compared to the total value of all the benefits you may have earned under the old plan as of December 31, 2001. As a result of this reduction, some employees will experience wear away periods even after the end of the five year transition period, meaning that they will earn no payable cash balance benefits until their cash balance account catches up to the value of their old plan benefits on the date it was frozen.

The failure to warn employees in this explicit fashion against the positive implications that the hypothetical examples collectively reinforce results in a violation of the maxim of quantity. That is, although the examples themselves are accurate in the sense that they depict how credits are earned and accumulate in employees' new CBP Select accounts, they are markedly incomplete and collectively misleading in relation both to what the employees reasonably would expect to know and in relation to what the company knew to a certainty would occur: some 1,500 employees would suffer wear-away periods after the end of the five-year transition.

So far, then, it may look as if El Paso did not disclose the existence of wear-away periods to any greater degree than CIGNA did. Before reaching that conclusion, however, it is necessary to examine El Paso's SPD and its one-page § 204(h) notice (see Appendix 2).

SPD and § 204(h) notice: Wear-way periods? As detailed, we saw that the court in *Tomlinson* did not examine El Paso's SPD because it accepted El Paso's claim that its precursors and other documents, including its § 204(h) notice, satisfied ERISA's disclosure requirements. In point of fact, just as El Paso did not disclose reductions to employees' future benefit accrual rate in its SPD, neither did it disclose wear-away periods there (see Table B.3). Instead, we see again that El Paso makes unqualified statements in its SPD regarding wear-away periods that simultaneously violate IMT's quality and quantity maxims:

> Your El Paso Cash Account Benefit from CBP Select is based on the value of a hypothetical 'account' that is established in your name when you become a participant in the Plan. Your account increases in value over time by being credited with quarterly pay credits . . . In addition, your account will receive quarterly interest credits. The value of your El Paso Cash Account Benefit will continue to grow as long as you maintain a balance in your CBP Select Account.
>
> After December 31, 2001, your Minimum Benefit will be frozen, and you will earn benefits only under your El Paso Cash Account Benefit.

As can be seen, these statements essentially repeat and reinforce statements in the precursor documents that once the conversion has occurred, employees can expect to see *continuous* growth in their new CBP Select Accounts; the company offers no qualification indicating that growth in these 'hypothetical' credits may not translate to any actual growth in future pension benefits.

The § 204(h) notice was disseminated sometime after the precursor documents quoted; the entire notice is presented in Appendix 2. As already noted, the *Tomlinson* court declined to review this notice in view of that court's strict interpretation of the version of § 204(h) in effect at the time. In the court's view, the defendants were not required by § 204(h) to disclose either reductions in future benefit accrual rates or wear-away periods but rather only required to "set forth" a summary of the cash balance plan amendment. Nevertheless, the notice is important to examine because it makes two statements that do not occur in any of El Paso's other documents and that might be contended to disclose the existence of wear-away periods. These two statements appear in the fifth paragraph of the notice and are ones that have no comparable counterparts in CIGNA's disclosures in *Amara*. To assess their significance and possible impact on El Paso employees' understanding it is critical to (a) consider statements that precede them in the notice, particularly those in the first, third, and fourth paragraphs (reproduced below) and (b) also consider the statements in El Paso's precursor documents that were just discussed (italics and sentence numbers added):

> **[1st Paragraph] (1)** Effective December 31, 2001, all participants . . . will cease accruing a minimum benefit under the El Paso Corporation Pension Plan (the "Plan"). **(2)** You have received a variety of communications describing this change since 1997 when the plan was amended to provide a cash account benefit. **(3)** This notice is simply a reminder of how the Plan was changed in 1997. **(4)** During a five year transition period that will end December 31, 2001, you have received benefit accruals under the Plan equal to the greater of the new cash account benefit and [sic] the existing minimum benefit formula.
>
> **[3rd Paragraph] (5)** An active participant under the Plan on January 1, 1997 who was an eligible employee or a vested terminated participant on December 31, 1996 is entitled to continue to accrue a minimum benefit after December 31, 1996 until the earlier of i) December 31, 2001, or ii) termination of employment after January 1, 1997. **(6)** The minimum benefit is based on a participant's final average earnings and credited service. **(7)** A participant's credited service and earnings that occur after the date the minimum benefit stops accruing will be disregarded when the minimum benefit is calculated.
>
> **[4th Paragraph] (8)** Each participant on December 31, 1996 who was an eligible employee on January 1, 1997 received an opening cash account balance in the Plan on January 1, 1997. **(9)** The participant's cash account balance grows with pay credits and interest credits. **(10)** The participant will be entitled to receive a benefit based on his or her cash account balance or the minimum benefit, whichever is greater.
>
> . . .
>
> **[5th Paragraph] (11)** After December 31, 2001, for a participant whose minimum benefit is greater than the cash account benefit, accruals under the Plan *may effectively* cease until the participant's cash account benefit exceeds the minimum benefit earned as of December 31, 2001. **(12)** This period of non-accrual will be more likely to affect individuals who elect early retirement.

As will now be explained, the claim that El Paso adequately disclosed the existence of wear-away periods in the fifth paragraph faces numerous problems that IMT maxims can help to illuminate.

First, the putatively key disclosive sentence (11) in the 5th paragraph violates the IMT maxim of quantity. The modal verb "may" together with the qualifier "effectively" implies the existence of conditions under which a cessation of benefits (wear away) would not occur. However, participants would be unable to understand these conditions here because no further description of them is provided. In particular, El Paso nowhere explains that the value of employees' new opening account balances may be significantly less than the total value of the benefits earned so far under the old plan. This lowering of the opening account value is what triggers the wear-away period, and without this crucial piece of information, the notion of a cessation or suspension in the accumulation of cash balance benefits would not likely be grasped by ordinary employee readers. Additionally, except to vaguely suggest in sentence (12) that individuals electing early retirement "will be more likely" to be affected, El Paso does not explain why; nor does it explain which groups of participants seeking early retirement would be affected, why or how these groups are at greater risk, or to what degree. The company had much more specific information available about age and service groups who would suffer lengthy wear-away periods but does not communicate any of that information here. Moreover, as we have seen, wear-away periods contribute directly to the overall reduction of the future benefit accrual rate following the date of plan conversion.

Second, the fifth paragraph also violates the IMT maxim of clarity in two distinct ways. First, it is referentially ambiguous. When participants read that "accruals under the Plan may effectively cease," they will not easily understand that the term "accruals" here refers to the pay and interest credits provided by the new cash balance plan. Participants will not likely understand the term this way because in El Paso's precursor documents the terms "accruals" and "accrue" are mostly used in reference to participants' benefits under their old plan.[5] For instance, in the "Program Highlights" precursor, participants would have read:

> The employee's benefits under the old plan formula will continue to accrue from January 1, 1997 until December 31, 2001.

The same restricted use of the term "accruals" to refer to growth in participants' old plan minimum benefits also occurs at the start of the § 204(h) notice itself, in its very first sentence, and then again in sentences (5) and (7) in the third paragraph:

> (1) Effective December 31st, all participants . . . will cease accruing a minimum benefit under the El Paso Corporation Pension Plan (the "Plan").
>
> (5) An active participant under the Plan on January 1, 1997 who was an eligible employee or a vested terminated participant on December 31, 1996 is entitled to continue to accrue a minimum benefit after December 31, 1996 until the earlier of i) December 31, 2001, or ii) termination of employment after January 1, 1997.
>
> (7) A participant's credited service and earnings that occur after the date the minimum benefit stops accruing will be disregarded when the minimum benefit is calculated.

Given this frequent use of the terms "accrual," "accruing," and "accrue" in connection with participants' old pension plan, they will not readily grasp in sentence (11) of the fifth paragraph that "accruals" refers to benefits accumulated in their new "cash account." Instead, they will likely think statement (11) simply refers to the cessation or "freezing" of their old plan benefits, which they had been told about repeatedly before in El Paso's precursors. Readers are normally conditioned to make the most spatially proximate parts of texts fit together as they construct meaning. They try to add the latest information in a segment to the *next* bit of information *unless* they are given some explicit cue not to do so (Vande Kopple, 1986). In this case, no such cue regarding the shift in usage of the term "accruals" is offered to readers. Participants may thus quite reasonably think that the phrase "accruals under the Plan" in the fifth paragraph means accruals only under the *existing plan*, especially given that (a) El Paso precursor documents repeatedly stated that accruals under the existing plan would cease at the end of the five-year transition period, and (b) the terms "accrual" and "accrue" were almost exclusively used in the precursor documents in reference to the growth of benefits under the old plan.

Also referentially ambiguous in the fifth paragraph is the use of the term "Plan" itself. Participants may reasonably think that the term "Plan" is still referring *only to their old or existing plan* because the very first sentence in the notice stipulates that the term "Plan" refers *only* to the "minimum benefit," which includes the five-year "transition benefit" employees would earn under their old plan, ostensibly to protect those nearer to retirement from harmful effects of the plan transition. And otherwise, the notice nowhere states that the term "Plan" includes the new cash balance plan.

Significantly, this analysis of referential ambiguity in the fifth paragraph is consistent with and illustrated by the deposition response of Mr. Muckelroy (plaintiff) to Mr. Nadel's (defense counsel) question concerning the term "accruals" as used specifically in the fifth paragraph of the § 204(h) notice:

Q. (Mr. Nadel)	Okay. Do you know what it means for accruals under the plan to effectively cease?
A. (Mr. Muckelroy)	I would assume that it means accruals under the old plan may effectively cease? Yeah, they could cease. (Deposition of Mr. Gary Muckelroy, January 30, 2008, p. 139)

Similarly, the depositions of Ms. Ballesteros (plaintiff) and Mr. Tomlinson (plaintiff) show that they cannot understand what the entire phrase "accruals under the plan may effectively cease" means:

A. (Ms. Ballesteros)	Well, the phrase ". . . accruals under the plan" is a little confusing because they don't specify which plan . . . I didn't understand what they mean by accruals would cease. (Deposition of Ms. Alice Ballesteros, February 25, 2008, p. 86)

A. (Mr. Tomlinson) I'm confused as to what plan we're talking about, cash balance plan or defined benefit plan. So the entire sentence doesn't make sense. (Deposition of Mr. William Tomlinson, January 31, 2008, p. 221)

Finally, the fifth paragraph also suffers from contextual ambiguity. The uncertainty expressed by these plaintiffs concerning the meaning of the fifth paragraph is understandable because the paragraph contradicts previous unqualified assurances in the precursor documents that CBP Select accounts would *only continue to grow*, as seen in parenthesis here:

> The employee's benefits under the old plan formula will continue to accrue from January 1, 1997 until December 31, 2001. (After this date, the employee earns pension benefits only under CBP Select.)

Given these previous assurances, employees might easily think the fifth paragraph simply informs them again about the "freezing" of their existing "minimum" transition benefit (i.e., their old plan benefit). The likelihood of this interpretation is reinforced given that at the outset, in sentence (3), the importance of the notice itself is misleadingly downplayed as being "simply a reminder." The characterization of the notice as "simply a reminder" violates the IMT maxim of quality, given that employees were *not* previously told anything about wear-away periods and therefore could not be "reminded" about them here. It is also an example of what Galasinski (2000) terms "metadiscursive deception" because it appears to be an attempt to conceal violations of quantity that occurred in the precursor documents (pp. 72–85). In this regard, IMT's Gricean cooperativeness principle requires that when later official disclosure documents present statements that contradict statements in, or implications generated by previous precursor documents, the documents provided later in time—in this case the § 204(h) notice—should explicitly call readers' attention to and explain these differences. In contrast with such 'reader-friendly' explanatory practice, the way this entire notice is framed works to inoculate participants against accurately understanding the seeming hint buried in its fifth paragraph.

Now some observers might contend that this analysis of the § 204(h) notice is faulty because it does not account for what readers would learn from the two paragraphs immediately preceding the fifth paragraph. Such observers' argument is that the existence of wear-away periods becomes clear when the information provided by all three paragraphs is properly combined. But this argument is, again, predicated largely upon expert hindsight bias, that is, upon the observer's prior knowledge regarding what a wear-away period is and what causes it. A careful 'step through' of what readers both do *and* do not learn in the third and fourth paragraphs will show instead that nonexpert readers must make highly implausible inferences from undefined terms and missing information.

To begin, ordinary readers would not likely understand why the old plan benefit as of December 31, 1996, is referred to as the "minimum" benefit. It is so termed in the first paragraph and then again in the third. Sentence (6) in the third paragraph states, "The minimum benefit is based on a participant's final average earnings and credited service." But why, readers would likely ask, is the old benefit referred to as the "minimum" benefit? Sentence (7) does not help to answer this question but cryptically and circularly says, "A participant's credited service and earnings that occur after the date the minimum benefit stops accruing will be disregarded when the minimum benefit is calculated." Readers would likely carry this puzzle forward, like a hangover, into the fourth paragraph, expecting some help.

But the fourth paragraph also does not answer this question. Instead, it creates another puzzling question for the reader to tackle. It instructs employee readers that they "received an opening cash account balance in the Plan on January 1, 1997," that this balance "grows with pay credits and interest credits," and that employees "will be entitled to receive a benefit based on [the]account balance or the minimum benefit, whichever is greater." But why would the "minimum benefit" be greater than the new cash account balance, especially given that El Paso *repeatedly* indicated before and without qualification that the new account would continue to grow? The presumption that ordinary readers could somehow leap past these prior indications of continuous growth to the conclusion that El Paso must have discounted their opening account balances, that is, so that these balances did not include the full value of their old, "minimum" benefit, clearly smacks of hindsight bias. In particular, notice the hiatus that occurs between sentences (8) and (9) in the fourth paragraph. Sentence (8) tells employees they will have a new account balance and then sentence (9) says this balance "grows with pay credits and interest credits." In between these two, El Paso might have directly told employee readers that the new account balance, contrary to their reasonable expectations, would be set up to contain much less than the value of their old "minimum" benefit, but they did not; nor did they do so in any of their disclosures. This clear quantity violation is what makes the hypothesis that readers 'could have learned' about wear away from El Paso's § 204(h) notice so implausible, despite the apparent accuracy of the notices' statements when they are decontextualized and then 'recoded' with the benefit of expert hindsight knowledge.

Post-transition individual benefit notices: Wear-away periods? Despite the contradictory messages that El Paso employees received about wear-away periods, the court in *Tomlinson* still concluded that El Paso had satisfactorily warned its employees. Without commenting upon *any* of these prior messages and considering their import *in context* for average plan participants, the court points to what it obviously considers El Paso's trump card, specifically the individualized pension benefit account statements sent to El Paso employees in 1999, just over two years into the five-year transition period following the plan conversion date of January 1, 1997. The court remarks that

> in 1999 . . . each employee received an individualized account statement which showed, in bar graph form, a comparison of the participant's benefit in the cash balance plan and the previous plan over time until age 65 . . . [T]he bar graph clearly shows the wear away effect, as it shows both the frozen old

> benefit and the growing cash balance plan at several intervals . . . [T]he bar graph shows that the cash balance benefit does not exceed the participant's frozen benefits even at age 65. I see no prejudice to Plaintiffs from the alleged failure to disclose in the SPD information that was already disclosed, and even illustrated individually, before the SPD was even issued. (*Tomlinson*, 2009, p. 23)

This bar graph, and the court's conclusion about it, must be taken seriously, for it might appear to be more compelling evidence of the disclosure of wear-away periods than the textual messages already discussed. By contrast, no such graphic depiction of wear-away periods was ever presented by CIGNA in its disclosures in the *Amara* case. The *Tomlinson* court clearly sees this bar graph in the same way that it views the statement about lower future benefit accrual rates contained in the initial "Employee Update" sent to plaintiffs in October 1996—as red-handed, *res ipsa loquitur* evidence of disclosure of wear-away periods.

But is it? The court says nothing more about the *context* of this bar graph, not only in relation to the earlier textual messages previously analyzed but also not even in relation to the text accompanying the graph within the individualized account statement itself. The concern, again, is that the court may have been affected by expert hindsight bias. It is therefore critical to look at the bar graph in the larger temporal and locative context in which average plan participants would encounter it.

A sample individualized pension account statement is shown in Appendix 4, titled "Your Retirement Benefits." It was prepared for a named plaintiff, and it is three pages long. The first page provides an estimate of the employee's retirement savings plan, which is based upon dollars that employees themselves contribute toward a separate retirement account. These savings, however, are distinct from the employee's pension account and do not need to be discussed further here. The second and third pages of the statement are the critical ones for examining the court's conclusion that wear away was adequately disclosed, with the third page containing the bar graph itself. It needs to be born carefully in mind that up to the point in time when El Paso employees received this individualized account statement, the only putative prior reference to wear-away periods is that discussed in the confounded fifth paragraph of the § 204(h) notice. In the middle of the second page of this individualized statement, the employee would read the following two paragraphs (boldface type appears in the original):

> **How Your Benefit is Calculated**
>
> When CBP Select was introduced, you were credited with an opening balance based on your accrued benefit under the prior formula. Additionally, you continue to accrue benefits under the prior formula (referred to as the Minimum Benefit) during the transition period which ends December 31, 2001. Therefore, up to that date, your pension benefit continues to grow under two formulas: the Minimum Benefit (the transition formula) and the Cash Account Benefit. Thereafter, only the Cash Account Benefit continues to grow.

> As an eligible participant during this transition period, your benefits under the "old" formula (Minimum Benefit formula) will continue to accrue through December 31, 2001. After this date, you will continue to accrue a pension benefit under the Cash Account Benefit while your accrued benefit under the Minimum Benefit formula will be frozen. When you retire or terminate from the company your benefits under the Minimum Benefit formula and the Cash Account benefit formula will be compared and you will receive the *greater* of the two amounts. **You do not need to retire or terminate on or before December 31, 2001 to receive the Minimum Benefit.**

The company contends, and apparently the *Tomlinson* court as well, that although the term 'wear away' is never used, the possibility of wear-away periods would be readily inferable from what is described in these two paragraphs. For a person who already knows about cash balance transitions and what a wear-away period is, such a contention might be plausible. But it is not plausible for someone without such prior knowledge for at least two reasons.

First and foremost, the initial sentence involves a crucial omission when it states, "When CBP Select was introduced, you were credited with an opening account balance *based on* your accrued benefit under the prior formula" (italics added). The employee is not told what the phrase "based on" means. In fact, just as occurred in *Amara*, El Paso significantly reduced employees' new opening balances in CBP Select compared to the benefits the employee had already earned under the old plan formula. Thus, for instance, if the El Paso employee had earned an annuity of $1,000 per month in pension benefits by the date of plan transition on January 1, 1997, the starting balance in the new CBP Select plan would not equal that amount but instead might be reduced so as to yield an annuity of only $486 per month, a drop of more than 50 percent (Deposition of Mr. Claude Poulin, F.S.A., April 15, 2008, para. 40–41).[6]

This up-front reduction to the new opening balance is the chief cause of wear-away periods; the employee must work long enough following the transition date of January 1, 1997, to 're-earn' benefits in the new CBP Select account that they already have earned and are entitled to under the old plan. Because the employee is *not* told about this up-front reduction, however, the likely default employee assumption would be that the phrase "based on" means that the new plan benefit amount would *equal* the total value of benefits already earned under the old plan—much as if one were taking one's savings from one bank account and putting them into another bank account. In other words, the natural and reasonable expectation on the part of an average plan participant would be that, even if future growth in the new account might be slower, one would still be starting from the old plan balance that the new account is said to be "based on."

Second, absent any indication that a reduction to the opening account balance is being effected, employees would have trouble grasping why in the second paragraph they are being told, "When you retire or terminate from the Company, your benefits under the Minimum Benefit Formula and the Cash Account Benefit formula will be compared and you will receive the *greater* of the two amounts."[7] To be sure, the employee is plainly told in the previous sentence that their old plan account will be "frozen" as of December 31, 2001. From this information, the company contends that employees should be able to make a complex, two-step inference. They contend that (a) employees will be able to connect the freezing of their old plan benefits with the statement affirming that they will receive the "greater of" their old plan or new plan benefits and thereby infer that their opening account balances were reduced; and then (b) employees will further infer from the opening balance reduction that from December 31, 2001, forward, they may earn no more pension benefits at all (i.e., that they will have a future growth rate of 0 percent in their pensions), while they are under a wear-away period.

When looking at very similar language in CIGNA's disclosures, the *Amara* court rejected this same contention. That employees could make the inferential leap in step (a) is highly implausible. Certainly employees could not conclude that because their old plan benefits are being frozen and will not further grow in value that their new opening account balances in CBP Select itself were being reduced. The freezing of the old plan benefit and the reduction to the new plan balance are entirely separate things: freezing simply means that growth in the old plan stops and does not imply that the value of the opening balance in CBP Select is being reduced. Indeed, El Paso employees were *never* told in *any* documents that their new opening account balances would be significantly less than the accrued benefit amount in their old plan balances.

In IMT's terms, the company discourse strategy in these two paragraphs involves violations of both the quantity and clarity maxims, with the latter violation serving to mask the former. That is, the company reserves a covert, ambiguous meaning for the phrase "based on" that it can try to argue does not involve telling any falsehood but that nonetheless hides crucial information it does not want to reveal. Despite the fact that no positive falsehood is being told with the phrase "based on" *per se*, used without any explanation for the average plan participant it is potently and materially deceptive all the same. It is being used here in the same way that the terms "reflect," "converted," and "transferred" were used ambiguously and deceptively in the *Amara* case for the same strategic purpose, that is, to hide the fact that CIGNA was significantly reducing employees' new opening account balances as part of its pension conversion.

In fact, these two paragraphs involve not only these quantity and clarity violations but a quality violation as well: they repeat false, materially misleading statements that the company made before. El Paso twice in these paragraphs tells the employee without qualification that after December 31, 2001, "only the Cash Account Benefit continues to grow" and that "[a]fter this date, you will continue to accrue a pension benefit only under the Cash Account Benefit." For the large number of employees under wear-away periods due to reductions in their new opening CBP Select balances, these statements are positively false: these employees are not "continuing to accrue" pension benefits at all after December 31, 2001. Contextually these statements serve to reinforce what El Paso misleadingly told employees in a previous precursor document, there also without saying anything about zero-growth wear-away periods (italics added):

> **You can't lose.** Your account will be credited with interest quarterly, so your account can only go up, never down.
>
> **You have your own personal account.** It's easy to watch your account grow; you'll always know how much your account is at any time.
>
> The employee's benefits under the old plan formula will continue to accrue from January 1, 1997 until December 31, 2001. (*After this date, the employee earns pension benefits only under CBP Select.*)

Without being told that their new opening account balances are being reduced relative to their accrued benefits under the old plan, average plan participants could not understand that all of these seeming assurances about continuous benefit growth are only true if the employee works enough years to escape the wear-away period. These assurances are materially misleading because those employees under wear-away periods will earn no new benefits after December 31, 2001, until their new CBP Select account catches up to the value of their old plan benefit.

Thus, just before reaching the third page of their individualized pension statements containing the bar graph, which the court sees as dispositive *by itself* regarding the wear-away disclosure issue, employees are once more denied material information and treated instead to misleading language that abrogates their recognition and understanding of the wear-away concept. Given the language just discussed, El Paso employees would certainly not expect to see what the court maintains the bar graph shows because they have been led to believe that wear-away periods would not occur. As will be discussed next, further violations of IMT's Gricean maxims on the third page where the bar graph appears cast even more doubt on the *Tomlinson* court's conclusion that the bar graph clearly discloses wear away in a manner that average plan participants could understand.

It is a bedrock principle in the graphic, instructional design, and reading comprehension research literatures that quantitative graphics are *not* self-explanatory, that they do not 'speak for themselves.' Instead, how people perceive them is greatly dependent on their prior conceptual knowledge, their cognitive state, and the larger discourse context in which such graphics are being presented (Cleveland, 1985, 1994; Cleveland & McGill, 1984, 1985; Kosslyn, 2006; Kostelnick & Hasset, 2003; Schriver, 1997). As Kosslyn (1989) explains, a major constraint on the ability to interpret quantitative graphic displays

> is a person's knowledge. The way a display will be interpreted, both at the level of semantics and pragmatics, depends on which stored information is most closely associated with the way the stimulus properties are categorized. If a person does not know the meaning of a word, or recognize a pattern of lines forming the framework of a display, he or she will have trouble associating the display with the correct information. (pp. 191–192)

In particular, the quantitative graphic literature shows that the prose material persons read prior to and accompanying the quantitative displays themselves may strongly affect not only how people interpret the displays but even what information they are able to 'see' in and retrieve from them (Tractinsky & Meyer, 1999). Nonexperts looking at quantitative graphics need and rely upon accompanying prose explanations to help them grasp the significance of the visuals or quantitative projections they see (Natter & Berry, 2005). The foregoing discussion of what the El Paso employees read in their precursor documents, in the company's § 204(h) notice, and on the page immediately preceding these graphics suggests strongly that participants could only have, at best, a confused picture regarding how El Paso's pension plan conversion would affect their future benefits. Their confusion, however, may become worse owing to a number of problems with the way graphics themselves are presented and annotated.

First, there is no verbal indication anywhere on this page that what the table and bar graph show is the existence and length of the wear-away period that the employee is under. As was the case on the preceding page, there is also no indication on this page that the employee's new opening account balance is being reduced. The employee would thus likely approach this page still assuming that the new opening account balance would equal the value of the old, frozen plan benefit. And importantly, because the old plan balance *as of December 31, 2001*, is *not* marked as such on either the table or the bar graph, the employee would be unable to recognize the figures they see or understand why these figures begin at the levels they do. They would be unprepared to grasp *why* the bar graph shows their "Minimum Benefit" is greater at their "Current Age" than the "Cash Balance" benefit.

Second, looking at the table display, the second row title on the left side uses the term "Pension," but *which* pension plan is being referred to is unclear: is it the old defined benefit pension plan or the new CBP Select cash balance plan? No prose within the table clarifies this term. The main heading at the top of the page says, "Pension Plan (CBP Select)," possibly leading the employee to think that the first row in the table labeled "Pension" refers to earnings under the new rather than the old plan. At the same time, however, a heavy black line separates the table from this heading and the bulleted text immediately above it, making the scope of the main heading unclear. This referential ambiguity violates the maxim of clarity and could only add to the employee's uncertainty about the figures being shown and their significance.

Third, there is no verbal explanation accompanying the table as to why the employee's "Pension" growth (whichever pension account it is) remains flat starting from age 60. Is it the case that the individual employee turns 60 in or at the end of 2001, and therefore the $2,548 benefit shown there represents the final frozen benefit under the employee's old plan? There is no way for the employee to tell if that is the correct interpretation both because which "Pension" account being shown is ambiguous (old or new?) and because the table does not indicate specific calendar years (e.g., 2001, 2002, 2003, etc.) along with the employee's advancing age to mark intervals. The omission of calendar years makes interpretation of the table data very difficult for average plan participants who lack prior knowledge about cash balance plan conversions. Along with prose explanations, it would have been easy for the company to add these calendar years to the table to aid employees' interpretation. The company may contend that the employee should be able to infer that the zero growth in the $2,548 means it is the employee's frozen, old plan benefit. But there is no legend or cue provided with the table to verify that interpretation. Given the fact that employees are never told about the up-front reductions to their new opening account balances and the fact that old plan balances *as of December 31, 2001*, are not marked as such on the table, any contention that the employee could understand why no growth occurs is implausible.

Similarly, turning to the bar graph, there is no verbal explanation accompanying it as to why the "Cash Balance" account lags behind the "Minimum Benefit" amount for at least seven years. It would have been easy for the company to add an explanation as to the nature and cause of wear away to this chart, that is, that the employee's opening account balance in the new plan was discounted relative to the value of the benefits earned under the old plan. Just as is the case with the table above it, there is no accompanying verbal explanation as to why starting from age 60 the "Minimum Benefit" fails to grow and remains flat; again, calendar years are not displayed along with the employee's advancing age.

Fourth, the page involves ambiguous language as to whether the employee's actual versus merely hypothetical projected benefits are being shown in both the table and the graph. On the one hand, the first sentence at the top of page 3 states, "Following are estimates of your monthly benefits from the Company." But, on the other hand, neither the table nor the bar graph is captioned with the individual employee's name. Adding confusion, a fine-print italicized "Note" below the bar graph states, "These figures are for illustration purpose only," which might lead the employee to wonder whether the projected figures are actually his or hers. Is this disclaimer simply a restatement of the fact that the figures in both the table and chart represent "estimates," as the first sentence on the page states, or does it mean something different? Collectively, these unexplained cues may lead average plan participants to believe that the figures shown are simply unreliable.

Fifth, and finally, there is no label or explanation as to whether the projected benefits in the table *are the same* as those in the bar graph below it. Research on quantitative data display has shown that bar graphs are not useful for persons who seek or need exact figures (Cleveland, 1985; Schriver, 1997). The physical properties of bar graphs can make the perception of measurements difficult. In this instance, if a straight edge is laid horizontally across the top of the age 60, 62, and 65 "Minimum Benefit" bars, the value of the benefit shown on the left side in these years appears to be $2,400, whereas the corresponding value for these same years in the table above is higher, at $2,548. To be sure, average plan participants might never compare the two displays with such scrutiny. Yet the lack of accompanying prose explanation could easily make them wonder what the distinct purposes of the two data displays are and why both are included.

To summarize, in view of these issues the *Tomlinson* court's conclusion that the bar graph, data table, and other information on page 3 clearly discloses the existence of wear-away periods and involves "no prejudice" toward the El Paso employees is very questionable. The court has not discussed or even mentioned any of the substantive explanatory issues with the table and bar graph, detailed above, nor considered how these could be viewed contextually in the checkered pattern of cues scattered across El Paso's preceding stream of prose communications. Instead, again, it would seem that the court's conclusion may be affected by expert hindsight bias that leads the court to lose sight of the average plan participant standard and the different context in which such participants would read El Paso's documents. The court is actively looking for some indication that wear-away periods will occur in contrast with employees who, not knowing how cash balance plan transitions work, would not likely know what a wear-away period is or that it does occur in such transitions. Rather, the court has a full picture of what is occurring in this cash balance transition; it can therefore readily identify and understand where each disconnected cue fits, including the quantitative graphics in the individual notices. But average plan participant readers are not offered, at any point, a 'big picture' of what is happening to guide their interpretation of each piece of information in the stream of employer communications, and thus it would be extremely difficult for them to integrate the quantitative information in the table and bar graph on page 3 with the disintegrated verbal information they previously received.

To complete this analysis of El Paso's communications, however, and given that the reduction of employees' new opening CBP Select balances is the chief cause of wear-away periods, the putative disclosure of these reduced balances must be further examined in El Paso's precursor documents, § 204(h) notices, and SPDs.

ARE OPENING ACCOUNT BALANCES IN THE NEW PLAN EQUAL TO THE TOTAL VALUE OF BENEFITS EARNED UNDER THE OLD PLAN?

Significantly, the court in *Tomlinson* nowhere discusses El Paso's statements regarding the initial value of employees' new cash account opening balances. Yet, as noted, understanding that these opening account balances are being reduced relative to the total worth of an employee's benefits under the old final average pay plan as of December 31, 1996, is crucial to the employee's ability to recognize that wear-away periods are being imposed and what causes them. As also noted, wear-away periods in turn contribute to reductions in employees' future benefit accrual rates.

As these next sections will show, El Paso's strategic approach to providing information about employees' opening account balances follows the same pattern used in its approach to providing information concerning future accrual rate reductions and wear-away periods. The apparent strategy, again, is to appear to disclose without actually or fully disclosing what is occurring, resulting in complex, interacting violations of IMT's quantity, quality, and clarity maxims.

Precursor documents: Opening account balances reduced? Table B.1.4 and Table B.2 display what, if any, language is relevant to employees' opening account balances under the new cash balance plan that appears in El Paso's precursor documents and § 204(h) notices, respectively. Specifically, Table B.1.4 shows that prior to receiving their individual pension benefit statements in 1999, El Paso employees could read statements in three different precursor documents purporting to describe how employees' opening balances in the new CBP Select plan would be set. For instance, starting with the "Employment Update" document in October 1996, which inaugurated El Paso's stream of disclosures, the company told El Paso employees the following (sentence numbers added for reference):

> **(1)** Employees' accrued benefit under the cash balance plan will not be less than what they have accrued under the current Pension Plan formula as of December 31, 1996.
> **(2)** This ensures that benefits employees have earned in 1996 will not be reduced in the transition to the new plan (p. 26).

It could not plausibly be contended that these two sentences, whether together or separately, informed employees that the opening balances in their new CBP Select Accounts would be *reduced* relative to the value of their old plan benefits as of December 31, 1996. Nor can it be validly argued that these statements clearly or unambiguously carry that implication for at least two reasons.

First, the second sentence appears to violate the quality maxim because it suggests that the value of the old plan benefits an employee has on December 31, 1996, will be preserved "in the transition to the new plan," that is, that the closing value of old plan benefits will become the starting balance under the new plan. The company might wish to argue that when saying "in the transition to the new plan," they were *not* referring to opening account balances but instead referring to what the effect of the entire plan change would be, that is, that the employees might never realize any further growth in their pensions after the date of plan transition due to wear away. But absent any further explanation on the company's part, and as discussed in the preceding section, it would be reasonable and natural for an employee to read this statement as saying that their new account balances open at the same value where the old plan accruals froze. Employees would not receive their individualized pension statements containing the bar graph for more than two years. Moreover, if employees understood that, under ERISA, pension benefits they have already earned can never be reduced or taken away, they might simply read the first sentence as stating no more than this fact—*not* that their opening account balances could be reduced or that wear-away periods could occur.

Second, the pronoun "This," which begins the second sentence, is vague. What, exactly, does "This" refer to? If it is taken as referring to the entire first sentence, the resulting (reconstructed) predication would go something like this:

> [The fact that employees' accrued benefit under the cash balance plan will not be less than what they have accrued under the current Pension Plan formula as of December 31, 1996] ensures that benefits employees have earned in 1996 will not be reduced in the transition to the new plan. (p. 26)

Even if the employee reader goes to the trouble of resolving the vague pronoun in this manner, which is uncertain at best, what does this reconstruction really tell the employee? The reconstruction appears to be almost tautological. It certainly does not undo what the second sentence seems to imply by itself. The company might wish to argue that the phrase "accrued benefit under the cash benefit plan" in the first sentence refers to the *ultimate benefit that the employee will have when beginning retirement*. But even apart from the fact that employee readers cannot be sure exactly what the pronoun "This" refers to, they could not jump to the conclusion that their benefits would not grow beyond what they already earned under the old plan unless they were informed explicitly about reductions to their opening account balances under the new plan. Effectively, these two sentences constitute another example of how clarity violations can serve to mask quantity and quality violations that have material consequences.

More baldly, in two subsequent precursors, the company appears to explicitly and categorically declare the very opposite, namely, that employees' new CBP Account balances *will* open at *exactly* the closing value of the employee's old plan account on December 31, 1996:

> The present value of your accrued benefit under the EPNG Pension Plan as of December 31, 1996 *will be* your opening account balance in your CBP Select account on January 1, 1997 (italics added).
>
> [and]
>
> Initial Balance: The present value of your accrued benefit under the EPNG Pension Plan as of December 31, 1996.

The company would argue that "present value" does not literally mean "current" value but instead a lesser value arrived at through certain "present value" actuarial calculations. But the phrase is not so qualified or explained anywhere in these two documents, and thus average plan participants would be unlikely to know or understand that the term "present value" was being used in this fashion. The term was not defined in any footnote or glossary attached to these documents. Again, in IMT terms the discourse strategy pursued here is to mask both quality and quantity violations with a violation of clarity; the latter violation is manifest in the company's covert and quite technical interpretation of a common phrase that average plan participants would not anticipate or expect.

§ 204(h) and SPD notices: Opening account balances reduced? Lastly, a close look at El Paso's § 204(h) notices and SPD shows that these documents consistently display a strategy of omission and ambiguity with respect to opening account balance reductions. Indeed, in the case of its § 204(h) notices, there are simply no statements at all concerning how the new CBP Select balances would be set up for any group of employees (see Table B.2, bottom row).[8] As can be seen in Table B.3, in the 2002 SPD employees would read the following (italics added):

> Your El Paso Cash Account Benefit from ***CBP Select*** is *based on* the value of a hypothetical 'account' that is established in your name when you become a participant in the Plan.

> **Opening Balance.** If you met the Minimum Benefit eligibility requirements, you had an 'account' established in *CBP Select* to *reflect* your accrued benefit under the Minimum Benefit Formula as of December 31, 1996.

The first statement would likely mystify average plan participants because El Paso never explains what is meant by the term "hypothetical 'account.'" In the company's expert understanding of the workings of the transition, this term conveys the fact that the pay and interest credits accumulating in the new CBP Select account will not translate into any dollar growth in pension if the employee is under a wear-away period. Thus the likely explanation for El Paso's use of this term, "hypothetical," is that it ostensibly allows them to claim they have disclosed the possibility of opening account balance reductions and wear-away periods. But it is simply untenable to maintain that average plan participants could share or somehow derive this understanding because no explanation of the term "hypothetical" is offered or cross-referenced.

Notably, in addition to saying that the new CBP Select balance would be "based on" the employee's old plan benefit, here El Paso also uses the term "reflect." Yet, just as occurs in the individualized pension statement examined here, El Paso offers no explanation of what the terms "based on" and "reflect" mean. Average plan participants could only naturally assume that if the new balance "reflects" the old, it would thus *equal* the old. Moreover, the earlier, seemingly categorical language in the company's precursor documents (i.e., "The present value of your accrued benefit under the EPNG Pension Plan as of December 31, 1996 *will be* your opening account balance in your CBP Select account on January 1, 1997" [italics added]) would only lead employees to read this 2002 SPD language in the same way. In *Amara*, as we have seen, the court called CIGNA to task not only for using for using such ambiguous language (i.e., "reflects" and "based on") ostensibly to disclose the reductions it was imposing on new opening cash account balances *but also* for *omitting* any direct, explicit statement that the new balances were reduced.

THE TENTH CIRCUIT REVIEW: DÉJÀ VU

To conclude this chapter, it is important to examine how the tenth circuit court treated plaintiffs' complaints on appeal about El Paso's disclosures (*Tomlinson v. El Paso Corp.*, 2011).[9] Did the circuit court attempt to address what I have argued are serious and disturbing deficiencies in the district court's review and analysis? As I will discuss here, it did not.

First, like the district court, the circuit court concludes that El Paso adequately informed El Paso employees that their future rate of benefit accrual would be reduced, and they do so based entirely upon the same original messages in the 1996 "Employee Update" document and the letter accompanying it that the district court treated as dispositive. Although the circuit court cites the ERISA requirement that a plan amendment (or summary of such amendment) must be "written in a manner calculated to be understood by the average plan participant," it never discusses the possible implications of this standard nor explains how it is being applied to El Paso's messages. Consider the court's remarks:

> El Paso informed employees of its planned transition in a "Business [Employee] Update" circulated in January 1996. It stated that the company would move from its traditional plan to a cash balance plan and noted that "employees will earn future benefits at a lower rate than under" the prior plan. El Paso provided more details in a letter in October 1996, warned that the new plan was "no longer at the top of the range," that "[t]he hard truth is that those who are not prepared may have to postpone retirement," and that after a transition period "the current pension plan formula will be frozen for [some] participants and they will not earn any additional benefits under the current plan." In the same month, El Paso distributed a brochure which summarized the cash balance plan and explained the transition in rosier terms. The brochure contained prominent statements such as "[y]ou can't lose," "[t]here's no risk," and "your account can only go up." (*Tomlinson*, 2011, pp. 4–5)

In my earlier analysis of these initial El Paso messages, I discussed how they might affect the understanding of average plan participants possessing little or no prior knowledge of cash balance plans and the possible methods involved in converting defined benefit plans to cash balance plans. In particular, I discussed how statements made by El Paso in subsequent documents, a few of which the court quotes, might seriously confuse older participants or even prevent them from understanding that their future benefits were being reduced. The circuit court acknowledges some of these other "rosier" messages but never considers or explains how they might affect average plan participants' understanding *in context*. Tellingly, these contrary messages are simply mentioned in passing and then conspicuously dropped from any further discussion in the court's opinion. Like the district court, the circuit court also never discusses the other misleading messages I have already examined. Again, this selectively decontextualized, 'flashlight' approach to cash balance plan disclosure texts is markedly different than the approach seen previously in *Amara*. There the court, recurrently referencing the "average plan participant" standard, carefully discussed individual messages in relation to the whole sequence of messages that CIGNA produced and further explained how CIGNA's disclosures, read as a whole, might adversely impact average plan participants' understanding (see *Amara*, 2008, pp. 88–97).

Second, regarding El Paso's wear-away periods, the circuit court at the outset states, "We hold that ERISA does not require notification of wear away periods so long as employees are informed and forewarned of plan changes," and then adds, "El Paso provided sufficient notice and warning" (*Tomlinson*, 2011, pp. 2–3). It's hard to tell for sure, but the court here appears to say that the creation of wear-away periods is not a "plan change." If that is indeed the court's position, the court never explains how it is that a wear-away period is *not* a plan change or part of a plan change. After all, wear-away periods were not a part of the employees' prior traditional defined benefit plans. Rather, quite plainly, wear-away periods were as much an *intentional feature* of El Paso's cash balance plan as they were *not* a feature of employees' old, prior defined benefit plan. Later in its opinion, however, the court backs up and explicitly declares that El Paso did adequately disclose the existence of wear-away periods. In doing so it relies upon the same 'connect-the-scattered-puzzle-pieces' reading comprehension theory that the district court relied upon:

> We conclude that El Paso's October 1996 letter and brochure provided all the notice required by ERISA § 204(h). Two months before the plan's adoption, El Paso circulated a letter regarding the upcoming plan change. It contained the effective date of the new plan. It warned plan participants that the new plan would be less generous than the old. It told employees that "the current pension plan formula will be frozen for [some] participants and they will not earn any additional benefits under the current plan." The brochure went further and explained the calculation of benefits and the transition period. *Knowing that their minimum benefit would freeze and knowing that they would have a choice between the minimum benefit and the more slowly-growing cash account benefit, employees were effectively on notice of the wear-away.* (*Tomlinson*, 2011, pp. 22–23, italics added)

As if to bolster its conclusion, the court adds that

> plaintiffs were explicitly warned that their benefits under the old plan would likely be "frozen," and that they would receive the greater of the frozen minimum benefit or the new cash balance benefit. *The brochure summarizing the plan, combined with the earlier letter which was quite direct about the potential downsides of the transition, provided adequate notice under ERISA § 204(h).* (*Tomlinson*, 2011, p. 23, italics added)

The expert hindsight bias problem is once more clearly on view in this reasoning. The circuit court assumes that average plan participants would be as able as the court itself to connect spatially disparate sentences that are located in two or more documents and situated in different contexts—i.e., as if those participants could have known what the court already (well) knows about cash balance plan transitions. The court sees these connections because, unlike the participants, it already sees the whole picture on the puzzle box. The court is also at least exaggerating, if not simply incorrect, to say that the El Paso letter was "quite direct" about potential downsides of the transition. If the letter was "quite direct," as the court says, there would have been no need for the employees to construct the complex chain of inferences that the court here implausibly supposes employee readers should be able to construct concerning wear-away periods. Rather, as discussed earlier, the unexplained statements in the initial letter when combined with the later statements in the precursor brochures would likely sow confusion and uncertainty about exactly what the changes in the plan amendment would be. In the end, the circuit court provides no more analysis or consideration of average plan participant comprehension abilities than the district court did. Nor does the circuit court feel any more need to analyze *in context* the statements that it points to than the district court did.

In fact, there are still worse problems with the circuit court's reasoning. First, the court's connect-the-scattered-puzzle-pieces theory does not explain how employees would know that their opening account balances under the new plan were reduced—a result, in part, of the fact that old plan benefits earned during the five-year transition period were not included when El Paso computed employees' new CBP Select opening balance. Like the district court, the circuit court never mentions let alone discusses these reductions; nor does the court discuss the language that El Paso uses to characterize the relationship between the value of employees' old plan benefits on the date of the transition and the value of the new opening account balances. As shown, this language was certainly misleading and prejudicial. If El Paso was communicating in a "quite direct" manner, as the court says it was, then the original announcement letter would have indicated that opening balance reductions would occur rather than leave readers to infer them from clues scattered across multiple documents or from covertly coded, ambiguous terms such as "based on" and "reflect." The letter would also have explained how such reductions contribute to the length of wear-away periods and then how the latter contribute to reductions in the future benefit accrual rate. As detailed earlier, absent any explicit, unambiguous indication of opening account balance reductions, it is highly implausible that average plan participants could complete the chain of inferences that the court supposes they could complete to ascertain the existence of wear-away periods. Average plan participants could not jump from the statements that the court flashlights to the conclusion that they would suffer wear-away periods precisely because participants *do not already have a picture of what a wear-away period is*; the very concept of a 'wear-away' period would be unfamiliar if not completely unknown to them.

Second, and inexplicably, the court does not mention or discuss the illustrative hypothetical employee examples of future benefits that El Paso included in its precursor documents. As discussed, none of these hypothetical examples offered any illustration of future accrual reductions, reduced opening account balances, and wear-away periods occurring after the five-year transition. Instead, all of these examples reinforce a neutral to "rosy" picture of the plan changes and their effects on employees' pension growth. The court's neglect to discuss these hypotheticals is especially disturbing given that the court, relying on the only tenth circuit precedent to consider disclosure of wear-away periods (*Jensen v. Solvay Chemicals, Inc.*, 10th Cir., 2012), declares that "wear away periods [do] not need to be explicitly disclosed *provided that the employer's notice [gives] sufficient representative examples of the effects of the plan amendment*" (*Tomlinson*, 2011, p. 20, italics added). One can only speculate why the court fails to review and discuss El Paso's examples in its opinion; yet it is hard to avoid the thought that the court knows these examples would fare poorly against, if not simply fail, this test. As demonstrated earlier in this chapter, it would be basically impossible to argue that these examples give average plan participants "sufficient notice" of lengthy wear-away periods.

Third, also conspicuous in the circuit court opinion is the absence of any mention or discussion of the post-transition bar chart sent to employees in their individualized pension account statements examined previously. As discussed, the district court uncritically took this chart as disclosing wear-away periods in a manner understandable to average plan participants. Again, one can only speculate as to why the circuit court does not mention or discuss this evidence. It may be because the chart is a post- rather than a pre-conversion document, distributed some two years after the January 1, 1997, plan conversion date. But it may also be that the court simply thinks the other evidence to which it points already provides sufficient grounds for its conclusion that El Paso adequately disclosed wear-away periods.

Ultimately, then, the circuit court analysis of El Paso's messages appears engulfed in expert hindsight bias. In sharp contrast, and has already been shown, the *Amara* court conducted its analysis in a very different and more recondite manner by repeatedly identifying and linking the separate misleading effects of CIGNA's strategic omissions of information with what that court concluded were CIGNA's "affirmatively misleading" declarations, carefully recognizing how each of these species of information manipulation compounds the effects of the others to produce an overall deceptive communication. Ultimately, both the district and circuit courts' analyses in *Tomlinson* not only miss the contextual effects of omitted information about reduced opening account balances *per se* but, further, fail to recognize the mutually compounding effects of omissions and related violations of quality (positive falsehoods) interacting with each other.

These problems are particularly apparent in the circuit court's discussion of El Paso's 2002 SPD, which appears in the final section of its opinion. Here the court again states that the sole tenth circuit precedent regarding wear-away disclosure concludes that wear-away periods resulting from plan transition need not be "explicitly disclosed" (i.e., citing *Jensen v. Solvay Chemicals, Inc.*). This time, however, the court does not even bother to include *Jensen's* crucial caveat noted above, that is, that "wear away periods [do] not need to be explicitly disclosed *provided that the employer's notice [gives] sufficient representative examples of the effects of the plan amendment*" (italics added). Nor does the court mention or discuss *any* of the illustrative examples in El Paso's 2002 SPD, none of which, again, show future reductions to employees' benefit accrual rates, reductions to new opening account balances, or wear-away periods. Instead, the court states:

> *Absent a finding of deceit on the part of the employer or a failure on the part of the employer to explain how benefits are calculated*, we will not invalidate an SPD that neglects to inform employees of a wear away period. Plaintiffs have presented evidence through their communication expert that the SPD and surrounding notices were somewhat confusing. *But they do not provide*

> *any evidence supporting an inference that the SPD was deceitful or failed to explain the manner of conversion to cash balance accounts.* (*Tomlinson*, 2011, pp. 26–27, italics added)

I disagree with these conclusions. Even a casual reading of my expert report would make clear that it presented evidence showing that El Paso's "SPD and surrounding notices" were far worse than "somewhat confusing." Rather, focusing on most of the same textual evidence that I have analyzed in this chapter, I argued in my report that these communications were misleading and deceptive both because they contained crucial omissions and because they offered contradictory, unqualified assurances to employees about effects of the new plan. At a minimum, by never disclosing the reductions to employees' opening account balances under the new plan, El Paso's disclosures can certainly be said to fail "to explain the manner of conversion to cash balance account." For the court to maintain that my report (not to mention El Paso's documents themselves) contains *no* "evidence supporting an inference that the SPD" and surrounding documents were "deceitful" or "failed to explain the manner of conversion to cash balance accounts" borders on the preposterous. The court does not trouble itself to discuss a single claim or argument from this report. Indeed, all of the evidence discussed there supported *exactly* the "inference" that the SPD and "surrounding notices" were "deceitful" and that they "failed to explain the manner of conversion to cash balance accounts."

Still more disturbingly, what the court appears to assume in these remarks is that deceit *only occurs* when the employer violates the maxim of quality, for example, by directly saying something like "Your opening account balance in CBP Select *will not* be less than the total value of your benefits under the old plan as of the date of conversion." In other words, in the court's view El Paso would only be deceitful if it directly made such positively false statements about the known effects of the plan transition. But, even taking this assumption seriously, and as I have shown in this chapter, El Paso *did make* these kinds of positively false statements, three of which the court quotes as being "rosy" but then fails at any point to discuss in relation to other ambiguous statements and omissions of information; for example, "Employees cannot lose any value in their accounts—accounts can only go up in value" (*Tomlinson*, 2011, p. 5).

What the court also misses is that El Paso makes materially misleading statements in ways other than direct falsification. For example, *without qualification or explanation*, El Paso tells average plan participants, that "[t]he present value of your accrued benefit under the EPNG Pension Plan as of December 31, 1996 *will be* your opening account balance in your CBP Select account on January 1, 1997" (italics added). As discussed, average plan participants would likely only assume that "present value" simply means "current" or "closing value" because the technical definition of the term "present value," which in reality involves a complex actuarial calculation, is not given or explained to them where this statement is made. Thus the average plan participant could only conclude from this statement that the two balances will be equal. And elsewhere, but again without qualification, El Paso states that the new balance will be "based on" and "reflect" the value of the participant's old account as of January 1, 1996. But the court provides no discussion of such ambiguous, restrictively coded language in context or in relation to the "average plan participant" standard.

The court's failure to recognize the deceptive communication produced by the *interaction among* omissions, false statements, ambiguous statements, and irrelevant statements is also suggested by its selective quotation of only a portion of the language of ERISA's implementing regulations. The court states that these "regulations further provide that an SPD must not be 'misleading' and should not 'minimize [or] [render obscure] other restrictions" on benefits (p. 26). The full text of the regulations actually reads as follows (italics added):

> The format of the summary plan description shall not have the effect of misleading, misinforming, or *failing to inform* participants and beneficiaries. Any description of exceptions, limitations, reductions, and other restrictions of plan benefits shall not be *minimized, rendered obscure*, or *otherwise made to appear unimportant*. (29 C.F.R. § 2520.102–2(b)

Looking at the full language, it would seem clear that Congress was concerned not only to prevent direct, positively false statements from being made in SPDs but also to prevent other more complex and sophisticated modes of deception about employees' future benefits as well. In particular, it is noteworthy that the court leaves out the regulation's phrases "failing to inform" and "otherwise made to appear unimportant," phrases that would respectively encompass omissions of information and more subtle violations of the clarity and relevance maxims that I have shown to be present in El Paso's documents. Indeed, when compared to the court in *Amara*, it is apparent that the *Tomlinson* court is motivated to read the scope of the terms in this regulation as narrowly as possible, if not simply to ignore them.

HOW DIFFERENT ARE THE DISCLOSURES IN *TOMLINSON* FROM THOSE IN *AMARA*?

Certainly it is reasonable that some lawyers and judges reading my analyses will feel that I have gotten *Tomlinson* wrong, that El Paso's disclosure documents are simply too different when compared to those that plaintiffs complained about in *Amara*. They would likely point to the fact that, unlike CIGNA, El Paso acknowledged the future accrual rate reductions its plan conversion involved, whereas as the *Amara* court stressed, CIGNA implied that their conversion was an unqualified "enhancement" of employees' pension benefits. They would also point out that El Paso, unlike CIGNA, provided a bar chart and table putatively revealing the wear-away effect in future benefit projections for individual participants. Given these seemingly clear differences, it would seem that *Amara*, beyond the circumstance that it was decided in a different circuit with different underlying precedents, must thus be distinguished and that both the district and circuit court decisions in *Tomlinson* are soundly reasoned.

This may be good lawyerly argument, but in the end, it is not very convincing. As I have stressed, this argument turns, not upon the whole effect likely produced by the pattern of maxim violations across El Paso's disclosures but rather upon the decontextualized salience that the *Tomlinson* courts choose to give to two particular messages in El Paso's disclosures. It turns on the unrealistic (and, I would argue, unjustified) presumption that average plan participants should and would similarly focus upon these parts *to the exclusion* of all the other contradictory messages about their future benefits and new accounts in the stream of disclosures they received. It may be unfair to say or imply that the district and circuit courts in *Tomlinson* simply 'cherry-pick' the evidence in the disclosures that they need to rule against the employees. But I think the analysis presented here shows highly relevant intra-textual interactions in the disclosures that the *Tomlinson* courts almost completely ignore in rendering their opinions. These interactions would make it very difficult for average plan participants to find the same meaning and significance in the judicially decontextualized and highlighted messages that the *Tomlinson* courts rest their judgment upon.

Equally important, the defense argument overlooks the quite similar misleading messages and omissions that the CIGNA and El Paso disclosures share. Both CIGNA and El Paso *omit any explicit or express reference to reductions to employees' opening balances in the new cash balance plans*—reductions that both plan conversions imposed. Both employers strategically deploy language designed to mask the occurrence of such reductions. This is the central deception worked upon employees in both cases. It constitutes an almost insurmountable roadblock to the employees' ability to learn about wear-away periods and to perceive the significant contributory effect of these periods on their lower future benefit accrual rate. The *Tomlinson* courts' scant attention to this omission while insisting, instead, that average plan participant readers should have figured out from El Paso's inconsistent messages that the opening balance reductions were occurring, sets an extremely low bar for what counts as disclosure. The similarity in CIGNA's and El Paso's stratagems in masking opening account reductions can be seen in the side-by-side comparison of their language in Table 5.2 below.

In neither case does the employer, when making these statements, elucidate what the italicized terms mean or imply; in neither does the employer show examples illustrating how the new balance is calculated and that it will be significantly reduced relative to the value of the old plan's frozen benefit. The vagueness and inconsistency of the italicized terms provide cover for the employers to claim 'disclosure' while also leading average plan participants into the mistaken inference that their new balance will simply equal the value of their old plan benefit as of the date of transition. In both disclosures, this omission of materially harmful information is similarly masked by violations of the clarity maxim.

What distinguishes the *Amara* and *Tomlinson* courts' reading of the employers' messages about opening balance reductions in these cases is that the *Amara* court ultimately discerns a consistent pattern of omission together with

Table 5.2 Comparison of CIGNA and El Paso Statements Regarding Opening Account Balances

CIGNA	El Paso
[Benefits] are fully protected [and] their value will be *reflected* in the new plan balance. Any benefits that you have earned under the CIGNA Pension Plan will be *converted* to an opening account balance in the new plan. If you are eligible for the new CIGNA Plan, all of your benefits earned under the current pension plan through 12/31/97 will remain yours. As of 1/1/98, those benefits will be *transferred* to the new plan (italics added).	**Opening Balance.** If you met the Minimum Benefit eligibility requirements, you had an 'account' established in *CBP Select* to *reflect* your accrued benefit under the Minimum Benefit Formula as of December 31, 1996. When CBP Select was introduced, you were credited with an opening balance *based on* your accrued benefit under the prior formula (italics added).

unqualified, misleading assurances. In sharp contrast, the *Tomlinson* court focuses upon chronologically and spatially separated messages that, although by themselves never explicitly mentioning reduced opening account balances, are implausibly presumed by the court to enable employee readers to infer this key feature of plan conversion. The latter interpretive approach rests on isolating and decontextualizing some relevant textual evidence while simultaneously ignoring other relevant text and apparently doing both things under the influence of expert hindsight bias. It is an approach almost completely divorced from any serious or meaningful consideration of the average plan participant's ability to integrate contextually disparate and unexpected messages. And still worse, it is divorced from the probability that these participants are unlikely to have any preexisting belief or notion that their opening account balance would not equal the value of their old plan benefit. On the contrary, they would be likely to expect the opposite and would not reverse that expectation without very clear and direct explanations and illustrations. It is simply implausible to suppose that they could infer the existence of something that they have no reason to expect would occur in the first place.

Ultimately, what stands out when comparing these two cases in light of IMT's Gricean maxims is that in both, the employers committed demonstrable clarity violations to help hide reductions to employees' new opening cash balance accounts. In discourse whose primary purpose is to reveal, without "obfuscation" and without "minimizing," material harms to employees, such stratagems would seem to constitute clear violations of ERISA's requirements. The *Amara* court recognized these violations; the *Tomlinson* court did not.

NOTES

1 Plaintiffs' subsequent petition for writ of certiorari to the U.S. Supreme Court was denied February 21, 2012 (Tomlinson v. El Paso Corp., 2012).

2 Importantly, on the basis of this reasoning the court refused to certify some 1,500 employees as part of the plaintiffs' lawsuit. These employees received the same disclosure documents that the named plaintiffs received.

3 CIGNA in *Amara* actually used a statement similar to that shown in the revision of sentence (4). CIGNA stated that "Your final plan benefits cannot be less than your old plan benefits *on December 31st, 1997*" (italics added). But the *Amara* court flatly rejected the idea that CIGNA employee readers could be reasonably expected to infer from this statement that either their future benefit accruals would be reduced or that they would be under a wear-away period.

4 As discussed earlier, this practice of presenting only "positive" examples to average plan participants was judged in 2002 to violate the ethical code of actuaries by the Actuarial Board for Counseling and Discipline (see Amoroso et al., 2001, 2002).

5 An exception to this pattern does occur in El Paso's initial "Employee Update" document of January 1996, where the company states, "Employees' accrued benefit under the cash balance plan will not be less than what they have accrued under the current Pension Plan formula as of December 31, 1996."

6 As plaintiff's actuarial expert Mr. Poulin further explains, the value of the employees' opening account balances was made lower by four distinct factors: (1) by "not including the values of early retirement benefits [previously available under the old plan];" (2) by not including "the benefits earned in the 5-year transition period;" (3) by applying a "pre-retirement mortality discount;" and (4) by "the decline in interest rates after opening accounts were established " (Deposition of Mr. Claude Poulin, F.S.A., April 15, 2008, para. 40–41).

7 The first paragraph also creates another terminological confusion that is never clarified. The company indicates in the second sentence that it refers to the "prior formula" under the old plan as the "Minimum Benefit." But then in the very next sentence, and without explanation, it refers (in parenthesis) to the "Minimum Benefit" as the "transition formula," suggesting perhaps that a special version of the old plan "prior formula" is in effect during the five-year period from January 1, 1997, to December 31, 2001. The truth is that the "transition formula" and the "prior formula" are no different: the "prior plan" formula is simply continued through the five-year period.

8 As a purely legal question, this omission is interesting given that the language of the version of § 204(h) applicable at the time requires the notice to "set forth the plan amendment." On its face, at least, this language would seem to require the company to disclose how the account balance in the new plan would be set up so that an average plan participant might understand it.

9 Plaintiffs' subsequent petition for writ of certiorari to the U.S. Supreme Court was denied February 21, 2012 (Tomlinson v. El Paso Corp., 2012).

REFERENCES

Amara v. CIGNA Corp., 925 F. Supp. 2d 242 (D. Conn. 2012).

Amara v. CIGNA Corp., 559 F. Supp. 2d 192 (D. Conn. 2008).

Amoroso, V., Flagg, D., Polisner, D., Rietz, R., & Segal, D. (2002). ABCD cash balance letter: Rephrasing the question. *Enrolled Actuaries Report, 27*(3), 1–7.

Amoroso, V., Flagg, D., Polisner, D., Rietz, R., & Segal, D. (2001). Pension professionalism. *Enrolled Actuaries Report, 26*(3), 4–6.

Bransford, J., & Johnson, M. (1973). Consideration of some problems in comprehension. In W. G. Chase (Ed.), *Visual information processing* (pp. xiv, 555). New York, NY: Academic Press.
Bruce, S. (1993). *Pension claims: Rights and obligations* (2nd ed.). Salem, MA: Bureau of National Affairs (BNA) Publishers.
Burke v. Kodak Retirement Income Plan, 336 F.3d 103 (2d Cir. 2003).
CIGNA Corp. v. Amara, 131 S. Ct. 2900 (2011).
Cleveland, W. S. (1994). *Elements of graphing data.* Summit, NJ: Hobart Press.
Cleveland, W. S. (1985). *Elements of graphing data.* Boston, MA: Wadsworth Publishing.
Cleveland, W. S., & McGill, R. (1985). Graphical perception and graphical methods for analyzing scientific data. *Science, 229*, 828–833.
Cleveland, W. S., & McGill, R. (1984). Graphical perception: Theory, experimentation, and application to the development of graphical methods. *Journal of the American Statistical Association, 79*, 531–554.
Declaration of Mr. Claude Poulin, F.S.A., April 15, 2008 (in Tomlinson v. El Paso Corporation, 2008, 2009).
Department of Treasury, Internal Revenue Service, 26 C.F.R. § 1.411(d)-6T, Q&A-10 (Matthew Bender & Company, 1996).
Employment Retirement Income Security Act of 1974, Employment Retirement Income Security Act of 1974, 29 C.F.R. § 2520.102–2(b) (Michie 1996).
Galasinski, D. (2000). *The language of deception: A discourse analytic study*. Thousand Oaks, CA: Sage Publications.
Jensen v. Solvay Chemicals, Inc. 625 F. 3d 641 (10th Cir. 2012).
Just, M., Carpenter, P., & Wooley, K. (1982). Paradigms and processes in reading comprehension. *Journal of Experimental Psychology, 111*(2), 228–238.
Kosslyn, S. M. (2006). *Graph design for the eye and mind.* New York, NY: Oxford University Press.
Kosslyn, S. M. (1989). Understanding charts and graphs. *Applied Cognitive Psychology, 3*, 185–226.
Kostelnick, C., & Hassett, M. (2003). *Shaping information: The rhetoric of visual conventions*. Carbondale, IL: Southern Illinois University Press.
Latin, H. (1994). Good warnings, bad products, and cognitive limitations. *UCLA Law Review,41*, 1193–1295.
Magliano, J. P., Trabasso, T., Graesser, A. P. (1999). Strategic processing during comprehension. *Journal of Educational Psychology, 91*, 615–629.
Mannes, S., & Hoyes, S. (1996). Reinstating knowledge during reading: A strategic process. *Discourse Processes, 21*, 105–130.
Morgan, M., Fischhoff, B., Bostrom, A., & Atman, C. (2002). *Risk communication: A mental models approach*. Cambridge, UK: Cambridge University Press.
Natter, H., & Berry, D. (2005). Effects of active information processing on the understanding of risk information. *Applied Cognitive Psychology, 19*(1), 123–135.
Otero, J., & Kintsch, W. (1992). Failures to detect contradictions in a text: What readers believe versus what they read. *Psychological Science, 3*(4), 229–235.
Register v. PNC Financial Services Group, Inc., 477 F.3d 56 (3rd Cir. 2007).
Schriver, K. (1991). Plain language through protocol-aided revision. In E. Steinberg (Ed.), *Plain language: Principles and practice* (pp. 148–172). Detroit: Wayne State University Press.
Schriver, K. (1997). *Dynamics in document design*. New York, NY: John Wiley and Sons.
Tomlinson v. El Paso Corporation and El Paso Pension Plan, 132 S. Ct. 1574 (2012).
Tomlinson v. El Paso Corporation and El Paso Pension Plan, 653 F.3d 1281 (10th Cir. 2011).
Tomlinson v. El Paso Corporation and El Paso Pension Plan, 45 Employee Benefits Cas. (BNA) 2534 (D. Colo. 2009).

Tomlinson v. El Paso Corporation and El Paso Pension Plan, 43 Employee Benefits Cas. (BNA) 1932 (D. Colo. 2008).
Tractinsky, N., & Meyer, J. (1999). Chartjunk or gold graph? Effects of presentation objectives and content desirability on information presentation. *Management Information Systems (MIS) Quarterly, 23*, 397–420.
Vande Kopple, W. (1986). Given and new information and some aspects of the structures, semantics, and pragmatics of written texts. In C. Cooper & S. Greenbaum (Eds.), *Studying writing: Linguistic approaches* (pp. 72–111). Beverly Hills, CA: Sage Publications.
van Dijk, T. (1999). Context models in discourse processing. In H. van Oostendorp & S. R. Goldman (Eds.), *The construction of mental representations during reading* (pp. 123–148). Mahwah, NJ: Lawrence Erlbaum Associates.
Wiedenbeck, P. (2008). *ERISA in the courts*. Washington, DC: Federal Judicial Center.
Williams, J., & Colomb, G. (2010). *Style: Ten lessons in clarity and grace*. (10th ed.). New York: Longman.

6 Comparing Experimental and Nonexperimental Analyses of Text Comprehensibility and Deceptiveness

Perspectives on Admissibility

In this chapter I will discuss how, guided by IMT's Gricean maxims, one may form and then experimentally test hypotheses about contested disclosure messages and the ways average plan participants would or would not understand them. To do so, I will discuss a modest but still useful experimental study that I was able to conduct on contested disclosure messages in another recent cash balance conversion case, *Mezyk v. U.S. Bank* (2009, 2012).[1] I originally reported the results of this experiment in my expert written report for plaintiff's counsel and also discussed these results in my oral deposition, along with other nonexperimental analyses of the defendant's disclosure texts in that case.

To date, direct, experimentally obtained evidence of surrogate readers' disclosure comprehension has been rarely produced or admitted into evidence in ERISA cash balance transition cases, a fact that may well seem surprising given the enormous monetary sums at stake in them. However, the reasons for this situation are not hard to find. The primary problems confronting a litigating party who wishes to conduct a reader comprehension study and introduce it into evidence are the conjoined problems of cost, risk, and feasibility. With respect to the latter, there is often simply insufficient lead time during attorney discovery for researchers to design and conduct appropriate comprehension experiments. Among other factors, university human research committees (internal review boards [IRBs]) take time to process researchers' applications for approval of their experimental protocols. And then there is the daunting cost–benefit question itself: attorneys and their clients do not want to pay for empirical studies whose results may be inconclusive or, worse, turn out to support the opposing side's claims. The longer and more complex the required study, the greater the risk of compromised or hard-to-interpret findings (Monahan & Walker, 1991; Shuy, 2006).

Further, as can be seen in *Amara* and *Tomlinson*, in ERISA cash balance plan disclosure cases the disputed communications to be tested are often lengthy and complicated. As a result, addressing the contentions of the parties will not often turn exclusively on the interpretation of one or two isolated employer statements or phrases. Typically, in fact, cash balance plan disclosure disputes potentially require testing many statements across diverse documents that are distributed to employees over a period of months to years, from pension transition announcement letters prepared by company CEOs and precursor brochures outsourced to pension consulting companies to legally required SPDs, § 204(h) notices, and technical benefit estimates sent to individual employees. Hence, any comprehensive experiment must try to replicate the original chronological presentation order of these documents and also, as far as possible, try to replicate the situational context, pension plan knowledge, and reading abilities of the original employees at the time these employees received these documents (see Perfetti, Rouet, & Britt, 1999). In particular, with the passage of time, some experimental research participants, through various media outlets, may have come to know more about cash balance plans and the controversies surrounding them than the original pension plan participants in a given case may have known or could have known, thus potentially biasing experimental findings. Such participants must be carefully screened.

Nonetheless, an arsenal of empirical methods exists for tackling these and related experimental challenges. Powerful, relevant methodologies are well developed in the scientific fields of reading comprehension, forensic linguistics, technical communication, psycholinguistics, sociolinguistics, persuasion, and decision science (e.g., Barnum, 2002; Bowen, Duffy, & Steinberg, 1991; Coulthard & Johnson, 2007; Just & Carpenter, 1987; Morgan, Fischhoff, Bostrom, & Atman, 2001; Pressley & Afflerbach, 1995; Redish & Dumas, 1999; Schriver, 1997, 1991, 1989). In this chapter, drawing in part upon the reader comprehension experiment that I conducted in *Mezyk*, I would like to explore some of the key benefits and issues that introducing such surrogate reader experiments into the judicial resolution of disclosure disputes may entail, including issues possibly arising under the U.S. Supreme Court's admissibility benchmarks in *Daubert v. Merrell Dow Pharmaceuticals* (1993) and Federal Rule of Evidence (FRE) 702.

EXPERIMENTAL EVIDENCE OF READER COMPREHENSION IN *MEZYK V. U.S. BANK*

To begin, in October 1998 Mercantile Bank, which later became a subsidiary of U.S. Bank, provided to its employees pre-transition (precursor) documents in which it touted its new cash balance pension plan as "[p]roviding an enhanced vehicle for retirement . . . [one that would] encourage employee participation and planning." It also stated that this change was being made "to enhance the Mercantile Retirement Plans for better understanding." Although it is not clear what Mercantile meant by an "enhanced vehicle for retirement" in these remarks, there were no qualifications included that might have indicated downsides to the plan transition, including an overall lower benefit accrual rate under the new plan. Thus, like *Amara* but unlike *Tomlinson*, at the beginning of the disclosure stream, employee readers were not warned or cued about negatives associated with the cash balance conversion but were instead encouraged to see it as an improvement.

Employer witnesses for Mercantile Bank in their depositions made interesting assertions concerning what participants would be able to understand about their future benefit accrual rate from certain statements subsequently provided in the defendant's § 204(h) notice of December 14, 1998. Two of these witnesses specifically asserted that the bank's § 204(h) notice informed plan participants of a reduction to their future benefit accrual rate. The statements on which they based their claim were as follows:

> **(1)** The cash balance plan is very different from the previous plan design. **(2)** Future benefits that you earn may be greater than, the same as, or less than what you would have earned under the previous plan design depending on your age at retirement/termination, as well as future service, pay, etc. (Boldface numbers added for reference.)

In the defendant's view, these sentences adequately disclosed that employees' future pension benefit accrual rate would be lower under the new plan, whereas the plaintiffs maintained that the two sentences constituted an equivocation and thus could not be considered meaningful or adequate disclosure. What experimental surrogate readers might conclude from the sentences, although certainly not legally determinative, could at least be probative for weighing both parties' contentions about how the text would be understood by average plan participants lacking technical knowledge about pension plans. As will be shown further, however, these two sentences hardly constituted all of the relevant, disputed discourse in the documents bearing upon disclosure of future accrual rates under the new plan. There was a good deal more of the disclosure texts that, given the limited time and resources available, could not be tested that would nonetheless need to be assessed together with the results of the sentences that were. In addition to many other concerns about the clarity of the disclosures, plaintiffs' counsel wanted to know if I thought the sentences could be shown to be equivocal and thus fail to disclose the reduction in the future benefit accrual rate that the company knew would occur for all of its transitioned employees, that is, relative to the accrual rate they enjoyed under the bank's prior defined benefit plan. I told counsel that I thought their contention could be supported nonexperimentally on two grounds, as follows.

First, consider a hypothetical participant's direct question to a Mercantile Bank plan administrator, for example, "Compared to the old plan, will my overall benefit accrual rate under the new plan be significantly reduced?" The second of these two statements, if left unqualified or unelaborated, simply puts the task of determining the answer to this question back upon the participant. In this regard, it is similar to case 2 in the crossing light example discussed in Chapter 1, in which the blind person asks about the color of the crossing light, but the bystander does not reply—in IMT terms, it is therefore a quantity violation. The Mercantile Bank statement implies that under a certain combination of factors, a reduction in the future benefit accrual rate *may* occur, but so also *may* an increase occur.

Even if putting this interpretive task back upon the participant reading a § 204(h) notice is acceptable, however, there was simply no other information provided in the § 204(h) notice about what different combinations of factors mentioned would yield which result. Nor was such information included in any other documents provided to Mercantile employees. There were no sample hypothetical illustrations, look-up tables, or calculation methods presented that would enable employees to compute their future benefit accrual rate for themselves or that would otherwise enable them to compare the old with the new rate. Participants would thus be incapable of making any determination on their own. It is true that the amount of accrual rate reduction that would occur would vary depending upon the individual employee's circumstances; to this extent the company's statement is truthful. However, the company knew that no employees moving from the old plan into the new cash balance plan would see a greater or equal benefit accrual rate as a result. The statement thus *omits* what the bank knows to be true and attempts to mask this omission behind an unexplained 'admission' of all the logical possibilities.

Another way to assess whether such a putative disclosure statement is equivocal is simply to ask whether removal of the statement from the document would provide *any less* disclosure than if the statement was retained (Bavelas, Black, Chovil, & Mullett,1990). In other words, is the statement's effect upon readers' understanding likely to be any different than complete silence regarding future accrual rates under the new plan? In this instance, such a test quickly suggests that plan participants could know nothing more about the answer to their question regarding the future benefit accrual rate with Mercantile's statement retained than if it were excluded. Indeed, without this statement, a plan participant might readily and logically assume that any one of the same three outcomes *might* occur as a result of the plan conversion—that is, their future benefit accrual rate might remain the same, go up, or go down—there simply are no other possibilities. Effectively, this statement might seem to offer disclosure, yet in reality it does not provide plan participants with any meaningful information. More fundamentally, the statement appears problematic because the specific purpose of a § 204(h) notice is to "set forth" a plan amendment that *has the effect of lowering* employees' future benefit accrual rate; the notice is *not* required if these rates will in fact remain the same or increase. Mercantile's statement, in the absence of any additional explanatory information, would seem to sidestep if not thwart completely the specific purpose of the statutory requirement.

Despite these arguments, the question should be asked: are these arguments sufficiently reliable without any empirical study of how ordinary readers would construe such language? Would experimental tests investigating how nonspecialized surrogate readers would interpret Mercantile's language support these arguments? And how might such an experiment be designed?

The defendant's witnesses adamantly maintained that Mercantile's statements *constituted disclosure*. Given that in these statements, they were plainly offering no assurances about the future rate, they contended that they *had* put employees on notice that they could not necessarily or reliably expect their future rate of accrual to be greater than or equal to their old rate. This argument should not be dismissed out of hand, because, importantly, the equivocation is overt rather than covert: a reader can plainly see that the statement is making no commitment as to what will happen. For instance, courts like those in *Tomlinson* might argue that although the defendant's §204(h) notice is indeed "somewhat confusing," it is not necessarily deceptive, because *surely some readers could and would infer from it that their future accrual rate would be lower*—else why would the employer expressly use such noncommittal language? In other words, a court might argue that when readers are confronted with such language, it is entirely reasonable *to expect them* to draw the inference that their future accrual rates *will* go down because the equivocality of the statement is itself explicit and is thus actually 'tipping' them off.[2]

However, this defense argument remains problematic because it overlooks the fact that the employer *knew* the future rate *would be lower*, that for all of its older employees it would *not* be higher than or equal to the old plan rate (Supplemental Deposition of Claude Poulin, F.S.A., December 20, 2011, in *Mezyk, et al. v. U.S. Bank Pension Plan*, 2012, para. 8, 10–12). There was no dispute about whether or not the employer knew future accrual rates under the cash balance plan would be lower. Just as occurred in both the *Amara* and *Tomlinson* cases, the employer structured the pension plan transition so that employees' new opening account balances would be lower than the value of their final accrued benefit under the prior plan; thus, they were fully aware that employees would experience lengthy wear-away periods.

Still, plaintiff's counsel was concerned about the defendant's argument regarding how the disputed text would function, practically speaking, and how it might be interpreted by ordinary readers. I thus discussed with plaintiff's counsel how one might experimentally test the disputed passage to see what conclusions surrogate readers may draw from it. I presented statements (1) and (2) together to a sample population of 37 college students in two different undergraduate courses in communication I was teaching at the time. Additionally, to test whether the equivocality hypothesized may be independent of the particular topics referenced, the statements were tested in two different scenario contexts. As shown, the first scenario is reflective of the present case (albeit camouflaged to prevent students from knowing that there is any legal case pending or involved). The second is an isomorph that, although containing the same underlying propositions, alters the situational context, that is, from a change in pension benefits to a change in pain medication. The inclusion of the isomorph is useful for estimating the generalizability and reliability of interpretations made by sample test readers in the pension plan conversion scenario. Importantly, however, individual students in this experiment did not receive both versions; each participating student randomly received one or the other, and the sheet on which they received the experimental question neither presented nor requested any other information.[3]

The two scenario questions are as follows:

> **Scenario 1.** Suppose that you have been working at the XYZ Company for 22 years, and that you are 49 years old. Your company has notified you that it is changing its pension plan to a new plan, called a "cash balance" plan. In the documents you have been sent, the company states the following about the

effect of this change on the value of your future pension benefits as compared with the value of your old plan (if the old plan was simply continued):

> The cash balance plan is very different from the previous plan design. Future benefits that you earn may be greater than, the same as, or less than what you would have earned under the previous plan design depending on your age at retirement/termination, as well as future service, pay, etc.

Now assume that the company provides you with *no other* information than this statement concerning the relationship between your age at retirement/termination, your amount of future service, and the value of your future benefits. Based only upon the statements above, which statement below best expresses the conclusion you would draw about the value of your future pension benefits (check one only):

____ I conclude my future benefits will be *greater than* the benefits I would have received under the old pension plan.

____ I conclude my future benefits will be *less than* I would have received under my old plan.

____ I conclude that my future benefits will be *the same as* (equal to) the benefits I would have received under the old pension plan.

____ I can draw *no conclusion* about the value of my future pension benefits compared to my old plan benefits.

Scenario 2. (Isomorphic Scenario) Suppose that you are 49 years old and that you have been experiencing pain in your left ear for almost three months from a stubborn infection. Your health care provider has notified you that it must change the pain medication it has been prescribing and that you have been taking. In the letter you have been sent, your health care provider states the following about the effect of this medication change on the amount of pain you will experience in the future compared with the pain you have been experiencing under the old medication:

> The new medication is very different from the old medication you have been taking. Future pain you experience may be greater than, the same as, or less than what you would experience using the previous medication depending on your age, length of time you have had your infection, and the dosage amount you have been taking with the old medication, etc.

Now assume that your health care provider provides you with *no other* information than this statement concerning the relationship between your age, the length of time you have had your infection, and the dosage amount you have been taking with the old medication. Based only upon the statement above, which statement below best expresses the conclusion you would draw about the pain you would experience with the new medication (check one only):

____ I conclude my future pain will be *greater than* the pain I would experience using my old medication.

____ I conclude my future pain will be *less than* the pain I would experience using my old medication.

____ I conclude that my future pain will be *the same as* (equal to) the pain I would experience using my old medication.

____ I can draw *no conclusion* about whether the pain I experience with the new medication will be greater, less or the same as that I have experienced with the old medication.

As can be seen, the basic question addressed by this modest experiment is to what extent the response patterns for each scenario favor the defendant versus plaintiff claims regarding the informativeness or equivocality of the § 204(h) statements and the conclusions, if any, that ordinary readers might draw from them. In the pension plan scenario, if the defense's argument about readers' inferential process is correct, we should expect to see some substantial percentage of surrogate readers mark the second choice; that is, they will infer that their future rate of accrual will be lower. In contrast, if the plaintiff's claim is correct, one would expect the majority of respondents to mark the fourth answer choice (*no conclusion*).[4] Similarly, in the pain medication scenario, if the defense's claim is correct, we would expect a substantial percentage of surrogate readers to mark the first choice because this choice reflects a *reduction* of medicinal effectiveness, that is, paralleling the reduction of accrual rate in the pension scenario. The plaintiff's contention would again be that the majority of respondents would choose the "no conclusion" response.

The results obtained support the contention that the § 204(h) statements regarding participants' future benefit accrual rate are perceived as an equivocation. As shown in Table 6.1, for both scenario questions, study participants overwhelmingly chose the "no conclusion" answer. Only one subject out of the 17 (6 percent) in the pension scenario chose the "less than" answer, and only 2 out of 20 (10 percent) in the pain medication scenario chose the "greater than" answer.

Despite these seemingly clear results, at least three caveats arise from the design and execution of this experiment. First, it should be noted that the sample

Table 6.1 Results for Perceived Informativeness versus Equivocation of § 204(h) Notice Statements (from Stratman, 2012, p. 11).

	Cash balance scenario (n = 17)	**Pain medication scenario (n = 20)**
No conclusion	82% (14)	90% (18)
Less than	6% (1)	0
Greater than	0	10% (2)
Same as	12% (2)	0

in this study is small and constitutes a convenience sample rather than a sample representative of the employee class certified in the lawsuit. There was no attempt made to match student surrogate readers' characteristics to those of the actual class members in the *Mezyk* lawsuit. There is thus some possibility that the actual participants originally exposed to the § 204(h) notice (circa 1998) might know somewhat more about pension benefits than the undergraduate students in this study and thus answer differently. However, these original plan participants, who included low-level bank employees, would likely not have known much, if anything, about the nature of cash balance pension plan transitions before encountering the Mercantile Bank disclosure documents. Given the amount of time that passed in the *Mezyk* case, it would be exceedingly important for judicial readers in 2012 to avoid expert hindsight bias regarding what original plan participants could understand about cash balance conversions in 1998—some14 years before. Differences between the student surrogate sample and the original population of Mercantile plan participants is of concern, and replicating these results in a larger, older population who might be more representative of the original Mercantile population is desirable. But this student sample is arguably better than no sample at all. And it is arguably useful (but obviously not determinative or conclusive) evidence for assessing competing claims regarding the equivocality or informativeness of the targeted § 204(h) statements.

A second caveat is that the experimental test could certainly be more robust, for example, by including more of the employer's § 204(h) text (if not the entire document) and asking more questions about other statements contained in it, that is, to help further camouflage the purpose and focus of the experiment. Indeed, it would be desirable to elicit surrogate readers' conclusions about what the *entire* notice meant, inclusive of the targeted statements. Doing so would enable one to compare the conclusions about future benefits that readers appear to draw from the two targeted statements in isolation with any conclusions they might draw from the whole document. This additional test condition would possibly enable one to discern how the surrounding text could influence readers' interpretation of the targeted statements. At the same time, it would also be an improvement to have varied experimental participants' response mode, for instance, by having a separate surrogate reader sample provide open-ended answers (either taped or written) expressing their conclusions in their own words rather than choosing from experimenter-constructed responses. Still another approach would be to have surrogate readers provide what is known as a concurrent read-aloud/think-aloud protocol: readers are tasked with reading the §204(h) notice aloud and, as they do so, saying aloud what they are thinking as they proceed (Ericsson & Simon, 1993; Krahmer & Ummelen, 2004; Pressley & Afflerbach, 1995; Stratman 1994, 2002, 2004; Van Den Hak, De Jong, & Schellens, 2003).

Finally, a third caveat is that the expert witness conducted the experiment himself and thus may have influenced the results through experimenter-participant expectancy (Rosenthal & Rosnow, 2007; Solan, 2010). Although I attempted to prevent any such influence by following a prewritten script when conducting the experiment, an arguably stronger method for preventing influence is having a third party uninformed about the purpose or issues involved in the experiment distribute and collect responses to the questionnaires used. All of these improvements, of course, do increase the cost of the experiment and extend the time it takes to complete it.

Despite these potential caveats, however, it would still be hard to hypothesize that surrogate readers given the entire § 204(h) notice would more frequently draw the conclusion that their future benefits would be lower. As I will suggest next, the protective stance or attitude collectively conveyed in additional § 204(h) statements made by the employer would likely point readers toward the opposite conclusion, that is, that Mercantile Bank was going to *prevent* employees future benefit accrual rate from falling by making certain adjustments to employees new opening account balances. In fact, participant readers' belief that their future benefit accrual rate would *not* be reduced was potentially reinforced by statements that followed shortly after the statements tested. These were additional statements that student surrogate readers in the small experimental study did not see.

Specifically, the § 204(h) notice also asserted that "[t]he Mercantile plan design avoids many of the issues that have been recently raised relating to cash balance plans." Considering this statement in the context of the rest of the notice, it is entirely plausible that plan participants, who may have been concerned about their future benefit accrual rate when they began reading the § 204(h) notice, would feel *less* concerned after reading this statement. Although this statement makes no specific mention of future benefit accrual rate as an issue, in context the assurance (i.e., "avoids many of the issues") could easily have the effect of reducing participants' concern about a future accrual rate reduction while simultaneously increasing their underlying trust in the communication itself. It also may reinforce participants' reasonable expectation that Mercantile would *expressly rather than impliedly* notify them of any factors causing reductions to their future benefit accrual rates, including reduced opening account balances and wear-away periods.

We can see how such expectations may be reinforced when, just below this vague assurance (i.e., "avoids many of the issues"), the § 204(h) notice touts the following putative protections against loss of future benefits, protections said to be built into the plan conversion:

- Generous annual company credits of 2%–7% of pay, based on age.
- Interest credit based on 10-Year Treasury notes, with a guaranteed minimum of 5.5%.
- Total benefit earned under old plan is guaranteed—your opening balance will be at least as much as the value of your benefit earned under the old plan.
- For employees 55 to 64, the early retirement subsidy was included in the opening balance. Additional transition credits were added to opening balances for any employees close to retirement age (ages 45–54) to avoid the potential loss of the early retirement subsidy in future years.

Significantly, two of these bullets actually represent falsifications or, in IMT terms, quality violations. In the third bullet, Mercantile can be seen to be claiming that participants' opening cash account balances *would equal* the value of their accrued pension benefit under the old plan. But these opening balances were reduced by the bank so that, in fact, they did *not* equal "the value of [the] benefit earned under the old plan" (Supplemental Deposition of Mr. Claude Poulin, F.S.A., December 20, 2011, in *Mezyk, et al. v. U.S. Bank Pension Plan*, 2012, para. 19–21). The fourth bullet also represents a falsification because the full value of the early retirement subsidy available under the old plan was not added to the opening account balances under the new plan—only a portion was included—and the unexplained "transition credits" that were said to be added were not sufficient to bring the opening balance up to the full value of the employee's benefits under the old plan (Supplemental Deposition of Mr. Claude Poulin, F.S.A., December 20, 2011, in *Mezyk, et al. v. U.S. Bank Pension Plan*, 2012, para. 19–21). All four of these bullet points are thus comparable to what the bystander says in case 3 of the crossing light scenario discussed in the introduction. In response to the blind person's question about the color of the light, the bystander says, "I think it's safe to cross now."

The main point here is that, contextually, the third and fourth bullets as well as the two preceding them may well affect what employee readers would infer from the experimentally tested language already discussed. The tested language could not plausibly be said to counterbalance or somehow 'cure' the implications of these bullets and the falsifications that two of them express. Indeed, one defense witness in his deposition twice acknowledged that *no statements* other than the demonstrably equivocal one already shown could lead participants to understand that their future rate of benefit accrual under the new plan would be reduced. But as we have seen in the experimental data, even in the absence of these other misleading statements, the claim that the equivocal statement *itself* would reliably lead readers to infer that the plan conversion will result in a reduction in their future pension benefits has little foundation.

WHAT ABOUT EVIDENCE ADMISSIBILITY?

Now, taking a full step back from this discussion, it nonetheless must be recognized that combining experimental test results of short disputed text segments like those from the §204(h) notice with IMT-framed analyses of other messages that are not tested raises important questions about the relevance and value of the linguistic expert's testimony and, ultimately, its admissibility. For instance, should only testimony presenting the experimental results be admitted, whereas the non-experimentally based testimony should be excluded? Or, should both kinds of testimony be included?

On one side, some might feel that no experiment was required in the first place because the tested § 204(h) passage was self-evidently equivocal, that is, on its face. In this view, the experiment merely 'confirms the obvious' and was a waste of time—as one of my former faculty colleagues might put it, "like cracking a walnut with a sledgehammer." It could thus be considered to fail Rule 702 of the Federal Rules of Evidence for expert testimony because a correct determination about the nature and effect of Mercantile's statement on employees' understanding could be made solely on the basis of the judge's intuition. Rule 702 states, "If scientific, technical, or other specialized knowledge will assist a trier of fact to understand the evidence or determine a fact in issue, a witness qualified as an expert by knowledge, skill, experience, training, or education, may testify thereto in the form of an opinion or otherwise." If the judge can *reliably* make a determination about the alleged equivocality of the Mercantile statement, then any linguist's experiment or other more theoretical textual analysis will be superfluous and fail to "assist the trier of fact."[5] Of course, it is a fair question as to how judges themselves actually make determinations about ordinary readers' probable understanding of legal documents, what concepts or evaluative criteria judges use to do so, and what theoretical basis they provide for applying them. As occurs in *Tomlinson*, judges may say little or nothing about how they draw these conclusions. In effect, how do judges (or anyone else) know that they are making *reliable* decisions about the ways ordinary readers would comprehend allegedly equivocal and other types of language?

In two interesting recent papers, Schauer & Spellman (2013) and Spellman (2007) argue that judges are not likely to be more reliable than jurors in making these kinds of factual determinations, and they draw upon careful empirical studies comparing judges' and juries' decision making to do so. In particular, they argue that the *Daubert* requirement, that experts must first demonstrate whether their theories or research are reliable by providing a known (and presumably experimentally and quantitatively derived) rate of error for them before their testimony can be admissible, creates a standard that judges themselves are never held to and one that usually they could not meet even if they were. As these scholars explain, the dubious consequence of many *Daubert*-based rejections of experimental findings produced by expert witnesses "is that [the] evidence that comes from an expert or is classed as 'scientific' will not be admitted even if non-expert and non-scientific evidence with no greater reliability, and often with less, would be admitted without question" (Schauer & Spellman, 2013, p. 8).

Similar to *Daubert*-based rejections on the ground that readers' understanding of the language in dispute would be 'self-evident' to the judge are rejections of experimental, surrogate readers' data as irrelevant. For instance, some courts may conclude that the only *relevant* data concerning how a disputed disclosure text would be understood must come from the plaintiffs themselves and no others. From one point of view, this claim makes sense, because how the participants themselves claim to have understood the texts is certainly relevant evidence. If there were devices wired to them that could record their exact thoughts and conclusions about their pension benefits *at the time* they initially read and pondered the disclosures, it might seem impossible to dispute the probity of their testimony. But in reality we do not have such devices, and thus the relevance of what plaintiffs may say long after their original experience would not be presumptively reliable.

Indeed, the chief problem is that, compared with an appropriately matched and properly recruited surrogate reader sample, the plaintiffs' testimony about their understandings may be affected by an obvious conflict of interest. They could be counted on to see the disputed text differently once a lawsuit is filed and the adversarial discovery process is under way than they *originally* saw and understood the text during their first encounters with it. They would be prone to reconstruct inaccurately their memories of their original understanding of the texts in ways congruent with their goals in the controversy. Collecting and presenting surrogate reader concurrent think-aloud or questionnaire response data in addition to plaintiffs' reported experiences could greatly mitigate this concern and thus be of considerable relevance.

On the other side, some observers may argue that, given the defendant's argument in *Mezyk* as to how average participant readers would take the tested § 204(h) statements, an experimental surrogate reader test of them was certainly relevant and needed. These observers might maintain that, after all, it is not intuitively or self-evidently clear how average plan participants would interpret them. In *Mezyk*, as in other cases, the conflicting claims of the plaintiffs and the defense clearly put the 'fact' of average plan participants' comprehension at issue. These same observers, however, may also feel that the experiment, as conducted, could have been made more reliable by addressing the design caveats already noted. They could argue, indeed, that multiple surrogate reader experiments were needed given the analyses I offered of subsequent Mercantile § 204(h) statements, that is, explicating how they violate Grice's maxim of quality. But do these design caveats make this admittedly modest experiment completely unhelpful or, worse, misleading to the court?

I would argue that they do not. To be sure, the experiment's results are not legally determinative and certainly do not constitute 'proof' regarding how the original employees would have interpreted the Mercantile statements. Nonetheless, the experiment does serve as a constructive test of intuition-based theories about the nature and potential deceptiveness of equivocation—the very kind of theories that judges would be forced to apply *in the absence of* any experiment. It does not make sense to exclude the experimental results simply because their reliability may have been improved when the judge's own methods for assessing the understandability of the texts to average plan participants will undergo no similar empirical test and have no known error rate and thus no known reliability at all (see Schauer & Spellman, 2013, pp. 20–23). In particular, the kind of readers that a judge might imagine in mentally running this or a similar experiment would likely be rather different than actual lay readers, and thus it cannot be harmful to admit data suggesting how ordinary lay readers may respond. Most importantly, this simple experiment, even with its caveats, may help to reduce the possibility of expert hindsight bias contaminating the court's view regarding how the disputed text would be interpreted.

But if such a rationale is deemed sufficient for admitting even improvable experimental evidence about ordinary readers' comprehension, then what about the expert analysis of those portions of Mercantile Bank's § 204(h) notice and its other disclosure documents that I offered but did *not* test experimentally? Should the testimony about these portions be excluded or included?

Ultimately, this question returns us to Professor Clark Cunningham's challenging question as to what, if anything, an expert's linguistic analysis can contribute to the judge's decision making (Proceedings, 1995, p. 935). Indeed, Cunningham's question has two different underlying motivations, one arising from understandings about the nature of linguistic analysis and the empirical science underlying theories of reading comprehension, the other arising from traditional understandings about judges' broad discretion in disputes focused upon legal language meaning and lay readers' comprehension.

Let's consider the issue of science first. In the symposium where Cunningham introduced his question, much of the skepticism directed at nonexperimentally based expert linguistic testimony focused upon the question as to whether linguistics is a science (Ainsworth, 2006; Proceedings, 1995; Solan, 1999). In particular, the skepticism that members of the legal professoriate expressed during that event focused upon whether linguists' claims about the ways readers may (or may not) comprehend or interpret a written text are *falsifiable*. An extreme form of this skepticism is premised on the assumption that the *only* scientifically acceptable method for falsifying such claims is with controlled laboratory experiments; other nonexperimental but still replicable, systematic approaches to language data analysis, comparison, and categorization simply do not count. It is not clear how much of the judiciary shares this latter view. As Ainsworth (2006) has pointed out, however, the present standards for admissibility of expert testimony under Federal Rule of Evidence 702 and the U.S. Supreme Court's interpretation of these standards in the so-called Daubert trilogy of cases (*Daubert v. Merrell Dow Pharmaceutical, Inc.*,1993; *General Electric Co. v. Joiner*, 1997; *Kumho Tire Co. v. Carmichael*, 1999) are clearly "based on a positivistic view of scientific expertise" (p. 655). As she notes, in deciding upon the admissibility of expert linguistic testimony, "the *Daubert*-governed judge" must consider "the degree to which the field in question is based on testable or falsifiable propositions, its error rate, and the degree to which the research has been subjected to peer review" (p. 656).[6]

But as Ainsworth (2006) further argues, falsification of competing claims about legal language and its interpretation by ordinary readers commonly does occur using nonexperimental but still rigorous, replicable, and peer-reviewed methods of textual analysis (see, e.g., Coulthard & Johnson, 2010; Cotterill, 2002; Levi, 1993; Mason, 2013; Schane, 2006; Shuy, 1998; Tiersma & Solan, 2002). Indeed, the potential value of these nonexperimental analyses is twofold: (1) they can help to focus and render more precisely the design of any experimental test of reader comprehension that may be undertaken, and equally valuable, (2) they can in many instances show that an experiment would be unnecessary because the analysis itself could be quite convincing as to what readers could or could not understand from a disputed text. Thus, a view that a relevant and reliable falsification of claims about ordinary readers' text comprehension can *only* be based upon results from controlled experiments would surely lead to some rather inconsistent, if not simply unreasonable, consequences for judicial decision making about the admissibility of linguistic expert testimony (Monahan & Walker, 1991). This extreme valuation of falsification by formal experiment implies, for instance, that (a) the only thing that may meaningfully distinguish the expertise of the judge from that of the testifying linguist would be whether or not the linguist conducted a formal experiment using appropriately sampled surrogate readers, and that (b) where no such experimental evidence was proffered by the expert, the judge would be equally as competent. That is, the judge could be expected to undertake *nonexperimental* textual and reader comprehension analyses that are just as relevant and just as reliable as those provided by the linguist. Perhaps that is sometimes the case, but considerable research now indicates that it is frequently not the case (Solan, 1999, 2010). Both the district and circuit court's treatment of the disclosure language and reader comprehension issues in *Tomlinson* clearly illustrates what can go wrong with this assumption.

Notably, in neither *Amara* nor *Tomlinson* were my nonexperimentally based expert reports rejected as inadmissible under *Daubert* or FRE 702. In *Amara*, the court stated:

> As part of their case regarding CIGNA's notices, Plaintiff's submitted an expert report by a communications professor . . . In that report, Professor Stratman presented his analysis of CIGNA's notices and suggested respects in which those notices might be considered deficient for their failure to communicate in a readily understandable manner certain features of the transition to Part B and the terms of Part B itself. CIGNA sought to exclude this testimony under Federal Rule 702, on the ground that the proffered report encompassed legal conclusions that experts are not permitted to make [citation omitted]. The Court denied CIGNA's motion to exclude and admitted the evidence subject to CIGNA's continuing objection [citation omitted]. The Court need not address CIGNA's continuing objection here, as the Court has not relied on Professor Stratman's report in its analysis of the disclosures at issue. (*Amara v. CIGNA Corp.*, 2008, p. 71, note 28)

These remarks are interesting, especially the final sentence. Although I am in no position to dispute whether or not the court "relied upon" my written report, my oral testimony in open court, which lasted about three hours, largely focused upon details of that report, and Judge Mark Kravitz asked me many questions concerning it while also taking notes on his computer. I can further state that his analysis, which I have discussed and quoted from extensively in Chapter 4, very closely reflected my own. In *Tomlinson*, there is no record of the court having rejected my written report either under *Daubert* or FRE 702. Rather, as discussed in Chapter 5, the tenth circuit court briefly refers to this report in its opinion and ultimately rejects it as unpersuasive (*Tomlinson v. El Paso Corporation and El Paso Pension Plan*, 2011, pp. 26–27). In *Mezyk*, it appears that the defendant U.S. Bank may have planned to challenge my report, but that challenge was mooted by settlement, and to my knowledge, the court never issued an admissibility ruling.

Now let's turn to the second, more legal motivation for Cunningham's question. This motivation can be seen in how it is framed. The burden for explaining the relevance of nonexperimental linguistic testimony about readers' likely interpretation (or misinterpretation) of a disputed text is clearly placed on the linguistic expert. In contrast, both the relevance and underlying reliability of the judge's analysis of ordinary readers' likely comprehension is apparently presumed. To be sure, text interpretation has long been the legal prerogative and responsibility of courts in many areas. The expression of this prerogative can be seen, for example, in the well-known stance that many courts take when faced with similar disputes over readers' likely understanding of contract and insurance policy provisions. Consider the court's oft-quoted declaration in a 1996 California case, *National Automobile and Casualty Insurance Company v. Stewart*:

> The interpretation of the terms of a written policy, in the absence of a relevant factual dispute, is typically a question of law. The opinion of a linguist or other expert as to the meaning of the policy is irrelevant to the court's task of interpreting the policy as read and understood by a reasonable lay person. (*National Auto. & Casualty Ins. Co. v. Stewart*, 1990, pp. 458–459)

This often-invoked presumption of judicial expertise and judicial reliability concerning lay readers' understanding has long troubled linguists and cognitive experts in reading comprehension in technical communication and technical document usability studies and in decision science, among other fields (Proceedings, 1995; Cunningham et al., 1994; Tiersma, 1993). The presumption is worrisome because it seems to fly in the face of what is known from research about expert hindsight bias in the interpretation of technically complicated legal texts that target nontechnically educated readers. In other words, if the statement from *National Automobile and Casualty Insurance Company* is accepted at face, courts are *de facto* experts on how contract and insurance policy texts would be understood by "reasonable lay" readers. And conversely, courts may consider any opinions about the likely understanding of "reasonable lay" readers proffered by linguists or similar experts to be just as presumptively *ir*relevant, regardless of whether or not the expert has experimental evidence of lay reader comprehension regarding the disputed text in hand.

Clearly, this *a priori* presumption of judicial reliability would be particularly disturbing if it were applied unconditionally in cash balance conversion cases under ERISA. In these cases, the court's presumptive expertise would extend to a very large range of decisions about average plan participants' comprehension of text meaning, including the following: decisions about whether or not such participants would find a disputed text to be ambiguous or vague; whether or not they would find it equivocal; whether or not it might be misleading or prove deceptive to them; as well as many other related issues of the sort encountered in the *Amara* and *Tomlinson* cases.

Indeed, the presumptive stance expressed in *National Automobile and Casualty Insurance Company* raises many interesting questions given that it seems to conflict, at least in part, with the current language of FRE 702 and the *Daubert* benchmarks cited. For instance, can judges themselves show that *their* methods and conclusions for determining what average plan participants could understand from a text satisfy the benchmarks of *Daubert* and Federal Rule 702's requirements? What is it that judges do, as textual analysts, that enables them to presume that their conclusions are "the product of reliable principles and methods" and that they have applied these "principles and methods reliably to the facts of the case"? I do not mean to imply any disrespect toward the judiciary. But it seems more than clear that judges do not often conduct surrogate reader experiments to test their conclusions about how average plan participants might interpret a text, even so modest as the one reported previously. At the same time, the overwhelming majority of judges do not have degrees in linguistics or in any of its numerous subfields, including cognitive studies of reader comprehension processes. It thus seems a fair question as to what knowledge, foundation, or training their presumptive expertise *in evaluating ordinary readers' comprehension* of allegedly ambiguous, equivocal, and deceptive texts actually rests upon.

By comparison, judges are not so presumptively empowered to substitute their medical knowledge and theories for those of medical experts, their knowledge and theories of hydrology for those of hydrological experts, or their knowledge and theories of engineering for those of engineering experts. Yet they *are* so empowered to deal with very complex questions concerning how ordinary, nontechnical readers would understand a disclosure and to determine, based largely upon their own intuition, whether such a text would be difficult for these readers to comprehend (Tiersma, 1993). This disparity in presumptive judicial expertise where ordinary readers' likely textual interpretation is concerned leaves the door open for expert hindsight bias to operate silently and unconsciously among judges when making decisions about ordinary readers' comprehension. And despite ERISA's comprehensive requirements for disclosures aimed at "average plan participants," this bias still seems to occur, as seen in the *Tomlinson* decisions.

The scientific field of text comprehension processes has grown exponentially since this particular presumption of judicial expertise became an accepted part of the common law. And before *National Automobile and Casualty Insurance Company*, Professor Lawrence Solan (1993), in his well-known book, *The Language of Judges*, shows that even distinguished judges can be demonstrably mistaken in their attempts to explain how the meaning of some disputed texts would be clear and plain to 'reasonable' or to 'average' persons whereas other texts are deemed ambiguous. He also shows that judges' use of linguistic theory and linguistic data when they introduce these explanations is sometimes naïve and even contradictory. Similar judicial misunderstandings of textual comprehension processes by ordinary readers have been meticulously researched in Cunningham et al. (1994) and Levi (1993).

Of course, it is crucial to point out how and why it is that the testimony of language and communication experts can similarly be flawed by confirmation bias (Berger & Solan, 2008; Sanders, 2007; Solon, 2010). Testifying experts, just like advocates, should be required to point out conflicting theories and data when making their court reports just as they do when they submit papers for professional publication, and they must do their best to explain why the opposing theories and data are not adequate or sufficient. However, I would suggest that there needs to be a balancing emphasis upon reducing the problem of expert hindsight bias that can be manifest in judicial pronouncements concerning what average plan participants, reasonable persons, and otherwise less-educated persons can understand in technical legal documents like ERISA cash balance plan disclosures.

Solan (1999) and other linguistic scholars (e.g., Levi, 1993) note that many judges do welcome and appreciate linguistic expert testimony and reject motions to suppress such testimony through strict or overly narrow application of the *Daubert* and FRE 702 standards. From all indications, the use of forensic linguists in trial courts deciding ordinary (or lay) reader comprehension questions has been steadily increasing (Ainsworth, 2006; Coulthard & Johnson, 2007; Gibbons, 2003; Tiersma & Solan, 2002). But more needs to be done to help the judiciary in complex disclosure cases appreciate how their own theories concerning the ways 'average readers' or 'reasonable lay persons' comprehend such technical documents may overly reflect judges' own specialized knowledge and abilities. In the next, final chapter, I would like to summarize how IMT and the Gricean maxims can help with the analysis of allegedly deceptive disclosures and increase judicial awareness of expert hindsight bias.

NOTES

1 This case settled before trial.
2 Recall that in *Tomlinson* (2008, 2009), the court was presented with deposition evidence of two named plaintiffs (see Chapter 5) concerning how they understood contested language in El Paso's § 204(h) notice. Their comprehension sharply deviated from what the defendant El Paso claimed the text to mean. But their testimony was never discussed by the court and, in that instance, the court apparently refused to consider that demonstrable textual ambiguity in the § 204(h) notice could also be considered to be deceptive (see Chapter 5, p. 170).
3 To reduce experimenter–participant expectancy effects, at the start of the test, I read to students the following orientation script: "To begin our class discussion of disclosure language today, you are asked to complete a brief nongraded exercise. You must be 18 years old to participate. Please do not place your name or any other identifying information on the exercise sheet I distribute; it contains a single question about some language that I would like for you to think about carefully and then answer. Note that you can only choose one answer. However, with your permission, I would like to use your response data in some research I am conducting on disclosure language issues. If you are willing to give me permission, you simply signify the fact by handing the sheet in to me at the end of class; if you do not wish to grant permission, then simply keep the sheet after marking your answer choice to the question. Either way, we will tabulate all of your responses on the blackboard at the front of the room and then discuss together the aggregate class results. There is no penalty to you if you choose not to turn the sheet in to me. Again, this is a nongraded exercise for discussion purposes." This research was otherwise conducted following the prior review and official approval of the university human subjects review board (IRB) at the university where the data was gathered.

4 To prevent any bias from the presentation order of the responses, four different response orders were rotated so that different response orders were equally present for both scenario questions.
5 In addition, Federal Rule of Evidence 702 also permits expert testimony if it meets the following criteria: (a) the testimony is based upon sufficient facts or data; (b) the testimony is the product of reliable principles and methods; and (c) the witness has applied the principles and methods reliably to the facts of the case.
6 *Daubert* (1993) requires judges to consider four benchmarks when evaluating the admissibility of scientific testimony, with the caveats that the benchmarks are non-exclusive and that a given expert's testimony need not necessarily meet all four to the same degree to be admitted: (1) whether the theory offered by the expert has been tested; (2) whether it has been subjected to peer review via professional publication; (3) whether the rate of error of the expert's conclusions is known and presented; and (4) whether the theory or hypotheses advanced are generally accepted in the scientific community. As Solan's (1999) discussion of the admissibility of expert linguistic testimony under *Daubert* suggests, however, it is not clear that courts necessarily would or should interpret these four benchmarks so narrowly.

REFERENCES

Ainsworth, J. (2006). Linguistics as a knowledge domain in the law. *Drake Law Review, 54*, 651–668.
Amara v. CIGNA Corp., 559 F. Supp. 2d 192 (D. Conn. 2008).
Barnum, C. (2002). *Usability testing and research.* New York, NY: Longman.
Bavelas, J., Black, A., Chovil, N., & Mullett, J. (1990). *Equivocal communication.* Newbury Park, CA: Sage Publications.
Berger, M., & Solan, L. (2008). The uneasy relationship between science and law: An essay and introduction. *Brooklyn Law Review, 73*, 847–855.
Bowen, E., Duffy, T., & Steinberg, E. (1991). Analyzing the various approaches of plain language laws. In E. Steinberg (Ed.), *Plain language: Principles and practice* (pp. 19–29). Detroit, MI: Wayne State University Press.
Cotterill, J. (Ed.). (2002). *Language in the legal process.* New York: Palgrave Macmillan.
Coulthard, M., & Johnson, A. (2010). *An introduction to forensic linguistics: Language in evidence.* New York NY: Routledge.
Cunningham, C., Levi, J., Green, G., and Kaplan, J. (1994). Plain meaning and hard cases. *Yale Law Journal, 103*, 1561–1617.
Daubert v. Merrell Dow Pharmaceutical, Inc., 509 U.S. 579 (1993).
Ericsson, K., & Simon, H. (1993). *Protocol analysis: Verbal reports as data.* Denver, CO: Bradford Books.
Federal Rule of Evidence 702 (Public Law. 93–595, §1, Jan. 2, 1975, 88 Stat. 1937; Apr. 17, 2000, eff. Dec. 1, 2000; Apr. 26, 2011, eff. Dec. 1, 2011).
General Electric Co. v. Joiner, 522 U.S. 136 (1997).
Gibbons, J. (2003). *Forensic linguistics: An introduction to language in the justice system.* London, UK: Blackwell Publishing Ltd.
Just, M., & Carpenter, P. (1987). *The psychology of reading and language comprehension.* Newton, MA: Allyn and Bacon.
Krahmer, E., & Ummelen, N. (2004). Thinking about thinking aloud: A comparison of two verbal protocols for usability testing. *IEEE Transactions on Professional Communication, 47*(2), 105–117.
Kumho Tire Co. v. Carmichael, 526 U.S. 137 (1999).
Levi, J. (1993). Evaluating jury comprehension of Illinois capital–sentencing instructions. *American Speech, 68*(1), 20–49.

Mason, M. (2013). Can I get a lawyer? A suspect's use of indirect requests in a custodial setting. *International Journal of Speech, Language and the Law, 20*(2), 203–227.

Mezyk v. U.S. Bank Pension Plan, 2012 U.S. Dist. LEXIS 97762 (S.D. Ill. 2012).

Mezyk v. U.S. Bank Pension Plan, 48 Employee Benefits Cas. (BNA) 1118 (S.D. Ill. 2009).

Monahan, J., & Walker, L. (1991, July/August). Empirical questions without empirical answers. *Wisconsin Law Review, 4*, 569–594.

Morgan, M., Fischhoff, B., Bostrom, A., & Atman, C. (2001). *Risk communication: A mental models approach*. Cambridge, UK: Cambridge University Press.

National Automobile & Casualty Insurance Co. v. Stewart 223 (Cal.App.3d 452, 1990).

Perfetti, C., Rouet, J., & Britt, M. (1999). Toward a theory of documents representation. In H. van Oostendorp & S. Goldman (Eds.), *The construction of mental representations during reading* (pp. 99–123). Mahwah, NJ: Lawrence Erlbaum Associates.

Pressley, M., & Afflerbach, P. (1995). *Verbal protocols of reading: the nature of constructively responsive reading*. Hillsdale, NJ: Lawrence Erlbaum Associates.

Proceedings. (1995). Northwestern University/Washington University Law and Linguistics Conference. *Washington University Law Quarterly, 73*(3), 769–970.

Redish, J., & Dumas, J. (1999). *A practical guide to usability testing*. Wilmington, NC: Intellect Publishers.

Rosenthal, R., & Rosnow, R. (2007). *Essentials of behavioral research: Methods and data analysis*. New York, NY: McGraw-Hill.

Sanders, J. (2007). Ethical considerations in the use of expert testimony: Expert witness ethics, *Fordham Law Review, 76*, 1539–1584.

Schane, S. (2006). *Language and the law*. New York, NY: Continuum.

Schauer, F., & Spellman, B. (2013). Is expert evidence really different? *Notre Dame Law Review, 89*(1), 1–26.

Schriver, K. (1997). *Dynamics in document design*. New York, NY: John Wiley and Sons.

Schriver, K. (1991). Plain language through protocol-aided revision. In E. Steinberg (Ed.), *Plain language: Principles and practice* (pp. 148–172). Detroit, MI: Wayne State University Press.

Schriver, K. (1989). Evaluating text quality: The continuum from text-focused to reader-focused methods. *IEEE Transactions in Professional Communication, 32*(4), 238–255.

Shuy, R. (2006). *Linguistics in the courtroom*. New York, NY: Oxford University Press.

Shuy, R. (1998). *The language of confession, interrogation, and deception*. Thousand Oaks, CA: Sage Publications.

Solan, L. (2010). The forensic linguist: The expert linguist meets the adversarial system. In M. Coulthard & A. Jamison (Eds.), *Routledge handbook of forensic linguistics* (pp. 395–410). New York, NY: Routledge.

Solan, L. (1999). Can the legal system use experts on meaning? *Tennessee Law Review, 66*, 1167–1199.

Solan, L. (1993). *The language of judges*. Chicago: University of Chicago Press.

Spellman, B. (2007). On the supposed expertise of judges in evaluating evidence. *University of Pennsylvania Law Review, 156*, 1–9.

Stratman, J. (2012). Expert report on U.S. Bank cash balance plan conversion: ERISA § 204(h) notices, summary plan description, and precursor documents. In Mezyk et al. v. U.S. Bank Pension Plan.

Stratman, J. (2002). When law students read cases: Exploring relationships between professional legal reasoning roles and problem detection. *Discourse Processes, 34*(1), 57–90.

Stratman, J. (1994). Investigating persuasive processes in legal discourse in real-time: Cognitive biases and rhetorical choices in briefs. *Discourse Processes, 17*(1), 1–57.

Supplemental Deposition of Claude Poulin, F.S.A., December 20, 2011. In Mezyk, et al. v. U.S. Bank Pension Plan (2012).

Tiersma, P. (1993). The judge as linguist. *Loyola of Los Angeles Law Review, 27*, 269–283.
Tiersma, P., & Solan, L. (2002). The linguist on the witness stand: Forensic linguistics in American courts. *Language, 78*(2), 221–239.
Tomlinson v. El Paso Corporation and El Paso Pension Plan, 653 F.3d 1281 (10th Cir. 2011).
Tomlinson v. El Paso Corporation and El Paso Pension Plan, 45 Employee Benefits Cas. (BNA) 2534 (D. Colo. 2009).
Tomlinson v. El Paso Corporation and El Paso Pension Plan, 43 Employee Benefits Cas. (BNA) 1932 (D. Colo. 2008).
Van Den Hak, M., De Jong, M., & Schellens, P. (2003). Retrospective vs. concurrent think-aloud protocols: Testing the usability of an online library catalogue. *Behaviour & Information Technology, 22*(5), 339–351.

7 Disclosure, Obfuscation, and Deception

Are IMT's Gricean Maxims Helpful?

In the penultimate section of Chapter 5, I focused upon remarks suggesting that the tenth circuit court in *Tomlinson* (2011) considers only quality violations (i.e., positive falsehoods or lies) to be deceitful while at the same time considering that omission of information, although perhaps causing confusion in disclosure readers, is not sufficient for a legal finding of deception. If the circuit court actually believes this to be true, then it has certainly put itself in a difficult position given what we have seen in ERISA's disclosure rules, where omission of material information about future pension benefit reductions in SPDs and SMMs is expressly forbidden (29 C.F.R. § 2520.102–2(b)). With this particular question about the *Tomlinson* (2011) court's beliefs regarding deception in view, we will first return to the question of inherent degrees of deceptiveness among the four Gricean maxims and then turn to the question of the usefulness of IMT's Gricean maxims in cases of contested disclosure language.

ARE QUANTITY VIOLATIONS INHERENTLY LESS DECEPTIVE THAN QUALITY VIOLATIONS?

In the introduction we explored the controversial notion that IMT's four Gricean maxim violations may be considered to involve less deception as one moves from quality violations (greatest deceptiveness) to clarity violations (least deceptiveness) (see Table 1.1). In particular, we focused attention on the question as to whether quantity violations may be *inherently* less deceptive than quality violations, and we examined several theoretical bases for holding such a view. As I suggested there, in addressing this question one key principle is not to confound the degree of material harm resulting from deceptive communication with the degree of deceptiveness of the maxim violation per se. Nor should one confound the degree of deceptiveness with the degree of intent to deceive that may be present in the communicator, because any of the four violations may be equally intentional; degree of communicator intention is thus not an inherent trait that distinguishes the maxim violations from each other. Rather, deceptiveness should be evaluated in terms of the degree of misunderstanding or distortion that a maxim violation works upon a receiver's comprehension of a situation or event as well as the degree to which the violation defeats the receiver's reasonable expectation of completeness and truthfulness in a communication.

However, as shown in the analysis of the *Amara* and *Tomlinson* cases in Chapters 4 and 5, we see some indications that courts may not view quantity violations as being as inherently deceptive as quality violations. Although these courts did not explicitly offer arguments in support of this view, we saw earlier that arguments that quantity violations are inherently less deceptive than quality violations appear to turn on one or more of three grounds: quantity violations are thought to be potentially more *detectable* by receivers than quality violations; they are thought to be *less causally responsible* for receivers' misunderstanding than quality violations when both involve the same information; and any misleading effects of quantity violations on receivers are thought to be *less foreseeable by the communicator* committing them than are the effects of quality violations. As discussed in the introduction, all three of these grounds suggest the idea that receivers are not complicit in their own deception when exposed to quality violations but that they are complicit, in varying degrees, when exposed to quantity violations.

In returning once more to this issue, consider the following statements. The first three show hypothetical variations of one of the actual El Paso's disclosure statements, that is, concerning how the employer will set the opening value of the employee's new account in the cash balance pension plan. The last shows (again) the actual statements that El Paso made:

Full Disclosure

(1) Opening Balance. If you met the Minimum Benefit eligibility requirements, you had an 'account' established in CBP Select whose balance is X% less than the value of your final accrued benefit under the Minimum Benefit Formula as of December 31, 1996.

Quality Violation

(2) Opening Balance. If you met the Minimum Benefit eligibility requirements, you had an 'account' established in CBP Select whose initial balance is equal to the value of your accrued benefit under the Minimum Benefit Formula as of December 31, 1996.

QuantityViolation?

(3) Opening Balance. If you met the Minimum Benefit eligibility requirements, you had a new 'account' established in CBP Select.

Clarity Violation + Quantity Violation (Two Examples from El Paso's Actual Texts)

(4a) Opening Balance. If you met the Minimum Benefit eligibility requirements, you had an 'account' established in CBP Select to *reflect* your accrued benefit under the Minimum Benefit Formula as of December 31, 1996 (italics added).

(4b) When CBP Select was introduced, you were credited with an opening balance *based on* your accrued benefit under the prior formula (italics added).

For the purposes of this discussion, statement (1) can be considered 'full disclosure.' It states unequivocally what El Paso knew would occur when its employees' opening accounts were set up under the new cash balance plan. It thus forms a useful base point for considering the other statements that follow and their potential comparative effects on employee readers. The second modifies El Paso's actual statement so that it explicitly denies the truth of what happens to an employee's opening balance and affirms the very opposite, and it does so without qualification. It would thus constitute a quality violation. Then in statement (3) we see another possible modification, one that says nothing at all about how the opening accounts under the new plan are set up; it gives no hint regarding whether the balance will be equal to, less than, or greater than the value of the employee's pension benefit under the old plan as of the date of plan conversion. Whether or not it constitutes a quantity violation, however, is controversial, as will be explained next. Finally, statements (4a) and (4b) show the two actual statements regarding opening account balances that El Paso made in its disclosures.

To think about the question concerning the relative inherent deceptiveness of quantity versus quality violations, the first question to be asked concerns their detectability. As noted in the Chapter 1, to the extent that an omission of some relevant information can be detected by a receiver, it may not be a quantity violation at all because, by definition, a deceptive omission must be *covert* and unknown to the receiver at the time the message in which it occurs is encountered (Galasinski, 2000). That is, the theory is that we are only deceived by an omission when we do not perceive any omission to occur at all, when we are completely in the dark as to its existence. Given this principle, should we then say that statement (3) above really is a quantity violation given the larger disclosure context situation? Had this statement been El Paso's *only* statement about opening account balances, is it plausible that El Paso employees would have failed to notice that *nothing is said about the amount of the opening cash account balance* and how that balance is computed?

There may well be some average plan participant readers who would not notice this omission. And perhaps many of these would fail to notice it simply because they presume the new balance would represent or equal the value of their old plan accrued benefit, that is, as of the date the old plan was discontinued. However, it also seems likely that many readers would notice it, just as it is likely that the blind person on the street corner in case 2 (discussed in Chapter 1) would recognize the omission of information about the color of the crossing light after she specifically asked the bystander about it. Most employee readers would likely wonder about and expect to be provided with *some* information about the value or amount of their opening account balances under the new plan. As manifest in statement (3), such a complete omission of *any* information about the amount of the opening balances would thus be conspicuous to many readers; the topical focus of this statement, given its presence in a document putatively created to explain new plan features, invites the reader to expect opening account information that should be 'there' but that in fact is not there. And if this had been El Paso's actual disclosure statement, one can readily conceive that the complete omission of information about the relative amount of the opening balance would quickly become an issue that El Paso employees might communicate with each other about.

Indeed, concern about the potential salience or conspicuity to employee readers of such a complete, overt omission may be the very reason that the employer (El Paso) did *not* pursue this particular disclosure strategy. It would be too risky. Rather, the employer may have sought some way to mask the complete omission of information about the relative amount or value of employees' opening balances under the new plan, some way to seem to provide information that they were actually hoping to conceal. Hence, in statements (4a) and (4b), those that El Paso actually made, we see a more subtle discourse strategy. The omission of information both occurs yet seems not to occur by masking the omission with a clarity violation arising from the terms "reflect" and "based on." Fundamentally, omission does still occur here because these crucial terms are, at best, vague and left unexplained. As discussed earlier, in fact, given the way they are commonly used, "reflect" and "based on" may readily be taken by substantial numbers of average plan participants to mean that their opening balances would equal the closing value of the employees' accrued benefits under the former, now-terminated plan. Given the unexplained way in which these terms are used, they could scarcely be said to prompt the inference that the opening balances *would be* significantly reduced.

This illustration should reinforce a point I made earlier: omissions, to become effective as a strategy of deception, almost always require and rely upon elements of the receiver's context and knowledge *as well as* other features of the text that accompanies and surrounds them. To effect deception, omissions have to be rendered covert in some way, although covertness may well be a matter of degree rather than a black-and-white issue. For instance, if we look again at CIGNA's strategy in *Amara* (see the statements in Table 5.2), we might well conclude that the discourse accompanying the company's omission of information about opening account balances renders their omission even more covert than El Paso's accompanying discourse. Indeed, it could plausibly be argued that the third of the three CIGNA segments shown is essentially a quality violation. The term "transfer," used as it is without qualification, seems unequivocally to mean that the total value of the employee's old plan benefits *is* the starting balance under the new cash balance plan. In this particular statement, the covertness of the omission becomes almost total by direct falsification; the term "transfer" explicitly contradicts what is actually occurring in the transition.

In the end, then, a claim that quantity violations are somehow *inherently* more detectable than quality violations seems very doubtful because all quantity violations occur in a specific discourse and receiver context that influences their particular degree of conspicuity or covertness. Even the rather complete omission of information about the amount of the opening account balance in statement (3) may not be noticeable at all to some employee readers and thus be deceptive. The differences between the particular examples of El Paso's and CIGNA's statements I have presented makes such subtle contextual variation in the conspicuity or covertness of omissions clear. It is therefore simply not meaningful to say that quantity violations always are *inherently* less deceptive than quality violations.

Can it then be said that omissions nonetheless are *inherently less causally involved* in producing deception than are quality violations and that receivers are more 'complicit' or causally involved in their own deception when omissions are used (Green, 2001)? The answer to these questions, at best, is 'sometimes yes, sometimes no.' The previous illustration and discussion would seem to make the "inherently" part of this claim doubtful. An omission that is fully covert and unknown to a receiver can readily be shown to produce as much misunderstanding in a receiver as an outright falsification about the same information, again, simply by virtue of features of the receivers' knowledge (or ignorance), their reasonable expectations, and the particular discourse context in which the omission occurs. Even in an instance like statement (3), where some receivers may clearly notice the omission of reasonably expected information, we cannot say receivers are in any sense *agents willfully contributing to, or complicit in*, their own deception. Perhaps it is entirely fair to expect that they ask questions about the omission if they notice it in the first place, but that is not to say that responsibility for the omission itself should not be fully chargeable to the employer. In situations of great knowledge and power disparity, as in employer-initiated cash balance pension conversions, one can thus argue that the less knowledgeable and less powerful interlocutors require strict protections against quantity violations. As ERISA § 102(b) states with respect to SPDs,

> the summary plan description shall not have the effect of misleading, misinforming, or *failing to inform* participants and beneficiaries. Any description of exceptions, limitations, reductions, and other restrictions of plan benefits shall not be minimized, rendered obscure, or otherwise made to appear unimportant. Such exceptions, limitations, reductions or restrictions of plan captions, printing type, and prominence used to describe or summarize plan benefits. The advantages and disadvantages of the plan shall be presented *without* either exaggerating the benefits or *minimizing the limitations*. (29 C.F.R. § 2520.102–2(b), italics added)

Finally, a third rationale advanced for considering quantity violations to be inherently less deceptive than quality violations is that the misleading effects of quality violations upon receivers are considered to be *more predictable by the communicator* than those of quantity violations. But this view again depends in part on the supposition, already shown to be unfounded, that quantity violations are inherently more detectable by receivers than quality violations. Once we understand that quantity and quality violations can contextually be made equally covert, and that degree of deceptiveness depends most directly upon the degree of covertness of the violation, the notion that the deceptive effect of quantity violations on receivers is inherently less predictable by communicators can be seen to be unsound.

HOW ARE THE GRICEAN MAXIMS USEFUL?

One of the most fascinating and perplexing things about studying written disclosure discourse is that such discourse is typically produced under the compulsion of legal rules. And the usual goal of such rules is not merely to prevent lying (quality violations) but other forms of deception as well, especially quantity violations. In particular, the goal of these rules is to force the communicator to reveal information that could cause material harm to certain receivers, harms that the communicator, for various reasons of self-interest, might prefer to keep secret or hidden. Thus, from one point of view, the whole notion of disclosure is antithetical to violations of the quantity maxim and to deception by omission. In the cash balance plan conversion controversy, to determine if such omission has occurred in the disclosure texts, one must first know what the nature of the allegedly concealed material harms may be, that is, against which to assess the particular information manipulations found in disclosure language.

As discussed in both Chapters 4 and 5, there were three distinct but also interrelated material harms to employees in the *Amara* and *Tomlinson* cash balance conversion cases: reduced future pension benefit accrual rates; the imposition of lengthy wear-away periods during which employees will earn no new pension benefits at all; and reduced opening account balances under the new plan. The latter two harms, as we have seen, contribute to the first, in stepwise fashion: reduced opening account balances lead to wear-away periods, and wear away-periods, in turn, contribute to reduced future benefit accrual rates. As many commentators on the cash balance transition controversy have pointed out, even if employees learn that their employer is reducing the future rate at which their pension benefits accrue, they may not also learn or understand that, due to wear-away periods, they may be earning no future pension benefits at all following the date of transition until the new cash balance account equals the frozen value of their accrued benefits under the old pension plan. Thus, for employers to only disclose that employees' future benefit accrual rate will be lower but not to inform employees about reduced opening account balances under the new plan and the consequent imposition of wear-away periods would not seem to constitute full disclosure of material harms occasioned by plan transition.

In both *Amara* and *Tomlinson*, these harms first become evident in the employers' official plan documents, which owing to their highly technical content and presentation, most average plan participants would never see or accurately understand if they did. From a linguistic perspective, of great interest is what happens to the material harm information as it moves (or is transformed) from employers' technical plan documents into their ERISA required disclosures. What may constitute an omission or quantity violation (or perhaps, more accurately, a suppression) between the two sets of documents is not quite a zero-sum game or simple 'yes versus no' question. As I have tried to show in my analysis of the disclosure language in *Amara* and *Tomlinson*, allegedly deceptive omissions always occur in a specific discourse and receiver context. Omissions may be more or less covert, and the degree of covertness is a function, in part, of their chronological and local context within the larger stream of disclosure documents. That is, the nature and potency of omissions as a means of deception will also vary depending upon the presence of *other* kinds of deceptive information manipulations in these texts, including violations of one or more of the other three maxims. I have been arguing that, when applied together, IMT's Gricean maxims may serve as useful heuristic categories for tracking manipulations of information concerning known material harms as this information travels from employers' technical plan documents into the 'plain language' disclosure documents prepared for average plan participants.

Absent reliance upon some such tracking categories, it should not be surprising that courts applying ERISA disclosure rules may sometimes struggle to recognize when deception has occurred and likewise struggle to offer a coherent basis for their conclusions. Judges' reasoning as to why deception has or has not occurred in a particular communication is often an opportunistic, *ad hoc* affair, with few or no clear theoretical definitions or precise criteria underlying it. It might seem that ERISA's disclosure rules make it exhaustingly plain what will count as deception in these documents or at least what will constitute 'inadequate' disclosure. However, we can see in the courts' reasoning about the CIGNA and El Paso disclosures what little distance toward consistent recognition of deceptive manipulations of information ERISA's rule language actually takes them. It was because of the gulf between these two courts' views, and particularly the gulf between each court's modes of reading and constructing meaning from the disclosure texts in view of ERISA's rules, that I originally turned to IMT and the Gricean maxims. I have done so as a way to make sense of how the actual disclosure documents may be comprehended by an audience of average plan participants relative to the actual impacts that the pension plan conversion involves.

So how are the maxims useful? My central conclusion in response to this question is that cataloging the larger pattern of maxim violations in a disclosure, including the ways that different types of violations may contribute to and amplify each other, is critical to clarifying whether and to what extent deception occurs and full disclosure of material harms may be confounded. That is, the emerging pattern of violations helps one to see what the disclosure texts do and do not communicate clearly and accurately relative to the plan conversion's actual material harms. Equally important, I have used the maxims to argue how each violation, once it is shown to occur, would likely impact employee readers' comprehension as they attempt to construct meaning from earlier and later disclosure messages over the full stream of employer discourse. Pursuing an analysis of the comprehension dynamics involved in disclosure texts with the use of the maxims, I would argue, thus results in a greater thoroughness in considering the issue of deception than courts may otherwise intuitively bring to bear. As Monahan and Walker (1991) have remarked, "the desire of courts to have empirical questions answered by empirical research often goes unrequited. The body of existing research on many questions of crucial interest to the law is either nonexistent or so plainly inadequate that judges are left to rely upon their own intuitions or forced to resort to plainly inappropriate procedures to transform unanswerable empirical questions into answerable doctrinal ones" (p. 570, citations omitted).

The *Amara* (2008) court, for instance, despite pointing out several seemingly blatant omissions on the part of CIGNA, nevertheless appears to wrestle with the question as to whether omissions alone can be as deceptive as outright falsifications. In strong contrast, the *Tomlinson* decisions, at both the district and circuit court levels, do not appear to consider omissions even as a potential form of deception but at worst as mere sources of "confusion." The *Tomlinson* courts do not seem to appreciate how omissions may alter the context in which average plan participant readers—unlike pension experts, judges, and lawyers—construct meaning from disclosure texts. As a guiding framework, IMT's maxims would help these courts identify what their largely intuitive, atheoretical approach to analyzing disclosure documents may overlook. In particular, I have tried to suggest how different the *Tomlinson* courts' conclusions about the adequacy of El Paso's disclosures might become were the maxims applied more carefully in view of ERISA's "average plan participant" comprehension standard.

At the same time, however, the preceding disclosure analyses using IMT and the Gricean maxims show how the maxims cannot, by themselves, serve as a panacea or complete account of how deception in disclosures 'works.' They simply provide a lens, a categorical framework. They cannot be sufficient for explaining in what ways disclosure texts can be deceptive when viewed as a totality or as wholes. I was thus led, as one of my theoretical purposes for this book, to consider how maxim violations interact with well-established principles and research findings in the areas of reading and graphical comprehension, persuasion, and, especially the phenomena of expert hindsight bias. With respect to the latter, I think the analysis of the disclosure texts I have presented shows rather clearly that even if the courts in these two cases were to use IMT and Grice's four maxims consciously as part of their investigation of their respective disclosures, they would not thereby automatically be rendered immune to this powerful bias. It might, however, make them more aware of how very different (and informed) their legal perspectives and comprehension processes as readers are when compared to the perspectives and reading processes of the average plan participant. The great irony is that, when looked at in its full historical context, ERISA's plain language rules for pension disclosure were born of the recognition that lawyers, judges, and pension actuaries are greatly advantaged as readers by their specialized knowledge. This knowledge prepares them to look for and then see in disclosure texts what average plan participants cannot. Both the district and circuit court in *Tomlinson* make no effort to explain why or how average plan participants, in *their* nonexpert knowledge context, could piece together El Paso's disconnected and contradictory cues in the same way that they, as court readers, do. Almost 40 years after ERISA's passage, it is distressing to see how inconsistently courts recognize and attempt to check the influence of expert hindsight bias in their reading of disclosures aimed at nonexpert readers.

For example, in Chapter 5 we saw that the tenth circuit court decision in *Tomlinson* (2011), in reference to my expert report, asserts that my analysis of El Paso's disclosures may have shown them to be "confusing" but not necessarily deceptive. The court, however, does little to explain this distinction. Surely part of the problem here is just what the court may understand by the concepts of "disclosure," "confusion," and "deception." Even if the claim of the circuit court regarding the upshot of my report is taken to be accurate, i.e., that my analysis merely shows some "confusing" language in El Paso's documents, the court nevertheless does not explain why or how a disclosure found in its own words to be "somewhat confusing" could still be revelatory and "calculated to be understood by the average plan participant," as ERISA requires. After all, ERISA's plain language rules themselves clearly proscribe any disclosure in which benefit reductions are "rendered obscure;" and therefore "obfuscation" becomes one possible basis for a legal complaint (29 C.F.R. § 2520.102–2(b)). Indeed, I think the foregoing analysis of the CIGNA and El Paso disclosures effectively shows much more occurring in them than "obfuscation" or merely "confusing" statements. Rather, IMT's maxims help to reveal a larger, strategically designed *pattern* of communication. Not only do we see how IMT's clarity maxim is repeatedly and cleverly violated in the reader–author disclosure 'conversation' but also that all three of the other maxims are demonstrably and repeatedly violated as well. And, perhaps most significantly, we can see how the cumulative impact of these violations on readers' comprehension, because of their mutually reinforcing interactions, is greater than the simple sum of them.

REFERENCES

Amara v. CIGNA Corp., 559 F. Supp. 2d 192 (D. Conn. 2008).

Employment Retirement Income Security Act of 1974, 29 C.F.R. § 2520.102–2(b) (Michie 1996).

Galasinski, D. (2000). *The language of deception: A discourse analytic study*. Thousand Oaks, CA: Sage Publications.

Green, S. (2001). Lying, misleading, and falsely denying: How moral concepts inform the law of perjury, fraud, and false statements. *Hastings Law Journal, 53*, 157–212.

Monahan, J., & Walker, L. (1991, July/August). Empirical questions without empirical answers. *Wisconsin Law Review, 4*, 569–594.

Tomlinson v. El Paso Corporation and El Paso Pension Plan, 653 F.3d 1281 (10th Cir. 2011).

List of Appendices

Appendix 1
Original and revised letter from CIGNA CEO Bill Taylor

(HIGHLIGHTING AFFIRMATIVELY MISLEADING TEXT)

I am pleased to announce that, on January 1, 1998, CIGNA *will significantly enhance* its retirement program. The changes include a new, simplified retirement plan for most employees, plus a new variable SIP match that rewards employees when corporate performance is strong.

These *enhancements* will make our retirement program highly competitive with those offered by other companies in our industry, helping us attract and retain the top talent we need going forward.

Just as important, the changes will strengthen the partnership between the company and employees. While the new Retirement Plan continues to provide a secure, company-funded benefit, the improved SIP plan gives employees *an even greater opportunity* to share in the company's success. Together, these plans help provide a solid foundation for your future.

The remainder of this newsletter provides more information on the coming changes. Please read it carefully. Your retirement benefits are an important part of your total compensation at CIGNA. The better you understand them, the more value you can gain from them.

LETTER FROM CEO BILL TAYLOR WITH AFFIRMATIVELY MISLEADING EXPRESSIONS REMOVED.

I am pleased to announce that, on January 1, 1998, CIGNA *will change* its retirement program. The changes include a new, simplified retirement plan for most employees, plus a new variable SIP match that rewards employees when corporate performance is strong.

These *changes* will make our retirement program highly competitive with those offered by other companies in our industry, helping us attract and retain the top talent we need going forward.

Just as important, the changes will strengthen the partnership between the company and employees. While the new Retirement Plan continues to provide a secure, company-funded benefit, the improved SIP plan gives employees *another opportunity* to share in the company's success. Together, these plans help provide a solid foundation for your future.

The remainder of this newsletter provides more information on the coming changes. Please read it carefully. Your retirement benefits are an important part of your total compensation at CIGNA. The better you understand them, the more value you can gain from them.

Appendix 2
§ 204(h) notice for El Paso employees

EL PASO CORPORATION PENSION PLAN NOTICE OF PLAN CHANGES

Effective December 31, 2001, all participants described below in item 1 will cease accruing a minimum benefit under the El Paso Corporation Pension Plan (the "Plan"). You have received a variety of communications describing this change since 1997 when the Plan was amended to provide a cash account benefit. This notice is simply a reminder of how the Plan was changed in 1997. During a five year transition period that will end December 31, 2001, you have received benefit accruals under the Plan equal to the greater of the new cash account benefit and the existing minimum benefit formula.

This notice is intended to satisfy the requirements of Section 204(h) of the Employee Retirement Income Security Act of 1974. Section 204(h) requires that all retirement plan participants be notified of plan amendments that freeze or reduce future benefit accruals. The following again summarizes how your benefit will be affected:

1. An active participant under the Plan on January 1, 1997 who was an eligible employee or a vested terminated participant on December 31, 1996 is entitled to continue to accrue a minimum benefit after December 31, 1996 until the earlier of i) December 31, 2001, or ii) termination of employment after January 1, 1997. The minimum benefit is based on a participant's final average earnings and credited service. A participant's credited service and earnings that occur after the date the minimum benefit stops accruing will be disregarded when the minimum benefit is calculated.

   Each participant on December 31, 1996 who was an eligible employee on January 1, 1997 received an opening cash account balance in the Plan on January 1, 1997. The participant's cash account balance grows with pay credits and interest credits. The participant will be entitled to receive a benefit based on his or her cash account balance or the minimum benefit, whichever is greater.

2. After December 31, 2001, for a participant whose minimum benefit is greater than the cash account benefit, accruals under the Plan may effectively cease until the participant's cash account benefit exceeds the minimum benefit earned as of December 31, 2001. This period of non-accrual will be more likely to affect individuals who elect early retirement benefits.
3. In no event will a participant receive a benefit which is less than the value of the benefit the participant accrued as of December 31, 2001 under the Plan.

Appendix 3

Hypothetical example in precursor document sent to El Paso employees

How It All Adds Up

Here are three examples of how your account can add up over the years. Of course, your personal situation and calculations may be different. All are based on the following assumptions:

- **Pay increases at a rate of 3% a year**
- **Interest rate is 6½% and remains constant**
- **Pay credits and interest are credited quarterly**
- **Retirement at age 62.**

Example 1:

Bob. Bob is 37 years old. He has worked for El Paso Energy Corporation for 15 years. His pay is $40,000 a year and he has an opening balance of $12,000. Here's how Bob's CBP Select account would add up over the years.

His account pay credit is calculated as follows:

* 37 (years of age) plus 15 (years of service) equals 52.

* The pay credit chart on the preceding page shows that the Company's annual contribution for Bob is 6% of $40,000 for the next 7 years. When he reaches age 44, he will have been with the company 22 years, and be eligible for the maximum 7% contribution until he retires.

Bob's CBP Select Account Growth

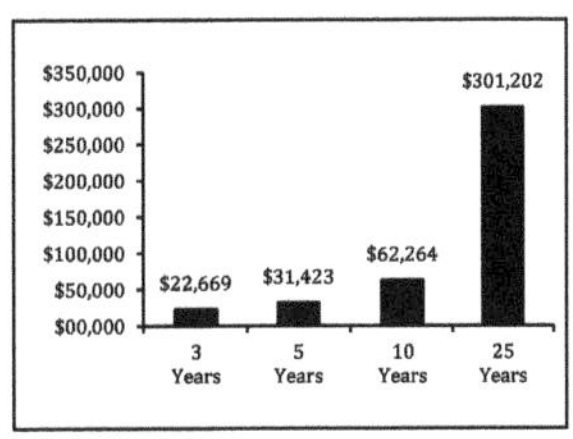

By the time Bob retires at age 62, he will have $301,202 in his CBP Select account.

Bob's First Year Account Pay and Interest Credits

Quarters	Opening Balance	Account Pay Credit	Interest Credit	Bob's Account Balance
First Quarter	$12,000	$600	$195	$12,795
Second Quarter		600	208	13,603
Third Quarter		600	221	14,424
Fourth Quarter		600	234	15,258

Appendix 4

Post-transition pension benefit notice sent to named plaintiff in *Tomlinson v. El Paso*, including tabular and bar chart displays

Your Retirement Benefits (continued)

CBP Select — A History

In 1996, El Paso Energy Corporation introduced our Cash Balance Plan (CBP Select), to become effective January 1, 1997. This changed the method of calculating your pension benefit from a traditional formula to a cash balance formula. Why a cash balance plan approach? First, business conditions at the time required El Paso to look for alternatives to our traditional pension arrangement, and a cash balance plan offered more favorable funding for the Company without sacrificing the Company's ability to continue to offer retirement benefits to its employees. Second, a cash balance plan is easier to understand and offers much more flexibility for employees in receiving benefits from the Plan.

How Your Benefit is Calculated

When CBP Select was introduced, you were credited with an opening balance based on your accrued benefit under the prior formula. Additionally, you continue to accrue benefits under the prior formula (referred to as the Minimum Benefit) during the transition period which ends December 31, 2001. Therefore, up to that date, your pension benefit continues to grow under two formulas: the Minimum Benefit (the transition formula) and the Cash Account Benefit. Thereafter, only Cash Account Benefit continues to grow.

As an eligible participant during this transition period, your benefits under the "old" formula (Minimum Benefit formula) will continue to accrue through December 31, 2001. After this date you will continue to accrue a pension benefit under Cash Account Benefit while your accrued benefit under Minimum Benefit formula will be frozen. When you retire or terminate from the Company, your benefits under the Minimum Benefit formula and the Cash Account Benefit formula will be compared and you will receive the *greater* of the two amounts. You do not need to retire or terminate on or before December 31, 2001 to receive the Minimum Benefit.

Early Retirement Supplement

Under the Minimum Benefit formula, you are eligible for an Early Retirement Supplement if you are at least 55 years of age but less than age 62 when you retire, and you have ten or more years of Credited Service.

If you meet the eligibility requirements and your Minimum Benefit plus the supplement is greater than the Cash Account Benefit, you will receive the Early Retirement Supplement in addition to your Minimum Benefit beginning on your commencement date and ending at age 62. At age 62, the supplement stops and your monthly annuity reduces to the larger of the accrued Cash Account Benefit or the Minimum Benefit (as of your commencement date).

If you retire after age 62, you receive no Early Retirement Supplement.

Note: Whenever you retire or terminate from the Company, the benefit you receive from CBP Select will be the greater of the Minimum Benefit or the Cash Account Benefit. You do not need to retire or terminate before December 31, 2001 to receive the Minimum Benefit.

Your Retirement Benefits

Another part of planning for your financial security is saving for your retirement. Although planning for your retirement is your responsibility, El Paso offers two retirement programs (RSP Select and CBP Select) which work together with Social Security to help you meet your retirement objectives. Through RSP Select, CBP Select, and Social Security, we're helping to provide the resources and financial support needed to help you meet your financial goals.

Retirement Saving Plan (RSP Select)

The future value of your Retirement Savings Plan account will depend on your contributions, the Company's contributions, and the returns on your investments. The following table illustrates the projected value of your account, based on these assumptions:

- Your current RSP Balance of $207,336 as of June 30, 1999 (excluding any outstanding loans);
- Your current base salary and bonus will remain the same over time;
- Company contributions of 75 cents on the dollar, up to 6%;
- You take no future loans or withdrawals;
- An investment return of 6%; and
- Projected amounts are based upon your current contribution rate of 15% (as of June 30, 1999), your current contribution rate plus 2%, and your current contribution rate plus 4%, subject to plan limits.

Contribution Rate		Estimated Value of Your Account			
Basic	Supplemental	At Age 55	At Age 60	At Age 62	At Age 65
10%	5%	$ 456,883	$ 716,447	$ 843,385	$ 1,063,810

Note: These figures are given for illustration purposes only. Plan limits have been taken into consideration where applicable.

Your Retirement Benefits (continued)

Pension Plan (CBP Select)

Following are estimates of your monthly retirement benefits from the Company and from Social Security. These estimates are based on the following assumptions

- Your service with the Company continues until the specified retirement ages;
- Your base salary and bonus remain level;
- The 5-year vesting requirement is met;
- Projected amounts are in the form of a Single Life Annuity; and
- A 4% Interest Credit.

Projected Monthly Annuity

Benefit	Current Age	At Age 55	At Age 60	At Age 62	At Age 65
Pension	$ 532	$ 2,293	$ 2,548	$ 2,548	$ 2,548
Early Retirement Supplement to Age 62	$ 0	$ 432	$ 480	$ 0	$ 0
Social Security	$ 0	$ 0	$ 0	$ 1,245	$ 1,561
Total	**$ 532**	**$ 2,725**	**$ 3,028**	**$ 3,793**	**$ 4,109**

Note: If you retire prior to age 62, call the Social Security Administration at 1-800-772-1213 for an estimate of your 62 benefit.

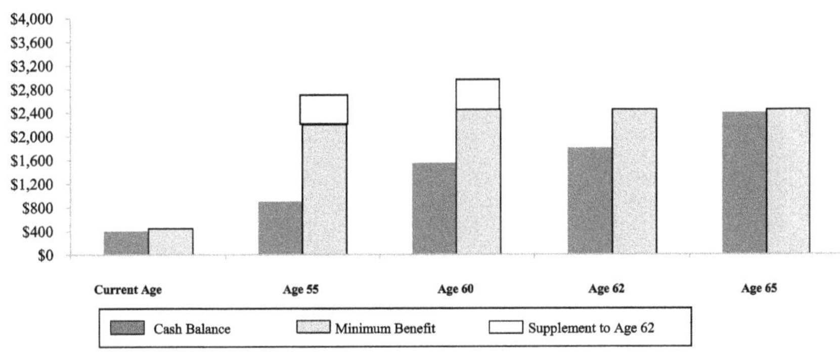

Note: These figures are given for illustration purposes only. Plan limits have been taken into consideration where applicable. If you have any questions about your CBP Select benefits call the El Paso Energy Benefits Center at 1-888-223-3338

Appendix 5

Table A, CIGNA textual data

Table A *Amara v. CIGNA* Disclosure Statements

Employee question:	**Precursor Documents: Newsletter (11/97) (Section 204(h) notice)**	**Precursor Documents: Information Kit (12/97)**	**Summary Plan Descriptions (10/98, 9/99)**
Compared to the old plan, will my benefit accrual rates under the new plan be reduced? **Note:** Statements with same superscript letter are from the same document section.	[nls] CIGNA will significantly enhance its retirement program.	[qa] [CIGNA] is not reducing the overall amount it contributes for retirement benefits, nor has the new program been designed to save money.	
	[nls] [Employees] will see an overall improvement in their retirement benefits.	[qa] **Q:** I was hired in 1989. Why wasn't I allowed to stay in the [old] Pension Plan? **A:** Our analysis showed that, in comparison to people with a higher age and service combination, you have plenty of time to take full advantage of the many attractive features of the [new] Retirement Plan.	
	[nls] [The] new plan is designed to work well for both longer- and shorter-service employees.	[qa] **Q:** Will my benefit be better under the new retirement plan? **A:** The new retirement plan is different from the current pension plan, so exact comparisons of benefits that cover all possible outcomes are difficult. Generally speaking, the new retirement plan, in comparison with the current pension plan, tends to provide larger benefits for shorter-term employees and comparable benefits for longer service employees.	

Table A (continued)

Employee question:	Precursor Documents: Newsletter (11/97) (Section 204(h) notice)	Precursor Documents: Information Kit (12/97)	Summary Plan Descriptions (10/98, 9/99)
Will a "wear away" period occur during which the employee will not earn any benefit at all? **Note:** Statements with same superscript letter are from the same document section.	[nls] [The new plan] provides steadier benefit growth throughout [the employee's] career.	[t] As of [January 1, 1998], the benefits you have earned under the Pension Plan will be converted to an opening account balance in the new plan. At the same time, you will begin earning retirement benefits under the new plan. [t] You will earn no further benefit under the Pension Plan after December 31, 1997. Starting in 1998, you will earn benefits under the new plan. [t] Keep in mind that this benefit comparison is intended to provide you with general information about opening balances and benefit growth . . . Your actual benefit will depend upon your age, future service, and salary history, and may differ from the benefits shown in the examples. [qa] [Y]our retirement benefit will continue to grow. [yp] **How Your Account Grows** Each dollar's worth of credit is a dollar of retirement after you are vested. Under the plan, your benefit will grow steadily throughout your career as credits are added to your account.	[spd] [Your quarterly statement will show] the amount of accumulated credited in your [cash balance] account. You'll see that amount continue to grow every year you are with CIGNA. [spd] Your final plan benefits cannot be less than your old plan benefits on December 31st, 1997. If this minimum benefits rule applies to you, you'll be notified by the Retirement Service Center when you request a distribution. [spd] Each dollar's worth of credit is a dollar of retirement after you are vested. Under the plan, your benefit will grow steadily throughout your career as credits are added to your account.

Table A (continued)

Employee question:	Precursor Documents: Newsletter (11/97) (Section 204(h) notice)	Precursor Documents: Information Kit (12/97)	Summary Plan Descriptions (10/98, 9/99)
Are opening account balances in the new plan equal to the total value of benefits earned under the old plan? **Note:** Statements with same superscript letter are from the same document section.		[t] Your normal pension benefit is an annual payment made to you for life, beginning when you turn age 65. To convert that annual pension benefit into an opening balance for the new plan, a calculation has to be made to determine how much that future stream of payments is worth today. This type of calculation is called a present value calculation. The method used to calculate the present value of a pension benefit is established by law. [t] Because of the relatively low interest rate, the amount [of plan benefits] available to you today is relatively large. In fact, to increase your opening balance, CIGNA has selected a much lower interest rate than the 7% or 8% rate adopted by most companies making similar pension plan changes. [t] [Benefits] are fully protected [and] their value will be reflected in the new plan balance. [t] Any benefits that you have earned under the CIGNA Pension Plan will be converted to an opening account balance in the new plan.	[spd] If you were an employee on December 31, 1997, or rehired after 1997, any benefit you earned under the Pension Plan through December 31st, 1997 was converted to an opening account balance in this Pension Plan. The opening balance was equal to the lump sum value of the pension benefit you earned through December 31, 1997 . . . The conversion formula used is based on guidelines established by the federal government for valuing pension benefits. If you have questions about the conversion formula, you may call [this number] [spd] Your final plan benefits cannot be less than your old plan benefits on December 31st, 1997. If this minimum benefits rule applies to you, you'll be notified by the Retirement Service Center when you request a distribution.

Table A (continued)

Employee question:	**Precursor Documents: Newsletter (11/97) (Section 204(h) notice)**	**Precursor Documents: Information Kit (12/97)**	**Summary Plan Descriptions (10/98, 9/99)**
		[t] [Benefits] are fully protected [and] their value will be reflected in the new plan balance.	
		[t] Any benefits that you have earned under the CIGNA Pension Plan will be converted to an opening account balance in the new plan.	
		[t] Keep in mind that this benefit comparison is intended to provide you with general information about opening balances and benefit growth . . . Your actual benefit will depend upon your age, future service, and salary history, and may differ from the benefits shown in the examples.	
Are opening account balances in the new plan equal to the total value of benefits earned under the old plan? **Note:** Statements with same superscript letter are from the same document section.		[qa] If you are eligible for the new CIGNA Plan, all of your benefits earned under the current pension plan through 12/31/97 will remain yours. As of 1/1/98, those benefits will be transferred to the new plan. [qa] **Q:** How do I know that the lump sum conversion is fair and accurate? **A:** The conversion factors we are using to determine your opening account balance are based on guidelines established by the government to ensure a fair transition for employees.	

Table A (continued)

Employee question:	Precursor Documents: Newsletter (11/97) (Section 204(h) notice)	Precursor Documents: Information Kit (12/97)	Summary Plan Descriptions (10/98, 9/99)
		[qa] If you are eligible for the new CIGNA Plan, all of your benefits earned under the current pension plan through 12/31/97 will remain yours. As of 1/1/98, those benefits will be transferred to the new plan. [yp] If you were an employee before 1998, any benefit you earned under the CIGNA Pension Plan through December 31, 1997 will be converted to an opening account balance in the Retirement Plan. The opening balance will equal the lump sum value of the pension benefit you earned through December 31, 1997.	

Appendix 5

Table B, El Paso textual data

Table B.1.1 *Tomlinson v. El Paso Corporation*: Precursor brochures distributed before §204(h) notices and the SPD

▼ **Employee questions** ▼	
Compared to the old plan, are accrual rates under the new plan reduced? **Note:** Statements with same superscript letter are from the same document.	[eu] Effective January 1, 1997, the current pension plan will be converted to a new type of plan called a "cash balance" plan. This type of plan provides employees with an individual cash account balance that increases each year with Company contributions and interest credits. Under the cash balance plan, employees will earn future benefits at a lower rate than under the current plan. Additional contributions related to Company profitability may be considered. Details of this new type of plan have not been finalized . . . Under the cash balance plan, employees will earn future benefits at a lower rate than under the current plan . . . Corporate Benefits will provide more details about this new program later in 1996. (Employee Update, 1/96).
	[cl] In the past, El Paso was able to provide employees with a very rich retirement benefits package. Our plans still provide excellent benefits, but are no longer at the top of the range. We are confident that the CBP Select, Retirement Savings Plan (RSP), and Social Security together can provide an adequate financial foundation for your retirement. However, your participation in the RSP and your own personal savings is [sic] now more important than ever. What does this mean to you? Planning will be key. The sooner you review your financial situation and take any necessary actions, the better. The hard truth is that those who are not prepared may have to postpone retirement. Or, they may have to retire with less money than they had anticipated. How can you be financially secure at retirement? Contribute at least 10% of your pay to the Retirement Savings Plan and start saving as much as you are able in addition . . . (10/96, p. 1).
	[cl] . . . active participants in the current pension plan as of December 31, 1996 will transition into the new plan over the next five years. What this means is that the current pension plan formula will remain in effect for all those plan participants until December 31, 2001. After that date the current pension plan formula will be frozen for those participants and they will not earn any additional benefits under the current plan of benefits. An employee who retires after December 31, 1996 will always be entitled to the greater of their benefit figured under the current pension plan formula or a benefit based on the cash balance under CBP Select. As a result, employees within five years of retirement are eligible to receive a pension benefit equal to what they would receive under the current plan.

Table B.1.2 *Tomlinson v. El Paso Corporation*: Precursor brochures distributed before § 204(h) notices and the SPD

▼ **Employee questions** ▼	
Compared to the old plan, are accrual rates under the new plan reduced? **Note:** Statements with same superscript letter are from the same document.	[mu] The Company feels very strongly that employees who are close to retirement should not be disadvantaged by this new plan. As a way to protect those employees who have worked for the Company for most of their careers and are now near to their retirement, we will transition to CBP Select over a five-year period. Here is what this means: the current pension plan formula will continue for all active participants as of 12/31/96 for 5 years. After 12/31/01, the current pension plan benefit for all participants will be frozen and employees will not earn any further benefits under the current plan of benefits. An employee who retires in the future will be entitled to the greater of their benefit figured under the current pension plan formula or the value of their cash balance in CBP Select. As a result, older, longer service employees are assured of a pension benefit equal to what they would receive under the current plan. (10/96, p. 3) [int] On the plus side . . . Employees cannot lose any value in their accounts–accounts can only go up in value. Employees may see some drawbacks too. Benefits will accrue at a slower rate in the future than under the current plan . . . This change in our pension plan may not be an easy one for some employees to accept. We have tried to balance employees' concerns with the Company's need to preserve financial resources. This led us to reduce the overall future benefits for employees and some employees will feel negatively about this . . . the bottom line is that the Company needs to make changes to our benefits if we are to survive and prosper in the future. (10/96, pp. 6–7). (10/96). **El Paso created the new CBP Select based on these primary objectives. We wanted to:** —Provide for long term service and older employees. —Provide adequate retirement benefits at age 60 and older. [ph] The employee's benefits under the old plan formula will continue to accrue from January 1, 1997 until December 31, 2001. (After this date, the employee earns pension benefits only under CBP Select). When the employee retires, his/her benefits under the old plan formula and CBP Select will be compared. The pension benefit paid will be the higher of the two formulas on the date of retirement.

Table B.1.3 *Tomlinson v. El Paso Corporation*: Precursor brochures distributed before § 204(h) notices and SPD

▼ Employee questions ▼	
Will a "wear away" period occur during which the employee will not earn any benefit at all? **Note:** Statements with same superscript letter are from the same document.	[int] **You can't lose.** Your account will be credited with interest quarterly, so your account can only go up, never down. [ff] **You have your own personal account.** It's easy to watch your account grow; you'll always know how much your account is at any time. [eph] The employee's benefits under the old plan formula will continue to accrue from January 1, 1997 until December 31, 2001. (After this date, the employee earns pension benefits only under CBP Select.) When the employee retires, his/her benefits under the old plan formula and CBP Select will be compared. The pension benefit paid will be the higher of the two formulas on the date of retirement.

Table B.1.4 *Tomlinson v. El Paso Corporation*: Precursor brochures distributed before §204(h) notices and the SPD

▼ Employee questions ▼	
Are opening account balances in the new plan equal to the total value of benefits earned under the old plan? **Note:** Statements with same superscript letter are from the same document.	[eu] Employees' accrued benefit under the cash balance plan will not be less than what they have accrued under the current Pension Plan formula as of December 31, 1996. This ensures that benefits employees have earned in 1996 will not be reduced in the transition to the new plan. [am] The present value of your accrued benefit under the EPNG Pension Plan as of December 31, 1996 will be your opening account balance in your CBP Select account on January 1, 1997. [eph] Initial Balance: The present value of your accrued benefit under the EPNG Pension Plan as of December 31, 1996.

Table B.2 *Tomlinson v. El Paso Corporation*: §204(h) notice

▼ **Employee questions** ▼	
Compared to the old plan, are accrual rates under the new plan reduced?	[g2] This notice is *simply a reminder* of how the plan was changed . . . This notice is intended to satisfy the requirements of Section 204(h) of the Employee Retirement Income Security Act of 1974. Section 204(h) requires that all retirement plan participants be notified of plan amendments that freeze or reduce future benefit accruals. The following again summarizes how your benefit will be affected: . . .
Will a "wear away" period occur during which the employee will not earn any benefit at all?	[g2] Each participant on December 31, 1996 who was an eligible employee on 1/1/97 received an opening cash account balance in the plan on 1/1/97. The participant's cash account balance grows with pay credits and interest credits . . . After December 31, 2001, for a participant whose minimum benefit is greater than the cash account benefit, accruals under the Plan *may effectively cease* until the participant's cash account benefit exceeds the minimum benefit earned as of December 31, 2001. This period of non-accrual will be more likely to affect individuals who elect early retirement.
Are opening account balances in the new plan equal to the total value of benefits earned under the old plan?	No statements

Table B.3 *Tomlinson v. El Paso Corporation*: Summary Plan Description (SPD)

▼ **Employee questions** ▼	
Compared to the old plan, are accrual rates under the new plan reduced?	No statements
Will a "wear away" period occur during which the employee will not earn any benefit at all?	[spd] Your El Paso Cash Account Benefit from ***CBP Select*** is based on the value of a hypothetical 'account' that is established in your name when you become a participant in the Plan. Your account increases in value over time by being credited with quarterly pay credits . . . In addition, your account will receive quarterly interest credits. The value of your El Paso Cash Account Benefit will continue to grow as long as you maintain a balance in your ***CBP Select*** Account. [spd] After December 31, 2001, your Minimum Benefit will be frozen, and you will earn benefits only under your El Paso Cash Account Benefit."
Are opening account balances in the new plan equal to the total value of benefits earned under the old plan?	[spd] **Opening Balance.** If you met the Minimum Benefit eligibility requirements, you had an 'account' established in *CBP Select* to reflect your accrued benefit under the Minimum Benefit Formula as of December 31, 1996.

Index

For Product Safety Concerns and Information please contact our EU representative GPSR@taylorandfrancis.com
Taylor & Francis Verlag GmbH, Kaufingerstraße 24, 80331 München, Germany

www.ingramcontent.com/pod-product-compliance
Ingram Content Group UK Ltd.
Pitfield, Milton Keynes, MK11 3LW, UK
UKHW022119190926
475702UK00013B/1527
9780367023492